# The CONTROL of
# CANDY JONES

# The CONTROL of CANDY JONES

## Donald Bain

ႷჯP

A Playboy Press Book

The facts related in this book are all true. Some names, locations and identities have been changed.

**Library of Congress Cataloging in Publication Data**

Bain, Donald, 1935–
    The control of Candy Jones.

      1. Hypnotism—Case studies. 2. Jones, Candy.
3. Nebel, Long John. 4. United States. Central
Intelligence Agency. I. Title.
BF1128.B34     154.7′092′6     76–7490
ISBN 0–87223–457–6

*For Candy Jones . . . an extraordinary woman*

# Contents

*Photos and Documents follow page 148*

# Foreword

I have come to know Candy Jones and John Nebel well over the last several years, both as an invited guest on their radio program and as a psychiatrist. As part of their efforts to unravel many perplexing questions about Candy's past, they asked me to examine her, especially in regard to her capacity to be hypnotized.

After a detailed clinical history, we evaluated her extensively, utilizing standard psychological testing, including the Thematic Apperception Test and the Rorschach. These indicated that she suffered episodic periods of stress, but not at the psychotic or schizophrenic level.

We then employed a clinical measurement of hypnotizability, the Hypnotic Induction Profile (HIP), in order to assess Candy's trance capacity. This test has been developed and standardized over ten years in a large population of patients, and seems to reliably indicate the extent to which an individual is hypnotizable. Such tests are important because hypnosis is a capacity which individuals possess to varying degrees, and which changes little in a given person with the passage of time. Hypnosis is not a quality projected onto someone by a hypnotist; rather, it is an ability inherent in the individual.

Candy's response to the Hypnotic Induction Profile indicated that she is extremely hypnotizable, and this outcome was confirmed independently by two other psychiatrists. Her trance

capacity places her in a small group of highly hypnotizable individuals, who comprise no more than ten percent of the population.

This high hypnotizability makes plausible her capacity to regress to earlier times in her life and to act as though she were
in the present. It is also consistent with her global amnesia—that
is, her complete "forgetting" of many events in her life. Such a
distinction is important because, as a rule, those who have a
lower capacity for hypnosis are far less susceptible to external
influence of the kind described in this book. For example, John
Nebel's response to the Hypnotic Induction Profile indicated
that he is at best minimally hypnotizable. Had he reported about
himself such a story of secret influences and amnesia for vast
portions of his life, and had he claimed to have experienced
spontaneous bursts of regression, I would have been quite skeptical.

Hypnosis, like many medical techniques, can be used for both
good and evil. A hypnotized individual has the ability to make
choices about complying with any suggestion. However, the
more hypnotizable a person is, the more inclined he will be to
comply with signals or commands, and to suspend his usual
critical judgment. Slipping into the trance state is something like
shifting into high gear in an automobile—any change in the
direction of motion is magnified. Thus, many individuals have
been helped considerably by learning about and by utilizing
their own trance capacities. At the same time, our research has
indicated that some highly hypnotizable people will do relatively
uncharacteristic things while in a trance state.

In one experiment, a highly hypnotizable subject entered a
trance state and was told to believe that there was a Communist
conspiracy to take over the television networks. Such a belief
was clearly contrary to his usual political orientation. Yet, after
leaving the trance state, he vehemently defended this belief
during an intense filmed interview with Frank McGee, the television news commentator, now deceased. The subject went so far
as to create names and places, and even began to openly suspect
McGee himself. Months later, when the subject viewed his performance on film, he was surprised and baffled at his own behavior. He had total amnesia of the entire filmed episode.

This and many similiar clinical experiences have led me to
believe that highly hypnotizable individuals are especially vul-

nerable to certain kinds of outside influence and manipulation. Such individuals may find themselves doing things which are, in some degree, at variance with their normal code of values. In the extreme, it is even possible that they may be manipulated into performing acts of physical violence. All people are prone to being molded by outside influence to some extent. The small group of highly hypnotizable people, when put in the hands of unscrupulous individuals, are even more vulnerable.

Another lesson of the filmed interview with the subject who'd been told to believe that the Communists had taken over the networks is that hypnotized subjects are also vulnerable to deception. Their desire to comply, both in and out of the formal trance, is such that they may convincingly invent information in an effort to give the hypnotist what he seems to want. They can even deceive themselves. Thus, interviews utilizing hypnotic age regression for the purpose of uncovering information must be performed carefully and dispassionately. Further, external corroborating evidence is crucial for verification of material produced in a regression study. Without external confirmation of data, the possibility of stress-hallucination is not ruled out.

It is well established, however, that under carefully controlled conditions, highly hypnotizable people can regress in time and uncover incredibly accurate and subtle factual and emotional experiences buried in the remote memory of the past.

*The Control of Candy Jones* is a fascinating and compelling book. I believe that John, Candy and the author, Donald Bain, have struggled to uncover the truth, although I share in their frustration at the difficulties involved in obtaining external documentation. I was not involved in the actual spontaneous and induced hypnotic age regression with Candy as reported in the book, but it is clear from my work with her that she is capable of such intense hypnotic experiences. Further outside evidence is important in evaluating Candy's story, and I view this book as an interim report, knowing that Candy, John and Donald Bain are determined to uncover as much information as possible. John's patience and sensitivity to unexpected cues is matched by Candy's persistent desire to surface all available memories.

Finally, I respect their courage in openly pursuing such a troubling and frightening personal story.

HERBERT SPIEGEL, M.D.

# Introduction

It has been almost two years since I was first invited to hear portions of tapes that had been recorded in the cramped East Side apartment shared by John Nebel and Candy Jones—Mr. and Mrs. Nebel. I recall sitting there on a hot and sticky August day in 1974, a drink in my hand, a yellow legal pad on my lap and a tightening knot of uneasiness in my stomach.

"I don't understand," I said. I was to say that many times during the long afternoon.

"Is it all right with you if I play this one?" Nebel asked Candy, referring to another cassette. He was to ask her that many times.

"If he's to be told any of it, he might as well be told all of it," she replied.

That was the beginning of my involvement with *The Control of Candy Jones*. As the afternoon progressed and I was barraged with information—a piece here, a slice there, a collage of material from John and Candy, and from the tape recorder on their coffee table, I found myself caught in a conflict of emotions. I am by nature a cynic, not a skeptic. But I was skeptical that day, not because of any conflict of information but because the story went beyond that which I wished to believe. I have always been able to accept evil as an abstract symbol but, like most people, find it more comfortable to deny evil's reality. To accept the evil displayed for me on the tapes would be to accept the resulting fear and anxiety real evil ultimately produces.

I preferred to be skeptical.

But skepticism is an intellectual act, forever at odds with the emotions. I found it impossible to ignore the potency of the Candy Jones tapes, and as they grew in number—I have listened to more than 200 hours of them—and began to consume my professional life, the urgency of their message exposed my skepticism as nothing more than intellectual cowardice. The clever skeptic is never wrong.

It took many months of research, writing and skepticism to complete *The Control of Candy Jones.* Each scrap of recall by Candy had to be placed within the framework of the puzzle. This was often difficult. At times, it was impossible. But as with any puzzle, when enough pieces are locked together, the picture is discernible.

There have been personal problems, too, in seeing this book through to publication. John Nebel has been a friend, and the difficulties this project have caused him have, to some extent, become my problems, too. John Nebel is 64 years old. He has cancer. He broadcasts six nights a week, six hours a night. He sleeps little. Most debilitating, however, has been the anguish of seeing in the woman he loves the tragic results of what others had done to her in the past. Nebel is, and has been for the past four years, engaged in a struggle to nullify the control over his wife gained by those other people during a 12-year period.

The amount of information contained on the tapes proved to be too unwieldy for transcription from the originals. Total transcription of the tapes would have produced 4000 to 5000 single-spaced pages. Instead, a system was devised in which as an original tape was played through earphones, I recorded on to another tape recorder my "play-by-play" of the events on the original. In addition, I used a stop-watch and called out the passing of each minute during individual half-hour segments. The built-in digital counters on the many tape recorders used for this project were calibrated against minute counts. Thus, I was able to go quickly to any point on any original tape, no matter which machine was used, by relating minutes to digit counts. My transcriber, Donna Pelini, transcribed my comments as opposed to the original tapes. Even at that, the condensed transcripts (my comments) numbered over 700 single-spaced pages. In addition to the tapes, there were approximately 60 hours of interviews with John and Candy.

A problem of another sort arose when I attempted to trace the pivotal physician directly responsible for the manipulation of Candy Jones. He wasn't found until I had begun writing the book, and his home and office addresses are now included in my secured files. I have, on the counsel of my lawyers, refrained from contacting him because of possible litigation.

The story of Candy Jones as presented on the tapes points a harsh and critical finger at the Central Intelligence Agency, for while Candy's story does not have the global impact of the CIA's Chilean folly or of the Cuban fiasco, it does level a powerful personal condemnation of that agency. One cannot help but consider it more important than those distant misadventures because it is the story of what happened, in a painfully personal way, to one person, Candy Jones, and left her with a nightmare with which to live, perhaps for the rest of her life. I have no quarrel with the CIA as a conceptual entity. I suppose such agencies are unfortunate realities in our tense and global society.

But when so large and powerful a government agency as the CIA fosters and encourages childhood fantasies of intrigue, adventure and manipulation within grown men and women, it must stand ready to accept the blame when this grown-up game of cops and robbers goes awry.

I have not met a more courageous person than Candy Jones. I refer not to her courage during the years from 1960 to 1972 when her adventures took place, but point with praise and admiration to her dedication to seeing that this book is published. She has expressed to me not only fear for her life, but also the fear that one day a reader of this book might look at her and wonder whether the attempts to control and manipulate her for all those years had marked her indelibly. May I simply say to them that Candy Jones, who nightly broadcasts beside her husband, Long John Nebel, on WMCA in New York City, is one of the sanest women I know.

Some final comments.

An understanding of hypnosis was a requisite to being able to write this book; and while texts provided my introduction to the subject, it was the kind, patient and generous willingness of experts in the field to explain it to me that provided the necessary understanding.

One such expert is Dr. Herbert Spiegel, a psychiatrist in private practice in New York City and an associate professor of psychiatry at Columbia University College of Physicians and Surgeons, where he has taught courses in medical hypnosis since 1960. His work in medical hypnosis has begun to revolutionize the field, not only as it applies to hypnosis as a therapeutic tool but as it relates to the entire concept of psychotherapy. The practice of short-term therapy has been dramatically advanced by Spiegel's work, particularly through his development of the Hypnotic Induction Profile (HIP). This technique has ramifications far greater than enabling a hypnotist to evaluate a potential subject's capacity for hypnosis. The HIP gives every physician an impressively quick and accurate insight into a patient's personality, an invaluable advantage when planning treatment strategies.

Three other fine physicians, all students of the Spiegel approach to hypnosis and his Hypnotic Induction Profile, added immeasurably to my grasp of the subject. One is Dr. Robert T. London, a New York City psychiatrist in private practice and also on the teaching faculty of New York University Medical Center. Another is Dr. Frederick Dick, an internist, perhaps the only one in New York City who regularly incorporates the HIP into routine physical examinations. The third is Dr. Barbara DeBetz, a psychiatrist in private practice in New York City and a colleague of Dr. London at N.Y.U.

Doctors Spiegel, London and Dick have all appeared with me on the "Long John Nebel Show," which, I must admit, was a comfortable and convenient way for me to pick their impressive brains over six-hour periods.

I also wish to extend my appreciation to my editor at Playboy Press, Bob Gleason, who offered a sensible blend of hard-nosed judgment and welcome encouragement.

Finally, I acknowledge my collaborators on this project, the myriad of tape recorders, large and small, without which there would be no book.

# PART I

PART I

# 1

## The Marriage

The marriage took place in New York City on December 31, 1972.

The bride was Candy Jones, born Jessica Wilcox in Wilkes-Barre, Pennsylvania, on that same day in 1925.

The groom was Long John Nebel, born Jack Zimmerman in Chicago, Illinois, on June 11, 1911.

Candy Jones had been America's most famous model during the Forties. Her photographs graced the covers of 11 magazines within a single month in 1943. She and Betty Grable constituted World War II's most potent pinup team; photos of Candy in a white bathing suit with coral dots had been affixed to the corrugated walls of Quonset huts throughout the South Pacific, promising better things to thousands of GIs once the battle was won. She traveled extensively throughout the war zone, her presence an injection of stateside softness into the reality of a hard war.

In 1946 Candy married one of the leaders in the American modeling field, Harry Conover, originator of the "cover girl" concept. With a matching investment of $500 from a young male model who was also his roommate, Gerald Ford, currently the president of the United States, Conover had formed the nation's most prestigious modeling agency. Their marriage was to produce three sons, grief, a divorce in 1959 and staggering debt.

Following her divorce from Conover, Candy managed to pull together the pieces of a broken marriage and a financially drained business and forge a new life for herself and her young sons. She created a corporation of her own, using the power of her name and reputation to get them moving. She entered the broadcasting field and became a fixture on NBC's network weekend radio service, Monitor. She devoted great amounts of time to charitable causes, was a familiar sight at Broadway openings and cabaret first nights, and maintained her close associations with leaders of show business, politics and the military establishment.

Candy's new husband, Long John Nebel, was New York's most successful radio talk-show host. He'd reigned for 20 years in the midnight-till-dawn slot, his caustic, strident voice as familiar to Manhattan's night people as sirens and honking horns. Six feet four inches tall and as slender as a model, he glided through his nocturnal world shrouded in controversial topics and an extensive wardrobe of fine clothes. Pale, he slept when the sun was up. Even his hair seemed colorless. An imposing figure in an imposing city.

John Nebel began his radio career at the age of 43 when WOR, the Mutual Network's New York flagship station, gave Nebel the all-night show. The time slot was known as a hopeless graveyard for announcers, but Long John built it into a lucrative program with a fanatically loyal following. Eight years later, after money hassles with WOR's management, he moved to WNBC where he remained for another eight years. He then switched to WMCA, another all-talk station, where he perpetuated the lure and lore of Nebel-at-midnight. Throughout his radio career, Nebel had pioneered in opening the airways to controversy. Possessing only an eighth-grade education, he brought with him to broadcasting an extensive background in selling. This along with an insatiable intellectual curiosity enabled him to generate real excitement and electricity, six hours a night, six nights a week. His interests, and the subjects he dealt with, were as varied as his background—jazz, flying saucers, psychiatry, law, ESP, the circus, gold, internal medicine and hypnosis.

John and Candy had met in 1941 when he was working as a free-lance photographer. At the height of her career he'd been assigned to photograph her for a major magazine advertisement. They bumped into each other around town over the ensuing years as they pursued their respective careers, but there was little communication. Candy admits to having carried a mildly flickering torch for Nebel in the Sixties but had assumed he was married. He was not, although he'd become involved in a series of long-term relationships with various women after his divorce from his first wife, Lillian, in 1960.

The courtship of John Nebel and Candy Jones was pursued at undergraduate speed. They'd gone together for 28 days prior to the wedding. Nebel's many friends, bemused at his decision to marry again, were unanimous in their favorable response to Candy. Her natural, guileless beauty and unaffected, warm personality captivated her husband-to-be's assortment of confidants without exception, this writer included. She was without the pretense one associates with models; nor, though a tall woman, was she the willowy, graceful model type—in fact she occasionally displayed a disarming awkwardness. Her personality was self-effacing: "I have good bones," was her embarrassed answer to well-meaning praise of her beauty, and a nervous laugh was generally added to soften even that comment.

The wedding was held at the lavish, sprawling contemporary apartment of attorney Kenneth Knigin, Nebel's lawyer. Approximately 40 of John's friends attended the ceremony. Candy's mother was there. A young lady who worked for Candy in her charm and career school was also present, although more as a companion to Candy's mother than as an invited guest.

"Strange that Candy has no one here," I commented to my wife.

Stranger yet was the change that came over Candy as champagne was poured into silver goblets and finger sandwiches were passed among the guests by uniformed waiters. As Nebel described it in retrospect: "Something happened that I really can't put into words. You'd have to have known Candy as I did to notice the change in her. She developed an expression on her face that wasn't Candy, at least not the Candy I'd come to love. I'd never seen that expression before—tense, angry, concerned. I asked her if anything was wrong and she gave me a curt 'No.'

I couldn't believe it was the same woman. I was upset to see her that upset."

I'd chalked it up to the tension of the moment. I'd worked professionally as a musician and had played at hundreds of weddings. Invariably, brides are tense, and often become angry at insignificant details.

At any rate, as she chatted with Nebel's friends, a tension, covert and unstated, became evident. Nothing major, nothing definitive, simply there. When it was time for the guests to leave, Candy and John stood at the door and bade gracious farewells to each person as he or she departed from the opulent apartment and prepared to go out into the unusually warm and hazy December day. Some of us would be joining the bride and groom that evening at Ho Ho, the Chinese restaurant where Nebel annually held court on New Year's Eve as a gesture to a longtime sponsor, and to his listeners.

John and Candy Nebel were a strikingly handsome couple as they stood side-by-side at the door. There was no question that Nebel was a happy man at that moment. And there was no reason to question whether Candy shared his pleasure.

But a larger and more tantalizing question might have been asked had the events that were to take place in the ensuing months and years been known to the gathered well-wishers.

Simply put, that question is: *Was the woman at John Nebel's side really Candy Jones?*

# 2

# The Wedding Night

Mr. and Mrs. John Nebel would spend their wedding night in a suite at the Drake Hotel, 56th Street and Park Avenue in New York City. First, however, was the party at Ho Ho. After a brief stop at the Drake to bathe and change clothes, they went by Smith's Limousine to the restaurant, which is located on West 50th Street, close to the WNBC studios from which Nebel had broadcast prior to his move to WMCA.

They were in good spirits as the guests began to arrive and joined them in the cocktail lounge, a lavishly colorful area of the landmark restaurant, softly lighted and dotted with table groupings and handsome club chairs. Candy, who owns an extensive collection of wigs, had persuaded John to wear a silver one, which caused much laughter around the tables. Faithful listeners, aware that he would be there, presented Nebel with an assortment of gifts, most of which had been personally sewn or baked.

At nine, those who were joining John and Candy for dinner accompanied them to the table in the main dining room, which is dominated by huge oil paintings of Chinese pastoral scenes.

As steaming platters of house specialties were served and listeners continued to approach Nebel at the table, I again sensed a change in Candy from her previous geniality. She seemed to detach herself from her surroundings, and her answers to questions were terse and without warmth. And again I thought I had a ready answer for this change in mood. After all, her husband of only a few hours was totally occupied with his fans. He was called to the telephone over a dozen times during the course of the evening to receive the best wishes of friends, and I understood the effect this preoccupation could have on a bride. Candy, no doubt, would have been happier alone with John on her wedding eve than sharing him with friends, fans and business cronies.

Actually, Candy was fortunate that New Year's Eve fell on a Sunday night that year. Had it not, she would have been forced to share her husband with a studio microphone following the dinner, because the show has always been Long John Nebel's life. There were no vacations, no nights off, no trips or honeymoons. When Nebel was hospitalized in January 1971, during which confinement his cancer was diagnosed following exploratory surgery, he arranged to leave the hospital each night by limousine and, with appropriate bags attached to his body, went to the studio where he did the six-hour show standing up.

The Nebels departed Ho Ho shortly after midnight and went to their suite at the Drake. Recalls Nebel: "There was a king-sized bed, and we went through the usual preparations for sharing that bed. Funny, but you can understand how 'romantic lovers' are reluctant to admit they even go to the bathroom or anything like that. I was tempted to go downstairs and use the john in the lobby. Anyway, Candy came out of the bathroom dressed in a beautiful negligee and I went in. I came out wearing my bikini shorts. . . . I always wear them. I didn't even bring a robe, so Candy gave me one of her caftans. I looked kind of faggish, I guess, but I put it on. We got into bed and talked awhile and then did what you'd expect newlyweds to do. When it was over, I casually asked whether she was happy. She reached over and grabbed a Fourth-of-July sparkler from the nightstand, lighted it and held it over our heads. I was thrilled, delighted, contented . . . I felt great."

But then, according to Nebel, something strange happened.

Candy had left the bed and gone into the bathroom, and when she returned she said something to him that he cannot recall. What she said is probably irrelevant, however, because it was *how* it was said that caused the reaction in Nebel. As he describes it: "She came out of the bathroom and I saw somebody who resembled the woman I'd married. I stress that word 'resembled.' I mean, I knew it was my wife because there were no exits from that bathroom. She was the same height and build as Candy. But she said something to me in an entirely different voice. I don't recall her words, but I do remember her voice was bitter, biting. It was frightening. I asked her what was wrong. She answered, 'Nothing's wrong,' in a deep voice that had the slicing effect of a razor. I didn't know what else to say so I went out into the suite's living room."

Nebel seldom drinks, but he poured a glass of bourbon from a bottle provided by the hotel's management, picked up half a chicken sandwich and turned on the television to see what was left of New Year's Eve celebrations from other parts of the country. He called into the bedroom and invited Candy to join him for a drink and a sandwich, which she did.

"She seemed to be Candy again," says Nebel, "the Candy I married. Warm and sweet and lovable. 'You're wonderful, John,' she said. 'You're a wonderful man and you've made me the happiest woman on earth.'"

They stood and kissed, and John Nebel tried to forget for the moment that other voice that had so jarred him in the bedroom.

# 3

# The Next Day

January 1, 1973, was a crisp, sunny winter's day. After a breakfast of eggs and bacon at the hotel, John and Candy took a walk,
hand in hand, along Park Avenue. They bumped into an old
Nebel friend, the noted attorney O. John Rogge, who offered
the couple his warm best wishes on their marriage.

"We were the happiest couple in the world," says Nebel as he
looks back at that day. "The change in Candy's behavior and
voice had been wiped from my mind."

The next day Nebel made a brief appearance as a guest on the
"Leon Lewis Show" on WMCA. He and Candy had dinner that
night at another of Nebel's favorite restaurants, Antolotti's, on
East 49th Street, near First Avenue. After dinner they picked up
the newspapers and retired to their suite at the Drake for a
leisurely evening of reading, sleeping and enjoying the novelty
of being alone together. Later that night they went to WMCA
where Nebel did his usual Monday night broadcast. Candy
watched with pride as her husband rolled through the evening
doing what he has always done better than anyone else in his
business.

On Tuesday morning they enjoyed a continental breakfast as they packed in preparation to leave the hotel to return to Nebel's apartment, which would become their home.

"I'll call the desk and have someone sent up for the bags," Nebel said after finishing his Danish pastry and coffee.

"Don't bother. I'll take care of everything," said Candy, her face molded into a stern, wrathful expression. John peered across the table. It didn't make sense to him. Why was she angry? What had caused such a sudden and drastic shift in her mood? He asked her about it.

"I'm not angry," said *the voice* through Candy's mouth. "But that doesn't mean I have to be happy about everything either." The voice was deep and cutting.

"What's wrong?" Nebel asked.

"Nothing." Candy looked beyond him with cold eyes.

Wishing to avoid a confrontation, Nebel fought the urge to question her further. Instead he suggested she go to the desk and pay the bill while he waited in the suite for the bellhop. Candy took the money he handed her and left the room.

The bellhop arrived and Nebel accompanied him downstairs where the limousine was waiting. He was apprehensive about getting into the car with Candy, afraid that what had occurred upstairs would repeat itself in front of the driver. It didn't. He was met by a smiling and loving Candy Jones-Nebel, who kissed her husband on the cheek and squeezed his hand.

Once in the apartment, Nebel changed into old slacks and Candy slipped into a frilly gown. They lay in bed and read the *Times* and *News* until it was time for him to go to the studio. He'd asked Candy to join him, but she'd declined; she was due at her offices early the next day for meetings. John kissed her goodnight and left to do his broadcast. Since he was early, he decided to call Candy from a phone in his office. After a brief chat, he went into the studio and greeted his longtime friend, writer and public relations consultant, Sandy Teller, who would sit in as a panelist on that evening's program.

At five minutes before air time, Nebel placed another call home. For some reason the events at the Drake had resurfaced and caused him to worry. Candy answered.

"Everything all right?" Nebel asked.

"Of course."

"I love you, Candy."

She sighed. They were silent a moment, and then *a voice* said, "Why do you always think something is wrong?" It was the same harsh voice Nebel had heard at the Drake. This time, there was a hint of mockery.

"Candy, what's the matter?"

"John, I'm fine." It was Candy's voice again, soft and sleepy.

"Candy, what's happening? Your voice is so different and angry sometimes."

"John, I've never been angry with you. I have nothing to be angry with you about."

"Then why do you *act* as though you're mad?"

"I don't know, John. I certainly don't feel mad at you for anything. I love you very much."

"And I love you. I want so much for us to work at this and make it a big success." Nebel continued to tell Candy how much he loved her and about his hopes for their future together. He became aware, however, that there was no response from the other end.

"Candy?"

Nothing. He hadn't heard her hang up, and it sounded as though the line were still connected and open. He called her name twice more. Still no response.

Nebel hung up and ran into the studio. The news was winding up; he'd be on the air with his familiar, *"Hi there, this is Long John Nebel,"* within a minute. Sandy Teller sensed his upset but didn't have time to ask about it because the red light flashed and Nebel was introducing the show. Once he had it under way, he slipped Sandy a note telling him he had to leave the station for a half-hour and to keep things moving. Teller, a veteran of over 200 Nebel shows, smoothly stepped into the host's role as Nebel hurriedly departed, took the elevator to the ground floor and hailed a cab at the corner of Seventh Avenue and 57th Street. The ride home took only five minutes, but it seemed much longer to him. Telling the driver to wait, he rushed into the building and up to the second floor, opened the door and went to the small bedroom at the rear. Candy was asleep on the bed, the receiver off the cradle and resting beside her. Nebel gently shook her shoulder.

"John?"

"Yes. I was talking to you and you just disappeared."

"What are you talking about?"

"We were talking on the phone and . . ."

"Is it six already?" She thought the night had passed and John had returned from work.

"No, and I have a cab waiting downstairs. Candy, you sounded so mad at me on the phone."

"John, that's ridiculous. I'm not mad at you."

"Don't you remember talking to me on the phone?"

"Yes, but I wasn't mad."

"Your voice was different and all. Candy, I . . . Look, I have to get back. You must have fallen asleep. Are you all right?"

"Yes, of course. I'm sorry."

"That's okay." Nebel kissed her, went downstairs and returned to the studio where he took over and guided the guest and panelists through the early-morning hours.

When Nebel arrived home from the show that morning and prepared to go to bed, Candy was in the bathroom. She entered the bedroom as he was getting into bed.

"How was the show?" she asked.

"Fine. How are you?"

"Fine," she replied.

"Look, Candy, I don't want to cause trouble or anything like that, but what the hell is going on here?"

"What are you talking about?"

"You know what I'm talking about. The changes in your moods. The anger. I never know what to expect from you. I mean that, Candy. One minute you're one thing, and then you become something else."

"That isn't true and you know it."

Nebel got up and stood close to her. He placed his hands on her shoulders and looked into her eyes. "Candy, something is wrong and I think we'd better get it settled right now before it goes any further. What is the problem?"

Candy was annoyed at the questioning. "I told you there wasn't any problem. You're imagining everything."

"Like hell I am." Nebel recited for her a list of times when he'd noticed her personality change. He concluded by saying, "I just wish you'd tell me what's causing it."

Candy busied herself at a small desk in the bedroom, and John climbed back into bed. They said nothing to each other for over five minutes. Finally, Candy walked to the bed, sat on it and touched her husband's face.

"John, there's something that maybe I should tell you."

"What's that?"

"It's just something that I never even thought was worth mentioning but maybe it is. There are times when I might have to take a trip."

"For what?"

"Oh, to give a lecture or something like that."

"I'm not sold on that idea," said Nebel, sitting up. He expanded on his negative reaction to her announcement. Candy listened patiently to his protests. When he was finished, she stood up and leaned against the bookcases that line one wall of the bedroom.

"John, there's more to it than just giving a lecture." She told him briefly and simply that she had in the past done some work for one of our government's agencies. Some of her travels had to do with that work.

Nebel lighted a cigarette and questioned her about what she'd just said. She seemed willing to answer his questions, and told him that after her divorce from Harry Conover in 1959 she'd been approached by the FBI.

"What did you do for them?" Nebel asked.

"Very little. They used my offices as a mail drop. And I carried a few messages for them."

Nebel found the revelation interesting, of course, but did not attach great significance to it. He asked whether she was still involved, and she said she wasn't.

After she left, Nebel lighted another cigarette and sat on the edge of the bed to think. At first he found the fact that his wife had performed undercover work for the FBI amusing. The circumstances under which she'd been approached were mundane, once you could accept the fact that such agencies as the FBI routinely enlist the part-time services of thousands of average citizens to accomplish its goals, goals with which Nebel had always been in philosophical agreement. But as he reflected upon the story Candy had told him about first being approached by the FBI agent, he began to feel uneasy.

"Was that all there was to it?" he wondered aloud.

# 4

## A Conscious Recollection of Childhood

Candy Jones's mother was named Jessica Wilcox, and she named her only daughter after her. The name, however, was not the only manifestation of Candy's mother's desire to leave her imprint on her daughter. There was also her harsh, unforgiving, stiff-kneed puritanism. Believing the world, and particularly its men, to be inherently evil, Mrs. Wilcox brought up her daughter on a tight rein. Had she had her way, Candy would have attended secretarial school, which, according to her mother's logic, would have headed off any notions her daughter might have had about venturing into more exotic and, by extension, more dangerous avenues.

The mother's attitude toward men was not without cause. Candy's father had left them when she was three. He was James Gordon Wilcox, preferring to be known as J. Gordon Wilcox to better reflect his status in the business world. Not that he was a financial titan. He'd met and courted Candy's mother while working as a ticket taker at the Capital Theatre in Wilkes-Barre, and their courtship was condemned by both families. J. Gordon Wilcox lived in Kingston, a less than desirable area according to the residents of Wilkes-Barre proper. He was also a Polish Catholic, a deadly combination for Ella Mae Jevons, Candy's maternal grandmother.

But there was undoubtedly more than simple snobbery and religious prejudice influencing Ella Mae. She'd divorced *her* husband, Arthur Rosengrant, when *her* daughter and a son, Eugene, were small; and while she enjoyed a more liberal and accepting view of life than did Candy's mother, she certainly showed the effects of her own broken marriage in the way she reacted to the pending wedding of J. Gordon and Jessie. She was firmly against it, which accomplished nothing more than to hasten the inevitable.

The couple wed, and after a brief stay in the grandmother's house, moved to Buffalo, New York, where J. Gordon became a car salesman for the Packard Company. Shortly thereafter, the firm sent him to their Atlantic City operation, which brought the couple closer to home and which introduced Candy's mother to that resort area, then a fashionable mecca of clean air, white sand, elegant hotels and a genteel *modus vivendi.* That latter attribute of Atlantic City was important to Jessie Wilcox for she did have pretensions, for herself and for the daughter who was born a year later. The fruits of those pretensions were not to be realized, however, with J. Gordon Wilcox at her side. He worked hard in Atlantic City and became Packard's top salesman. He simultaneously took advantage of the many available women in the convention city. Tall and slender and with a penchant for gab, he came home to his bride less and less. Finally, when Candy was three, her mother moved back to the grandmother's house on Carey Avenue.

"I never knew my father until I was older," Candy reflects. "In fact, I don't recall any men in my life when I was very young. My mother's brother visited once in awhile, but only to see how much money he could get from my grandmother. He was a jeweler in San Francisco, and had driven an ambulance during World War One. That's all I know about him. When he did arrive, my mother would usually say, 'Well, here he is. I wonder how much he's going to ask for this time.' "

The first visit by Candy's father that she recalls occurred when she was about four, one year after her mother's split from him. He had dinner at the house, following which the mother and grandmother left him alone with his daughter. They sat together in the living room. The child perched demurely on the couch and shyly watched her father, a figure as imposing in the large, dim room as the bulky, dark pieces of furniture.

"I have to leave now," he told the child after 15 minutes. She didn't respond. "Aren't you sorry that I'm leaving?"

"No," Candy answered.

"Good little girls would be sorry when their daddy leaves," said Wilcox. Candy didn't know what she was supposed to say, or do. She did know that the term "daddy" bothered her. She'd referred to him as Mister during the meal, and although he tried to hide his displeasure at having his daughter use so formal a term, it was evident to her.

"Won't you cry when I leave?" Wilcox asked.

"No."

If he was angry at her answer, he concealed it. "Of course you'll cry," he said.

"No, I won't."

"Well, I do have to go." He rose from his chair and held out his hand to her. She took it and allowed him to lead her toward the kitchen. Instead of going into the kitchen, however, he opened the door that led to a butler's pantry. Inside, he opened a drawer and pulled out a silver nutcracker. "I can make you cry," he said.

"I don't cry," Candy said.

Wilcox placed one of Candy's fingers in the nutcracker and squeezed. She closed her eyes against the pain and fought against the tears. He sandwiched another finger into the nutcracker and squeezed harder. Candy would have cried had not her mother opened the door to the pantry.

"What are you doing?" she asked.

"Just playing a little game," Wilcox replied, tossing the nutcracker into the drawer. "Weren't we, Doll?" he asked Candy, using a nickname that had been with her since infancy. His tone carried the ring of warning to the child.

"Yes," Doll answered, pressing her bruised knuckles against her side.

"Just having fun," said Wilcox. "Come on, Doll, give daddy a kiss before he leaves." Candy kissed his cheek, and he gave her a hug.

After he left, Candy went to a Victorian chest in the dining room and picked up a framed photograph of her father that he'd given her at dinner. She threw it to the floor and smashed her heel into it.

"Stop that!" her mother screamed, picking up the frame of cracked glass and holding it away from Doll.

"I've never understood why my mother saved that photograph," says Candy. "She supposedly hated my father, and was always ready to take him to court for nonpayment of child support."

Candy's exposure to her father was minimal over the next ten years. At five, she was invited to visit with his parents in Kingston, Pennsylvania. A man picked her up and drove her to their home which, Candy recalls, was impressive. Her grandfather raised Doberman pinschers, and Candy was allowed to pet them. Her father had many brothers and sisters, and they seemed young and carefree compared to the older atmosphere of her own home. "They all were wearing tennis clothes," says Candy, "and there seemed to be dozens of cousins. I was introduced to all of them and loved it."

Mostly Candy remembers sitting on her grandfather's knee. He held her away from him and stared at her for a long time. People commented that she looked like her father; others said she would grow up to look like her grandmother, who according to Candy had the face of a porcelain doll, blonde, with brown eyes. Everyone seemed to have red hair and blue eyes in her father's family except his mother. And they were all fair-skinned.

When the same man drove her home early that afternoon, there were fire engines in front of her house, and her mother was standing outside, arms crossed. Candy ran to her, eyes wide with excitement. "What happened?" she asked.

"There was a fire," her mother replied. "It's all over now." A few minutes later, Candy was taken to her room and shown the results of the fire. The furnace had ignited and sent flames racing through the ductwork. Candy's bed was scorched where flames had flashed from the register on the wall next to her bed.

"Did you enjoy your day?" her mother asked.

"Yes."

"It's just as well you went. The fire happened when you would have been taking your nap."

During her courtship with Long John Nebel, Candy had little

to say about her childhood. She did discuss her father with John, and, naturally, he met her mother, with whom she lived at 1199 Park Avenue. But in response to his questions about the general quality of her early years, she seldom said more than "It was lonely."

"Didn't you have any friends?" Nebel would ask.

"No. My mother didn't like my having friends."

The loneliness of Candy Jones's early life was tempered by her love of animals, and by her grandmother, Ella Mae Jevons. Divorced before the turn of the century, unconventional behavior for the era, Ella Mae set about supporting her two children, as well as other family members. A younger brother, who worked in one of the paint stores owned by Ella Mae's side of the family, was forever dipping into the till to pay gambling debts. Her younger sister, Kate, prone to hypochondria, married an unambitious employee of the Pennsylvania Railroad. Brother and sister, and their families, lived in two of the more than twenty houses owned by Ella Mae. There was always talk of paying rent, but it never materialized. Candy, to this day, has notes for as much as $5000 each, signed by various family members to her grandmother.

When the Depression embraced Wilkes-Barre in 1929, Candy's grandmother lost virtually everything except the house on Carey Avenue and the house on Lake Nuangola. Her cash had failed with the banks, and all the remaining houses owned by her were repossessed when she failed to pay taxes. Despite these reverses, Ella Mae survived by virtue of her own foresight and resourcefulness. She had, at the time of her divorce, taken an unusual step for a woman in those pre–Fem Lib days. A nurse by training, she enrolled in an osteopathic college in Philadelphia and earned her degree. She then opened offices in Wilkes-Barre's finest downtown office building, which overlooked a square.

Occasionally Candy was allowed to watch as her grandmother, whom Candy always called "Ma-Má," manipulated her patients' arms and legs in search of a cure for their elusive ailments. A proud and handsome woman who wore high heels which increased her already greater than average height (she stood about five feet seven inches tall and looked taller because of her rigidly erect posture), Ella Mae, in Long John Nebel's argot, knew how to "turn a classical buck." With her patients as a captive market, she organized them for summer tours of Europe to support her own yearly, month-long jaunts to the Continent, Depression be damned. She took random medical courses at the Sorbonne in Paris, and attended for three consecutive decades performances of the Passion play produced every ten years in the Bavarian village of Oberammergau. She would return from her European trips with expansive tales of the people and places she'd seen—and always with gifts for Doll. By the age of five, Candy owned two fur coats, one black and one white, gifts from Ma-Má. She had also learned rudimentary French from her grandmother, who spoke French and German fluently.

The house on Carey Avenue in which Candy grew up had 16 rooms and was painted battleship gray. Deep, graceful porches ran the length of the front of the house and along one side. Neighboring houses were of a similar size.

The first floor parlor was the largest room. It was dominated by a black piano decorated with rococo carvings that were a source of frustration for Candy whose Saturday chore it was to polish the piano. A black lacquer rolltop desk stood next to the piano and was precious to Candy's mother. Nothing was ever to be placed upon it.

Three floor-to-ceiling windows were hung with heavy gold and purple festooned draperies. The colorful drapes caught the bright hues of the huge oriental rug that, too, was sacred to her mother. The draperies were always closed.

The square dining room whose windows overlooked a garden was separated from the living room by sliding panels. Candy much preferred this sunny room to the darkness of the living room. The table could seat 12, but it seldom served more than Candy, her mother and her grandmother. Mother and grand-mother sat at opposite ends while Candy sat on the long side between them that faced the windows.

The upstairs front bedroom was shared by Candy and her mother. Wallpaper bouquets of violets against a buff back-ground covered the walls, and five large windows overlooked the roof of the front porch. The mother's portion of the room contained a highboy, another dresser and a vanity table with a frilly-shaded lamp and a tray holding bottles of perfume, a tortoise set of brush, comb, shoehorn, nail buffer and round powder box. Each item was positioned carefully and never varied.

Candy's bed was on the far wall, next to the furnace register. She had a child's dresser, a coat tree and a small clothes closet.

"It was a sunny, pleasant room," Candy recalls, "the floors polished to a high gloss by Pearl's elbow grease. Funny, but I actually believed that Pearl had some magic ingredient in her elbows that made wood shine. I asked her about it one day and she straightened me out."

Adjacent to the front bedroom was a narrow hall that ran 20 feet and then made a sharp left into Ma-Má's area. Sconces with amber, flame-shaped bulbs lighted the hallway. Ceiling-to-floor purple velour drapes covered bookcases that ran the length of the hall, their shelves bulging with Ma-Má's extensive collection of medical books, journals and file folders.

Ma-Má's bed was brass, and the air was heavy with the scent of lilac; she soaked little cotton pads in lilac perfume and pinned them beneath her bed bolster and to the curtains. A large half-hemisphere of amber glass covered the triple ceiling bulbs. There were more file folders, medical journals and travel brochures piled everywhere, and a massive dressing table with mirrors that pulled out and surrounded you on three sides. Seated before it, you could see seven images of yourself.

Ma-Má's area of the house held for Doll a mysterious and foreboding quality, as well as a magnetic force that drew her to it almost daily. Ma-Má could be stern, but she seldom scolded Doll for playing with her clothes or arranging tea parties on her massive dresser for the cadre of imaginary friends created by Doll to fill her reclusive hours.

Her mother, on the other hand, perhaps resenting her child's growing closeness to her grandmother and diminishing closeness to her, became an increasingly demanding taskmaster. A nervous woman, Jessie Wilcox established and maintained a smothering hold on her daughter. She insisted that Doll become proficient at sewing and painting by the age of six, and enforced this demand with a riding crop that was always within arm's reach. A wrong stitch or a carelessly drawn line would bring a sharp crack across the back of Doll's knees with the crop. Doll's mother was careful, however, not to use the crop when Ma-Má was present because the grandmother would intercede on Doll's behalf. To cover the welts made by the crop, Doll was made to wear long skirts and lisle stockings that reached over the knees.

"My mother was an excellent swimmer and horsewoman," Candy recollects. "She loved the outdoors, and I learned to love it, too. She also sailed and played tennis. I never played tennis, but I could swim by the time I was three, and was riding horses by the time I reached five."

Summer and the outdoors provided Doll with an escape from the confining atmosphere of the large, creaking house and from her mother's unbending discipline. With her dog and cat, Doll would often spend the entire day outside. She loved to fish, or to simply sit at the edge of Lake Nuangola and daydream about her life as it would someday be. She would stay out until dark, or until called by her mother. When summer waned, a profound sadness engulfed her for it meant a fall and winter inside, with only Ma-Má's comforting presence to soften the routine and to temper her mother's nervous outbursts.

During the school term, Doll was expected to come directly home, sit down and complete all homework. Then she was to do her chores. She would dress for dinner, which was always served at five, and would speak only when spoken to during the meal. At six she was to be in bed. It wasn't until she turned 12 that her bedtime was extended to seven o'clock.

"My mother didn't want me to bring any friends home from school because they would mess up the house. She was very nervous about that."

Doll's only real playmate during the winter months was a black girl, the daughter of their laundress, whom the laundress affectionately called Snowflake. They were allowed to play together for only brief periods, and even those times were infrequent because Snowflake only came to the house with her mother on rare occasions. In the summer, there were a few other children to play with, particularly when Doll and her mother ventured to Lake Nuangola. But in the winter, there were only the occasional meetings with Snowflake. And, of course, there was Ma-Má's huge dressing table with its three mirrored panels in which Doll could see her imaginary friends when they joined her for tea.

"Ma-Má always enjoyed my having tea parties at her dresser," says Candy, "but only if I didn't dress up in her mules. She was always bringing back new mules from Paris, and I loved wearing them when I had my imaginary tea parties. My mother hated me daydreaming like that, though, and got very mad when she caught me at it."

Doll was caught by her mother at many things, and when the leather riding crop was out of reach, or Ma-Má was within protective proximity, Doll was often punished by being locked in a small bedroom on the third floor. Daytime punishment of this type was not nearly as traumatic as when it occurred at night, because her mother often removed all light bulbs from the room prior to remanding Doll to it. Doll would sit in the dark for hours, at times quiet, at times crying and pleading with her mother to unlock the door. Ma-Má lost patience with this form of punishment, too, however, and would release Doll from the room over Jessie's vehement objections.

It became an increasing game of tug-of-war between mother and grandmother, with Doll in the middle. Doll faced each day with the hope that Ma-Má would be home, and her mother away. Jessie's absences were infrequent, however. She was not a social person, preferring to remain at home and sew. She was particularly fond of sewing dolls' clothing, and often chastised Doll for her indifference to dolls. She belonged to the local church, and played cards one evening a week—an evening which, unknown to her, was precious to her daughter.

"My grandmother was Catherine the Great, Katharine Hepburn and Tom Mix (she rode a mean saddle while in her sixties) all rolled up in one to me," says Candy. "I used to stand for what seemed hours and watch her brush her long chestnut hair, and then I'd go to my room and do the same, pretending to be her. I loved her very much, and was in awe of her. She was such an imposing woman, but could turn right around and come up with the most marvelous stunts, usually to my mother's horror."

One "stunt" Ma-Má enjoyed was to flip a dinner plate out the dining-room window to see if she could scale it across the driveway and have it land without breaking.

"Let's open a window and invite the sunshine in," Ma-Má would say to Doll, smiling at the child's knowledge of what was coming.

Out went the plate, a china Frisbee catching the sun as it skimmed over the driveway and slid to a stop unbroken on the soft green grass.

"Me, too, Ma-Má," Doll giggled, reaching for a plate. But her mother was quicker. She raced to the window, slammed it shut and drew the curtains. "What will the neighbors think?" she asked angrily.

"They won't think because they don't think," Ma-Má answered. "They won't because they can't." It was a stock routine between Doll's mother and grandmother, and it invariably caused the mother to stomp off in a rage. Once she'd left the room, Doll and Ma-Má would look at each other and laugh.

"Everything was different when I was with Ma-Má," Candy reflects. "There always seemed to be love and laughter when she was around. When she wasn't, there was anger and nervous outbreaks by my mother. And threats, always threats, that she'd do something bad to me if I made her nervous again. One of her worst threats was that she'd give me away to the orphanage."

The orphanage was on South Franklin Street, across the avenue from one of the houses owned by Ma-Má. It was a three-story red brick building surrounded by a ten-foot iron spike fence.

One day Candy's mother planned to take some fudge to the orphanage, as well as some of the clothes Candy had outgrown. She did this three or four times a year, but on this day she insisted Candy accompany her. Candy was six at the time.

"Why do I have to go?" Candy asked her mother.

"To give you an idea of how it looks in case I have to give you to them," was her mother's reply.

Candy was frightened. But when her mother asked whether she'd said goodbye to her dog, Sandy, and to Tommy, her cat, the child really panicked. She raced upstairs, found the cat and cradled him in her arms on the floor of her bedroom: "Jesus loves me, this I know . . . 'cause the Bible tells me so," she crooned to Tommy, tears streaming down her cheeks.

"Come down here," her mother yelled from the foot of the stairs.

Candy put the cat back in the hatbox in her closet and joined her mother in the downstairs hallway. They took a bus to the orphanage, rang the bell at the gate and were escorted into the building by the superintendent, a fat, greasy woman with straight pencil lines for eyebrows. Candy's mother followed the superintendent into her office, leaving Candy in a large dining room. A girl of ten came in with a pail and mop to clean the floor, and nervously eyed Candy as she went about her chore.

After a few minutes, Candy walked to the large windows that looked out over the rear yard where children were playing. A small girl cried because she'd been hit by the "ball," an old sock with an orange inside it. Candy watched until the girl with the pail and mop asked quietly, "Are you new here?"

"No," Candy replied, avoiding the girl's eyes.

Moments later, her mother and the superintendent entered the dining room. "It's time to go," her mother said.

Candy burst into tears and hugged her mother's silk-clad legs. "I promise to be good," Candy said.

"I'm sorry for this display," her mother told the superintendent. "She's a very nervous child. She takes after me." They left the orphanage, the acrid smell of ammonia from the scrub pail etched into Candy's nostrils, and mind.

"Losing my grandmother was the worst fate that could have befallen me," says Candy as she reflects on the days leading up to Ma-Má's death. "I knew she was dying one day, and I sneaked into her bedroom and sat at her bedside. She'd been very ill, and when I saw her looking so sick, I began to cry."

"Tears are best for washing out embedded eyelashes," said Ma-Má as she took the child's hand. "Besides, Doll, I shall always be close to you. I shall be watching over you just as you, one day, shall watch over those whom you love."

Later, when Ma-Má's death was imminent, she told her granddaughter at her bedside: "Take care of your mother. She needs help, love and affection." Doll brushed Ma-Má's hair in anticipation of a visit by the doctor, and when he arrived she waited outside the bedroom door.

"How is Ma-Má?" Doll asked him when he emerged from the bedroom.

"Just fine," replied the doctor. "Your grandmother will be fine."

Six months later, at age of 65, Ma-Má succumbed to cancer. Doll was 11.

In the late summer of 1936, Jessie Wilcox packed up and moved herself and her daughter back to Atlantic City, where

Doll, now too old to be called that, enrolled in high school.

"I was only five feet tall when we moved to Atlantic City," says Candy, "but I grew eight inches during my four years of high school. My mother said it was the air, and maybe it was. There was a lot of foul air in Wilkes-Barre because of all the coal mining, a lot of tuberculosis. I had diphtheria when I was a child. Atlantic City was a nice place to grow up."

At 16, Candy, then called Jessica in school, decided she wanted to go to college. "I wanted to be a doctor, like my grandmother." But her mother refused to spend money on such frivolity. Without telling her mother, Candy wrote a letter to her father, J. Gordon Wilcox, who had left the auto industry and was working in the sales and publicity department of Paramount Pictures in Chicago. She told him of her plans to attend college and asked him to send her money. Two weeks later she received a package from Chicago. In it was a bank draft for $200 and a large doll. The doll, he said in the accompanying note, was for her sixteenth birthday.

"I knew that even in 1941 two hundred dollars wasn't going to get me to college," says Candy. "My mother cashed the bank draft and used it to pay bills, and I shifted gears and tried to decide what to do after graduation. My mother was adamant about my attending secretarial school, although she had included nurse's training as an option. I did neither, because I made a move that was, I suppose, pivotal in terms of leading me into the modeling field. I entered the Miss Atlantic City contest that year as the Girl Scouts' entry and won."

Although Miss Atlantic City was not an entrant in the Miss America contest held in that city each year, she did act as official hostess at the beauty pageant, and received substantial publicity during the weeklong affair. Sixteen-year-old Candy was thrilled. Her mother was not. She sat silently in the Traymore Hotel as the contestants, led by her daughter, Miss Atlantic City, made a grand sweep of the vast ballroom before such luminaries as the governor of New Jersey; the mayor of Atlantic City; network broadcasters; Jimmy Dorsey and his orchestra, which featured the singers Bob Eberle and Helen O'Connel; modeling czar John Robert Powers; Twentieth Century-Fox fashion commentator Vivyan Donner; and opera singer Conrad Thibault. Thousands packed the ballroom and watched as Candy did her best to walk gracefully in glass slippers several sizes too small for her, which had been placed on her feet by an official "Prince Charming." The booming tones of the Steel Pier's official announcer filled the room as Candy tried to catch her mother's eye and, hopefully, a smile. But her mother sat impassively, eyes straight ahead as the excitement of the moment, the music, the overzealous announcer, the applause, the smiles of the thousand guests in the room swelled to a crescendo that left the young girl dizzy.

At the completion of the grand parade, Candy was swamped with newspaper men and women asking for interviews. A reporter from the *Atlantic City Press Union* asked, somewhat hopefully, whether her unusual manner of walking stemmed from a childhood bout with polio. The public-relations man from the Atlantic City Press Bureau stepped in and tried to establish an orderly system for interviewing his city's reigning queen. Candy looked over the heads of the reporters in search of her mother and spotted her leaving the ballroom. Candy broke away and pushed through clusters of guests until she reached the doors and finally the lobby, where she caught her mother about to depart the hotel.

"Where are you going?" Candy asked as she caught up with her.

"This is the beginning of the end, Jessica," her mother said resolutely. "This is the start of your downfall. Goodnight and goodbye."

With her mother gone, Candy went about her chores as hostess to the Miss America pageant. She was interviewed by all the media, including coast-to-coast network radio. At three the next morning she was accompanied home by her official chaperone. Her mother was awake.

"Hang up your dress because you may wish to wear it again sometime," she told her daughter. "And set your hair."

"Goodnight, mother," Candy said.

Her mother did not respond.

"I hadn't felt that bad since my eleventh birthday," Candy recalls of that night and morning in Atlantic City. "It was all so clean and pure and innocent, but my mother made me feel so dirty."


The eleventh birthday Candy referred to had been celebrated in Wilkes-Barre. It fell on a Saturday that year, which meant there were additional chores for her to do since Pearl did not work on the weekends, and Candy was expected to fill the gap. She came down the back stairs on the morning of her birthday and dusted the dining room, living room and hallways. She knew there would eventually be some celebration of her birthday because she'd seen a wrapped package in the dining room.

Her mother came downstairs at ten and went directly to the kitchen. She called for her daughter to join her there.

"Here," said her mother, handing Candy a scrub brush, a pail and a bar of naphtha soap. "You're old enough to clean a kitchen floor. I want it spotless."

Candy got down on her knees and scrubbed the floor, which was large enough for roller skating. It was dirty with cinders and coal soot, and it took her almost two hours. The job completed, she called her mother in to inspect.

"It looks all right," said her mother, returning quickly to the sitting room where she'd been writing a shopping list. Ten minutes later Candy was summoned to the dining room. Her mother had set the table for breakfast; Candy's gift package was at her place, along with a large gray envelope. They sat at the table and her mother picked up the envelope and handed it to her, saying, "Well, here's your first present of the day."

Candy looked at the envelope. It had been mailed from New York and was addressed to her mother in Wilkes-Barre. Candy opened the envelope and withdrew the hardcover book it contained—a teen-age instructional manual about sex and pregnancy.

"It's for you," her mother said. "Go to your room and read it. If you ever have a baby, I'll kill you!"

Candy stayed in her room until early afternoon and read her gift book. She didn't want to read it, because of what it represented: a threat from her mother. But she was afraid not to read it in case her mother asked questions about its contents.

After lunch, Candy was allowed to open her other gifts. She received a pair of pajamas and two Nancy Drew books. Her birthday cake was maple walnut, with thick, creamy icing.

She was allowed to listen to the radio that night until nine, but pleaded with her mother to be allowed to stay up to see the new year in. Reluctantly, her mother agreed to wake her a few minutes before midnight. She did as she promised, saying to her daughter, "Your birthday is ending, Jessica." Candy got up from bed and went to her window, which looked out over the street in front of the house. Lights were burning brightly in other houses as celebrants poised for the sound of the miner's whistle that would herald midnight. The whistle was used to signify changes of shifts at the mines, but there was no midnight shift on New Year's Eve.

Candy had made confetti from yellow and orange wrapping tissue, and took the brown paper bag filled with it from her closet. She opened the window and looked down the sloping black roof, patched with ice, and at the giant maples and elms that dominated the front lawn, their branches shadowgrams against the snow on the ground.

The whistle blew and Candy leaned out the window and tossed her confetti and banged together two kitchen pans she'd brought to her room after dinner. A neighbor's door opened and people spilled onto the front walk.

"Happy New Year," Candy yelled to them, banging her pans. They looked up, saw her and returned her greeting. Tommy, the cat, slipped past her and onto the roof. Candy watched as he carefully navigated the ice and sniffed the colorful confetti that had stuck to the icy patches.

"Tommy, come back in," she said. "You'll fall." She made coaxing noises and the cat returned to the window and leaped inside. Candy closed the window and slipped beneath the covers on her bed. The cat joined her. She said her prayers. Always, her prayers were long, and included hopes for peace and love for all poor and sad people, and for all four-legged animals.

And *always* her prayers ended with ". . . and please, God, make me a better girl tomorrow so that mother won't be so nervous with me."

# 5

# The First Tape

The marriage between Candy Jones and Long John Nebel moved smoothly through the first five months of 1973. Nebel's all-night show on WMCA prospered, becoming New York's top-rated program in that time slot. This came as no surprise to anyone, for he'd enjoyed the same success on both previous stations, WOR and WNBC. There was a difference, however, in the way he viewed his success on his new station. At WNBC Nebel had become disenchanted with management, particularly after a new managerial team had been brought in to bolster the station's overall sagging ratings. The new bosses decided to try to capture the rock-music market, and began to come down heavily on Nebel to alter his approach to better appeal to that music's audience. He balked, which led to his departure from WNBC.

John Nebel's style had always been free-wheeling. With six hours a night within which to stretch out, he enjoyed a rambling, casual approach that his many listeners had responded favorably to over the years. That isn't to say that he ran a slow, uninspired program. To the contrary, the typical Nebel show was a spark-filled, electric experience. His knack for probing a guest's hidden weaknesses was legendary in broadcasting. Fledgling announcers at broadcasting schools around the country were played tapes of Nebel shows as part of their course study. He was the acknowledged master of the controversial interview, although he credited the man whose show led into his at WMCA, Barry Gray, with being the finest interviewer in radio.

Nebel's guests ran the gamut of interests, and they participated at their peril. Nebel could spot a phony before he ever began questioning him, and it was not unusual for a guest to storm from the studio in a rage over what he considered unfair and overly harsh treatment by the show's host. At times it *was* unfair, although from Nebel's viewpoint anything that contributed to the success of the show was justified. There was a time when Nebel's producer would approach a guest as he or she sat in the waiting room and ask casually, while the guest was signing release forms, whether there were any areas of discussion the guest would prefer to avoid. A hidden microphone carried the answer to Nebel, listening in another room. The moment the red light came on in the studio, the guest could count on that forbidden area of discussion being the basis for Nebel's very first question.

Throughout his career John Nebel stirred controversy. He was hated by many listeners who resented his grating, often vicious handling of guests for whom they felt an affinity, and they railed against his handling of these guests when they called in during open telephone segments of the program. Still, they listened, a faithful flock for whom the Nebel voice was an integral part of their families. Nebel knew his following was solid, and it was for that reason he chose to structure his deal at WMCA along the lines of Barry Gray's arrangement with the station—no salary, but 50 percent of all advertising revenues generated by his show.

Within months, Nebel was making more money than he'd ever made at WNBC or WOR, and his salary at WNBC had been in excess of $100,000 a year. Sponsors were turned away for lack of time to accommodate them. In all, John Nebel's financial base was solid, a satisfying situation for a man who had been happy to earn a dollar or two on the streets of New York in his youth selling orange-juice extractors to whatever crowd he could gather around him.

Candy's financial fortunes were not as solid. She was, by her own admission, a poor businesswoman. Her charm-and-career schools, respected fixtures in the modeling field, were not profitable. Nebel suggested she close the schools and join him on the show. She agreed, and Nebel's attorneys and accountants instituted the long and involved process of phasing out her business activities.

Candy's shifts in mood that had so upset John still occurred, although never with enough regularity or intensity to create an open rift between them. They were both extremely busy and saw little of past friends. According to Nebel, the only real anxiety in their lives at that juncture was the result of Candy's worsening insomnia. She simply could not sleep, despite an increasing need for it. She was living a double shift—days grappling with the myriad of problems in her business, nights as part of her husband's life. She was exhausted, but attempts at sleep resulted in shallow, restless catnaps, no matter what the hour.

On Sunday morning, June 3, 1973, John and Candy returned to their apartment from WMCA. She'd been cohosting the show on a regular basis since May, and was still involved in the phasing out of her own businesses. She tried to sleep that morning but, according to Nebel, just tossed and turned in the double bed in their cramped bedroom. Her face was drawn, and dark circles beneath her eyes caused them to appear sunken. She was near tears as she sat up in bed and told her husband of the effect her fatigue was having upon her. Nebel offered to help.

"How?" asked Candy.

"I'll hypnotize you."

She forced a laugh. "I can't be hypnotized, John."

"Well, let me try. I've never done it before, but I think I can do it. It'll just be to relax you, like meditation."

Although he had never before attempted to induce an hypnotic trance in anyone, Nebel was confident he could accomplish it because of his extensive reading on the subject. But he had apprehensions about putting theory into practice. He knew, of course, that his friends in the medical profession who practiced hypnosis frowned upon anyone dabbling in the science without solid medical grounding. He also knew, however, that unless a hypnotist deliberately used the trance to "accomplish mischief," as his friend, Dr. Herbert Spiegel, psychiatrist and associate professor at Columbia University College of Physicians and Surgeons, prefers to term it, little harm could befall the subject.

The situation of the moment was certainly conducive to successful trance induction. Candy was, and is, a suggestible person, and much of her business failure resulted from this personality trait. She had great faith in her husband, an extremely helpful requisite for anyone practicing hypnosis. Most important, Nebel did not intend to manipulate her while in the trance. He intended only to induce relaxation, the most common benefit from hypnosis, particularly self-hypnosis, and further intended to employ an induction technique called "progressive relaxation." There are as many induction techniques as there are hypnotists (the scientific community prefers to call hypnotists "operators," but the term "hypnotist" will be used throughout this book). Progressive relaxation, in which the hypnotist *suggests* that each part of the body is going into a relaxed state, is a favorite method of lay hypnotists who conduct clinics for smoking and weight control. Physicians seldom use it because of the length of time it takes to induce the trance. Other methods, which will be explained at various stages in this book, are faster and, in general, more effective.

Nebel's only goal, however, was to relax his wife and help her sleep. Although this first session with Candy, and the two that followed shortly thereafter were not taped, Nebel re-created the induction process for me late in 1974, and I taped it. During the first session with Candy, they were both in bed. All lights in the bedroom were out because John wasn't sure whether lights would inhibit the trance. They would not have, and most subsequent sessions were done with at least one light burning in the room. The following is a verbatim transcript of John Nebel's simulated trance induction. My comments appear in brackets.

■

. . . I want you to close your eyes and I want you to think of your forehead and I want you to relax your forehead. . . . You are going into a deep, relaxing natural sleep. . . . [He gently places his fingertips on her forehead, and then on her eyelids. Touching can be used to focus attention on those areas of the body that are being relaxed.] I want you to relax the muscles around your mouth [places his fingertips on her mouth] . . . and now I want you to relax your cheekbones. [It is necessary to touch only the initial body areas. There was no further touching involved.] And now your neck . . . I want you to relax your neck muscles, and then your right shoulder. . . . The feeling of relaxation is traveling down to your elbow, down to your wrist, right down to your fingertips. . . . And now we will do the same thing with your left arm. . . . Relaxed . . . deep, pleasant relaxation. . . . Deeper and deeper . . . You're going into a deep, deep relaxing natural sleep . . . deeper and deeper. . . . And now I want you to relax your abdomen and your hips. . . . Relaxed, relaxed . . . [Nebel commented that Candy shifted in bed to feel more relaxed in her abdominal and pelvic areas.] And now your legs, all the way down to your feet and to your toes, each toe becoming more and more relaxed [Nebel's voice throughout is calm and natural, flat in tone]. . . . And now your whole body is completely relaxed, and I want you to think about floating on a puffy white cloud on a hot summer's day . . . magnificent blue sky . . . the sun beating down on your body. . . . You're resting . . . deeper and deeper . . . drowsier and drowsier and drowsier [these words were said deliberately and were elongated] . . . deep, deep, relaxing natural sleep. . . . And now I'm going to lift your left arm. [Nebel had observed that Candy's breathing had become slow and regular, one sign that a trance state had been entered into. He knew, at least, that a state of relaxation had been achieved. But he wished to test further, and decided to see whether her trance was sufficiently deep for him to suggest limb catalepsy—that is, the hypnotist suggests that the subject's arm, for example, is rigid and cannot be moved without permission of the hypnotist. If a trance has been induced, the subject should accept such a suggestion. Nebel placed his fingers around the wrist of her left arm and raised it above her.] . . . Now that I've lifted your arm, you find that it is becoming rigid and wishes to stay in that raised position. . . . You cannot lower it. . . . It is impossible for you to lower your arm . . . it is rigid and will stay in its present position. . . . I'm going to count from three down to one, and when I reach one, you will find it impossible to put your arm down. . . . Three . . . you're going deeper and deeper into a relaxed natural sleep . . . deeper and deeper. . . . Two . . . your arm is becoming more and more rigid . . . deeper and deeper. . . . One. . . . Put your arm down. [Nebel could feel the muscles tighten in Candy's arm as she exerted pressure to lower it. It remained above her, however.] . . . I'm now going to allow you to lower your arm . . . in fact, your arm is now so relaxed it is impossible for you to hold it above you. . . . Relaxed . . . deep, deep relaxation . . . You cannot hold your arm above you. [Candy's arm came down, Nebel lifted it, but it simply fell to the bed each time he took his hand from it.] . . . And now you have reached a state of deep, relaxing, natural sleep. . . . You are sound asleep; and when you awaken, your body will be completely relaxed . . . no tension . . . no problems . . . just deep, relaxing, natural sleep . . . your body floating on a white cloud in the blue sky, the warmth of the sun beating down on you . . . deeper and deeper . . . and when you awaken, you will be refreshed, relaxed and rejuvenated. . . . [Nebel allowed her to remain in the trance and to eventually drift into a natural sleep state.]

■

This first attempt at hypnosis by John Nebel was an unqualified success, and he was heady with satisfaction. He'd succeeded in helping Candy achieve her first full night's sleep in months, and had proven he was capable of inducing a trance. He didn't give any thought to the fact that, despite her assertion that she couldn't be hypnotized, she'd proved to be a good subject. Estimates vary, but it is commonly held that approximately 70 percent of the population is capable of entering the trance state, in varying depths.

Inducing only a relaxed, natural sleep, as did Nebel in his experiment with Candy, is one of the reasons a hypnotic subject needn't fear what would occur should the hypnotist disappear, or die following trance induction, a common fear of neophyte subjects. In almost all cases the subject will simply pass from the hypnotic trance into the natural sleep mode, and will awaken a normal number of hours later—shocked, perhaps, at seeing a dead hypnotist at his feet, but no worse for the trance experience.

Had John Nebel been prudent in hypnotizing Candy? He'd had no formal training, either in hypnosis or, more important, in psychology and psychiatry. He did not, of course, intend to delve into such weighty waters. His original goal was only to encourage general relaxation and, he hoped, sleep.

But this well-intentioned use of hypnosis by John Nebel was soon to turn into a much more profound and tricky situation. Candy began to spontaneously age-regress during subsequent sessions. This provocative phenomenon of hypnosis, which can occur only in those subjects with an extremely high trance capacity, is best left to the professionals. That is not to say that a nonprofessional such as John Nebel is incapable of fostering age regression in a good subject. To be more correct, it is the subject who fosters the regression to times and places in the past, the nonprofessional hypnotist is often nothing more than an interested bystander while the subject "does his or her thing." Such was the case with the age regressions experienced by Candy and recorded by John over the many months of their adventure with hypnosis.

In a medical setting, in which a physician uses age regression as part of his treatment strategy, there is a more structured approach, one in which the physician, usually a psychiatrist, applies very specific techniques and principles in order to direct the patient's flow of regression in an attempt to reach repressed memories considered vital by the psychiatrist.

I asked Dr. Herbert Spiegel, one of the nation's leading experts in hypnosis and age regression, and who wrote the foreword to this book, whether a trained professional in hypnosis, particularly a psychiatrist, might have been more effective in retrieving the information from Candy that forms the core of the book.

"Probably," responded Spiegel. "I would prefer to have seen a professional deal with Candy, someone detached from the situation and who perhaps would have been more selective in following and directing the regressions. There might have been less inadvertent cues given by the hypnotist in a more detached, structured exploration. Also, a professional has a repertory of corrective actions should the subject experience an abreaction, which is an unexpected emotional outburst. This is the most compelling reason why highly hypnotizable people need protection from nonprofessional intervention."

But Spiegel went on to comment about the time and money factors which would have virtually ruled out the use of a professional throughout the many months of hypnotic sessions with Candy. There now exist over 200 hours of tape taken during her age regressions. "I suppose you could view it as a trade-off of sorts," says Spiegel. "John's intense interest and patience in pursuing this project was necessary if such an abundance of material was to be gained. He was with Candy day and night, an impossible task for any outsider."

It was suggested by the publisher during the recent prepublication phase of this project that an outside psychiatrist attempt to retrieve some of the material recorded by John Nebel during Candy's age regressions. Dr. Spiegel was asked about the potential value of such an experiment.

"To do it properly at this stage would take exorbitant amounts of time and money," was Spiegel's response. "It would have to be done over a prolonged period of time, and may or may not be fruitful. And to do a brief sampling regression with Candy would prove nothing. Any outside professional hypnotist would probably recover much the same material, valid and invalid, that has already come out and been recorded by John."

There is, of course, a question of propriety regarding John's continuing use of hypnosis with Candy, particularly after the sessions began to result in her age regressions.

"Let me explain it this way," comments Dr. Speigel. "If someone does an appendectomy on a kitchen table and it works, you have to recognize that it worked. But such an experience should not become the model for all appendectomies. That John Nebel was able to gather so much recorded information during Candy's regressions is not, and should not become the model for similar adventures with others."

Spiegal's final comments regarding the value of bringing in an outside psychiatrist reflect, to some extent, his own extensive experience as a consultant to various law enforcement agencies, including the FBI. He recently went to Ann Arbor, Michigan, where he hypnotized some of the surviving patients in the Michigan Veterans' Administration hospital in which eleven patients had died of respiratory arrests. It was suspected that someone on the hospital staff had injected the dead patients with Pavulon, a variant of the lethal South American plant toxin, Curare. Dr. Spiegel hypnotized one patient who, while in the trance state, recalled events in the ward that were not remembered during prior questioning of him in the nontrance state. Based upon this information, the FBI was able to expand the scope of its investigation and, eventually, two suspects were named, both nurses.*

"The point is," says Spiegel, "that information recovered through the use of hypnosis is not, in itself, legally valid. What it is, however, is a further broadening of potential areas in which to seek external validation. In the Michigan VA hospital case, it gave the FBI more material with which to work. The incredible amount of material recorded by John Nebel while Candy was in the hypnotic mode should be viewed in the same way. The tapes contain a rich field from which to draw leads for the continuing investigation of her past. I'm pleased that such investigation is taking place."

I asked Dr. Spiegel whether he was surprised that a non-professional such as John Nebel could have gained so much material from Candy while she was under hypnosis.

"Not at all," he replied. "Most trance states, especially in someone with Candy's demonstrated high-trance capacity, oc-cur spontaneouly anyway. Lovers go into a trance; it's not termed that because there wasn't a third party around to label the experience. One of the biggest myths about hypnosis is that all the power rests within the hypnotist. That's not true. The trance capacity is carried through life by the subject. Candy is one of perhaps five percent of the population with an extremely heightened capacity for trance. In fact, when dealing in a thera-peutic situation with such patients, the problem is not one of inducing trance, but of teaching the patient how to avoid going into spontaneous trances in their daily life."

Nebel repeated the experience the following morning after they'd returned from WMCA, and again after a few days. It was on this third attempt that he encountered something more than simple progressive relaxation. During this third session, Candy began talking in a strange voice, not the harsh, grating voice of the "other person" that had jarred Nebel on his wedding night and on subsequent occasions, but that of a child. She engaged in an imaginary dialogue with an unnamed person, and Nebel, acting on instinct, slipped into the verbal role of that other person.

The conversation between them lasted only a few minutes; but when it was over and Candy was sleeping soundly, Nebel

*As reported in the March 22, 1976 issue of *Time*.

went to the living room, lighted a cigarette and pulled out one of his many books on hypnosis. Turning to a chapter on age regression, he began to read. He didn't know whether what had just happened in their bedroom was significant or not, but he did know that his wife had, for a few moments, moved backward in time. He was interested and wanted to learn more in case it should happen again.

It did. Candy's next regression to childhood occurred on June 15, 1973. By that time a series of nonchildhood regressions far more dramatic and bizarre had occurred, prompting Nebel to purchase, from his friend Irving Miller of Bryce Audio, a Sony TC-142 cassette tape recorder. Nebel chose this particular machine because, besides its versatile features, it was small enough to fit into the headboard of their bed. He began recording selected hypnotic sessions, one of which was the June 15 regression to childhood.

It took place at approximately 8 A.M. They'd done the show, and Candy asked John to help her relax. She still didn't believe she was being hypnotized, preferring to chalk up her recent successful attempts at sleep to "just being relaxed." Her reaction is common: Many people undergo hypnosis and later refuse to believe they were hypnotized. These people will do almost anything suggested by the hypnotist and, after being wakened, insist they only did what they did to please the hypnotist. While that may be true, it points up exactly what hypnosis is—a level of heightened concentration and suggestibility. It is no more mysterious than that, and those who expect bizarre or tangible evidence of having been in a trance will forever be disappointed. And they will continue to "please the hypnotist."

On that Friday morning Nebel again put Candy into a relaxed state, a trance, and moments later, she began to speak in the little girl's voice he'd heard in the earlier session. He reached up, turned on the recorder and held the microphone close to her.

■

JOHN: Where are you now?
CANDY: I don't know where to go.
JOHN: Where do you want to go today?
CANDY: Fishing.

JOHN: Where do you think you'll go fishing?

CANDY: Down by the swamp.

JOHN: Who'll go with you?

CANDY: Tommy.

JOHN: Who's Tommy?

CANDY: Tommy's my cat. *(She laughs.)* You better watch him, he'll eat the fish.

JOHN: Does Tommy like fish?

CANDY: *(giggling)* Not really.

JOHN: He just likes to play with them.

CANDY: I have to get some worms. . . . I can't take them in the house.

JOHN: Do you dig them up yourself.

CANDY: Yes. *(whispers, and sounds pleased)* I have some in my bedroom.

JOHN: *(laughing along with her)* Where do you have them in the bedroom?

CANDY: *(still delighted with her secret)* Under the bed.

■

Nebel played along with her and they laughed together in whispers. It should be pointed out that the dialogue in this scene, as well as in all other scenes taken from hypnotic-session tapes, does not flow as it might appear in the reading. It is very natural dialogue, and as such, is punctuated by long pauses, sometimes as a natural result of what is being said, and sometimes because Nebel has trouble in pushing the conversation forward, or in grasping who and where he is in a given situation.

■

CANDY: Ssssssssssh, don't tell her *(meaning her mother. Nebel promises he won't. He asks her what time of year it is).*

CANDY: July.

JOHN: That's a lovely month.

CANDY: *(laughs like a child; then, following a long pause, complains of having hit her head on the boat. It evidently was a canoe that was upside down on the shore, and she'd been underneath it.)*

JOHN: Do you ever pray?

CANDY: Sure.

JOHN: Does God answer your prayers?

CANDY: I never heard [him].

JOHN: Why don't you try a little prayer to ask God to stop the
    pain in your head?
CANDY: *(after a very long time, during which Nebel tries to get her to make
    up a prayer)* Dear God . . . ah . . . *(she laughs)* make the pain
    go away . . . please!

■

Candy then suggests that her grandmother, Ma-Má, will get
rid of the pain for her. She tells John, whose identity is unknown
in this session, that everyone is asleep in the house and that it
is 6 A.M. She mentions that she has an Airedale, and John says
it's the same kind of dog Little Orphan Annie has. She laughs
at that. He then asks her what she is wearing.

■

CANDY: My ducks, no shoes.
JOHN: What's your blouse like?
CANDY: It's red. I wore it yesterday.

■

Nebel asks her what she wants for her birthday, but she only
laughs. He then suggests that God has answered her prayer and
that her headache is gone. She reluctantly agrees, and the session is over. It had lasted seven minutes, and Candy simply
drifted into natural sleep.

This first recorded example of Candy regressing to an earlier
age was a pleasant experience, for both of them. John played the
tape for Candy, and hearing it caused her to consciously recall
having hit her head on a canoe one morning when she was a little
girl.

"You regressed yourself," he told her. "That sometimes happens under hypnosis."

Candy laughed. "It was just a dream. I wasn't hypnotized. I
*can't* be hypnotized."

John laughed, too, and placed another blank cassette in the
machine.

Hundreds of hours later, he would not be so liberal in his use
of cassettes. Nor would he look forward with such anticipation
to future regressions, for he soon discovered that there was
more to his wife's former life than Airedales, worms and canoes.

# 6

# Conover('s) Girl

Among the judges at the June 1941 Miss Atlantic City contest won by 16-year-old Jessica Wilcox was John Robert Powers, the famous model agent. Following her crowning, she paid her respects to the three-judge panel, including Powers. "You'll be hearing from me," he told her.

In September of that year young Jessica received a telegram from Powers. It read: Would like to meet with you in my office to discuss possibility of a Chesterfield ad.

Candy's mother did not respond favorably to Powers's telegram, but agreed to stop off in New York with her daughter on their way to Boston where, over Candy's objections, she intended to enroll her in the Katherine Gibbs secretarial school. Mrs. Wilcox decided to make the New York stopover a two-week holiday, and on the second day in Manhattan, Candy, still known as Jessica Wilcox, visited John Robert Powers's office. After having her walk around the room for him, and after instructing her to sit in a chair with her back to him and then turn her head to face him, he said, "You have wrinkles in your neck."

"I'm sorry," she replied.

Powers then launched into a sell for his school. "Many contest winners come to New York and use their contest winnings to take advantage of the training I offer," he said.

Candy told him that her winnings from the Miss Atlantic City contest included a wardrobe, part of which she was wearing, and $20, 16 of which were tucked in her bra. Powers sadly shook his head, and Candy anticipated the bad news.

"What about the Chesterfield ad?" Candy asked.

"I've already booked a model for that."

Candy displayed spunk for a 16-year-old in suggesting she might call the Miss Atlantic City people and inform them of the game Powers seemed to be playing. Her mild threat worked, because Powers picked up his phone and instructed his secretary to allow Candy to sit in the models' waiting room for the next two weeks in case an order came in for "her type." She thanked him profusely and took her place alongside six other models in the bullpen.

That two-week New York holiday turned into gold for Jessica Wilcox, although John Robert Powers had nothing to do with her success. Instead, it was Powers's biggest competitor, Harry Conover, who launched Jessica Wilcox on a career that was to take her to the peak of the modeling field.

She went to Conover's offices at the end of her second week in New York, after having achieved only two modeling assignments through Powers, each paying five dollars. Her mother, furious at Jessica's vehement refusals to go to Boston and the Katherine Gibbs School, resigned herself to the inevitable decadence of her only daughter.

The Conover offices were located on the eighth floor at 52 Vanderbilt Avenue, and reflected their founder's expensive tastes. Conover, a handsome and meticulous man with carefully styled dark hair and dazzling green eyes, had used his stature as New York's leading male model, as well as an inherent, astute public-relations sense, to build his agency into a worthy rival to the Powers empire. His offices were lavishly decorated, furnished with valuable French Provincial furniture, and he moved through it all with the assurance of a man born to this environment. But perhaps the most memorable aspect of Harry Conover's outward appearance was his hands—perfect hands, model's hands, displayed through gesticulation as a buxom woman might display her breasts while concealing the act of display.

"I didn't go to the Conover agency looking for a job," Candy recalls. "I'd promised a girl in Atlantic City that I'd look up her sister while in New York. Her sister was a model and worked out of the Conover office."

The model's name was Jewel Lindsay, and she was out on an assignment when Jessica arrived. The receptionist suggested she wait in the models' reception room. Twice, the receptionist, a model herself, asked Jessica whether *she* wouldn't like to model. "You could, you know." Jessica was confused. She felt committed to Powers, but responded to the more positive atmosphere at Conover. Her confusion disappeared an hour later, however, when a young photographer named Eliot Clarke came in. After studying Jessica for what seemed an eternity, he disappeared into the inner offices. A few moments later Jessica was asked to go in and meet Mr. Conover.

"Hello, I'm Jessica Wilcox," she said, extending her hand. Conover remained seated behind his desk.

"You're . . . Johnson," he said. "Candy Johnson, I think."

"Candy Johnson?"

"Yes, and your rate is five dollars an hour. The photographer who was just here wants a girl of your type."

That was all it took. Conover wrote a letter to Powers informing him that his client would from that moment forward work for the Conover agency, and the buildup began in earnest. Conover built an entire image around the name Candy. Her new wardrobe and accessories were designed to incorporate a candy-stripe design. There were matchbook covers, earrings and even a bicycle in the red-and-white-stripe motif. Conover ordered 10,000 steel-engraved business cards in red and white which said—*Candy Jones Was Here.* (Candy Johnson became Candy Jones because she couldn't remember the name Johnson and kept referring to herself as Jones, which Conover finally accepted.) The cards were left all over town, in cabs, restaurants and on receptionists' desks. Warner Brothers fell for the publicity and signed her to a contract, despite their reservations about what they considered her excessive height. She took acting and voice lessons, and soon joined the New York celebrity crowd at openings and parties. Her natural, wholesome tanned beauty began appearing with regularity on magazine covers and in full-color ads for national products. One such ad, for the Borden Company, was photographed by a young fledgling photographer named Jack Knebel, later to become Long John Nebel of radio fame and Candy's husband. She was voted Model of the Year in 1943 because, according to Loretta Young, one of the judges, "You looked like a real girl with a sunburned face, not at all like a model." All in all, things were good professionally.

They were not so good personally. Candy's mother moved to New York and they shared an apartment on the Upper East Side. Her mother's nerves, so controlling in Candy's childhood, continued to dominate her existence as a young adult. She was incapable, even with maturity, of fighting her mother's domination, and she chose instead to run from it. At the time, 1944, the avenue of escape she chose, a USO tour of the Southwest Pacific to entertain war-weary GIs, did not represent escape to her. It is only in recent years that she has realized in retrospect what her true motivations were, particularly her decision to extend her six-month tour to almost eighteen months. She traveled to the Pacific war zone in a show especially written for her, *Cover Girls Abroad,* and was listed as Captain Candy Jones until an altercation with a general resulted in a demotion to lieutenant.

She did not travel to the Pacific as a stranger to the troops. In addition to the ubiquitous polka-dot-bikini pinup, another photograph of Candy in a floor-length gown made of parachute nylon was equally popular, perhaps receiving greater barracks exposure because the chaplains preferred its relative modesty to the bathing-suit shot. She was also the model used in the official recruiting posters for the WACS and the WAVES.

"I was very comfortable performing in the show," says Candy. "I'd just finished eight months on Broadway in Mike Todd's show, *Mexican Hayride,* and didn't mind the rigors of a hectic show-business schedule. We broke in the show at Fort Dix, New Jersey; Cherry Point, North Carolina; Fort Benning, Georgia; and in a number of veterans' hospitals. It was like breaking in a Broadway show in Boston and Philadelphia. For us, Broadway would be New Caledonia, New Guinea, Leyte and the Philippines. We had to be good because after every performance the special-services officers filed a report with the army and with the USO—theater critics in khaki."

Candy's adventures in the South Pacific during World War II are fascinating, and provide a substantial portion of the subject matter for one of eleven books written by her, the one titled *More than Beauty,* published by Harper and Row in 1970. She loved the experience, and basked in the freedom of being away from the New York apartment and the Conover agency. She met the challenges of performing in an alien climate and of surviving away from the comforts of the States. In fact, she enjoyed the hardships and resulting need to live by her wits on a day-to-day basis.

But there was little she could do to fight the combination of ailments that suddenly attacked her in April 1945 in Morotai. She'd enjoyed a quart of milk flown in from Australia by an army air corps pilot, the first fresh milk she'd tasted since leaving the States. Unfortunately it was not pasteurized, and she developed a severe case of undulant fever. At the same time she contracted malaria, despite her daily intake of Atabrine pills. Those two ailments were enough to convince her special-services officer, Bill Talman, who later appeared as the D. A. in the Perry Mason TV series, to put her into a field hospital in the Philippines. Two days after checking into the facility and enjoying what she assumed were clean sheets, she developed a contagious fungus, commonly referred to in that area of war as "jungle rot." Within a week, her hair had begun to come out in patches. Coupled with a greenish-yellow complexion, the loss of hair was not heartening to a woman who made her living as a model. A nurse finished the job by shaving Candy's head, and medics worked to rid her of the malaria and undulant fever.

Candy became friends with a number of medics, including an officer we will call Gilbert Jensen, who gave her a picture of himself and wrote his military APO address on the back in the hope she would write him. Within six weeks she was feeling well enough to travel, and accepted the invitation of a staff general to attend a theater opening in Manila. She'd made some unofficial trips to that city after MacArthur had won it back and released the prisoners of war from Santo Tomas in February 1945, and she eagerly accepted the general's invitation.

She remained in the Southwest Pacific until August 1945, then, with great ambivalence, boarded the *Charles H. Muir* and sailed home via the Panama Canal. It was another eight months before her hair and skin were sufficiently restored to face a close-up camera. In the meantime she accepted a role in a Broadway musical, *Polonaise,* based upon the life of Chopin. In the show she wore a wig to cover her wartime wounds, and heavy theatrical makeup to shield from the public the hue of malaria. And on July 4, 1946, she married her boss, Harry Conover.

It was not a marriage made in heaven.

Two thousand people attended the wedding of Harry Conover and Candy Jones. It was held in a cathedral in Hamilton, Ontario, and Candy's wedding rings were red, white and blue. Immediately after the nuptials the couple traveled across town to judge the Miss Canada contest. Canada was celebrating 100 years of progress.

That evening, Candy put her mother on a plane for Niagara Falls where Mrs. Wilcox had wished her daughter to spend her honeymoon. Instead, Candy and Harry stayed in Hamilton, while Mrs. Wilcox spent her daughter's honeymoon in America's traditional honeymoon haven.

The newlyweds occupied the presidential suite in Hamilton's finest hotel. It was a warm, listless night, and as Candy sat in the window and listened to the sounds of a carnival band as it performed in a park across the street, fireworks from the park snapped through the humid air and caused her to wince. Her husband was asleep. He had told her he loved her during a telephone conversation prior to the wedding.

"Do you love me now?" she'd asked him that afternoon as they drove from the beauty pageant to their hotel.

"As much as I can," he answered. "But don't pin me down. Nothing is forever. I don't like to be tied down."

Candy stayed awake the entire night. They flew to New York the next morning and moved into his apartment.

"We consummated the marriage sometime between the wedding day and Christmas," Candy says. "It didn't matter. At first I wanted to be held and caressed. Harry didn't like that, and I soon didn't care one way or the other."

Candy Jones was a disappointment to Harry Conover. For one thing, he disliked her relatively large bosom, preferring more boyish women: "Your large bosom is revolting," he told her.

For another, she was a virgin: "I don't want to break in a virgin," he proclaimed.

Six months after their marriage, Candy Jones opened her own offices next door at 52 Vanderbilt Avenue. She'd left the Conover agency because some of the other models began to complain that she was receiving favored treatment from her husband. When John Powers heard of her move, he invited her to work for him; but though she wanted to accept his offer, she felt it would be disloyal to Harry. Instead, she continued to serve those clients for whom she'd worked as a model, and also developed new business for her enterprise. Her most impressive new account was Colgate-Palmolive, but Harry wanted the prestige of that account for his agency. Candy serviced the account, but all billings went through the Conover group. The same arrangement held for other prestigious accounts that followed.

Three sons were born during the 13 years of their marriage —Harry, Cary and Chris. Two subsequent pregnancies were aborted, on Harry Conover's insistence. Oddly enough, Harry had also insisted that Candy pay all the medical bills for the birth of her three sons herself, from her own earnings.

As the marriage declined from the low point from which it had started, Harry spent less time at home. When he *was* there, he spent hours in the bathroom, temper flaring if anyone questioned him about this habit. Most nights he was "out with the boys."

"I didn't realize that Harry Conover was bisexual until we'd been married twelve years," says Candy. "That may sound naïve, and perhaps it was, but once our relationship became one of simply sharing living space, I didn't much care that he almost never made sexual advance toward me. In fact, I was relieved, thankful. The only time he came into my bedroom with those intentions was after he'd been drinking heavily."

Candy's mother was aware that all was not well in her daughter's marriage, but assigned the wrong reason to it: She constantly told Candy that Harry was running around with glamorous women. It was easy to come to this conclusion. Conover was a charming gentleman and enjoyed being in the company of beautiful females. His manners were exquisite, and he had an infectious laugh and keen wit, attributes that had attracted Candy to him in the first place—that, and a desperate need for approval from a man of Conover's stature. She viewed him as a father, and when he proposed shortly following a divorce, Candy was flattered, thrilled and somewhat dazzled.

But Conover's real pleasure in life came from the ego-boosting attention of his many male friends. He spent entire nights on the telephone, and his monthly restaurant bills often ran as high as a thousand dollars. He entertained anyone who came close to him, including waitresses, bartenders and hat-check girls. He adored attention, often at the expense of his wife. Moreover, on more than one occasion according to Candy, he smuggled male friends into his bedroom and hid them in the closet while he made sexual overtures to Candy.

"I detested our marriage," says Candy, "but I adored the three beautiful, loving sons that resulted from it. They became my life, and I didn't care whether Harry Conover even existed."

On May 18, 1958, Conover disappeared.

"I did all the usual things a wife would do when her husband has disappeared," says Candy. "I checked the hospitals and the morgues, and eventually reported him missing to the missing person's bureau of the New York City Police Department. I didn't hear a word from him until August."

Conover's disappearance was news in New York, once the word got out. Candy isn't sure where he initially went to so effectively vanish, but he eventually took a suite in the Plaza Hotel. The suite was the scene of nightly parties, and included two teen-age models who worked for Candy. Conover had always enjoyed young girls, and Candy sensed it (she was only 21 when they'd married). But discovering that two teen-age models with whom she'd so diligently worked were engaged in raucous parties hosted by her husband was a bitter blow. To add insult to her injury, Conover sent a friend to his offices over a weekend and cleaned out all the furniture, which he used to furnish an expensive East Side apartment where he continued to live the high life.

But as painful as the blows to her heart might have been, it was the series of financial blows to the head that drew the most blood. Conover had wiped out their joint bank accounts, including a savings account in which $125,000 of Colgate-Palmolive fees had been deposited. Candy didn't know this until Conover's departure; she hadn't made a withdrawal from that account in

13 years of marriage, and hadn't even checked the account's balance during that time. Instead of seeking professional help immediately (the accountants and lawyers for their businesses were Conover confidants), she made a series of unilateral decisions that proved disastrous. She willingly assumed all debts of the Conover agency out of an admirable, albeit misguided, sense of duty, and even signed a new lease on his offices, which came due shortly after his departure. When she did finally get around to checking her resources, she discovered she didn't have any. The joint savings account in which the Colgate-Palmolive money had been deposited held a grand total of $36.

Conover visited his offices only once again, and that visit came as a shock to Candy. She was conferring in the office with three attorneys, two of whom were counsel to the business, the other retained by Candy for her personal legal problems, when the door opened and Conover walked in, as confident and well dressed as ever. It was the first time Candy had set eyes on him in slightly over a year. His timing, usually flawless, was slightly off that day, however. At the very moment of his arrival, Candy and the attorneys had been discussing plans to sue for divorce on the basis of abandonment. There would also be legal judgments brought against Conover for the Colgate-Palmolive money, and for back alimony and child support.

Those lawsuits made headlines in New York, and the legal battle was long and bitter. The three boys, all in private schools, were kept out of the fray as much as possible. Finally, the courts handed down their various rulings, and Harry Conover was sent to Hart Island for a prison sentence of two years. It was pay or go to jail, and he'd spent every cent he'd taken with him.

The marriage had been dissolved, and resolved; the emotional war was over, the battlefield cleared for whatever would come next.

"I was relieved to settle it," Candy says. "But then I faced the ultimate truth about my situation. I was not only broke, I owed what seemed like everybody in town for Harry's other debts, and my own. My sons' tuitions were big. I had my mother to support. I had a business that needed bailing out if it was to have a chance to grow in the future. I really didn't know what to do. I hated to admit it but I was afraid and desperate."

# 7

## The Setup

Candy continued to run her school, and the remains of the Conover agency, from the seperate Conover offices at 52 Vanderbilt Avenue. "There wasn't much progress," she says, "just a daily finger-in-the-dike operation."

The offices occupied most of the eighth floor. The school—actually a series of individual rooms, 807 through 812, for group makeup, private makeup, consultation, drama lessons (France Nuyen, Julia Meade, Leslie Parrish, Joyce Bulifante and Sandra Dee were among her students), hair-styling, closed-circuit television (hers was the first agency to use this technique) and wardrobe storage. Candy spent most of her time in room 808, a huge office across from the office that was leased to the former heavyweight champion of the world, Gene Tunney. According to Candy, Tunney was a very private man, and all the years they spent across the hall from each other resulted in little more than casual pleasantries. Tunney did not seem to be conducting a business from the office, and Candy surmised that he used it as a convenient location from which to handle his personal investments.

Unlike Candy, who conducted classes for her students on Tuesday and Thursday nights, Tunney seldom spent evenings in his office. She knew when he arrived and departed because she kept the door to her office open when she was there, day and night. Tunney's office door, like all the others in the building, had two large panes of thick, opaque, waffled glass, through which indistinguishable shadow figures could be seen. Candy often saw Tunney move within his office, or at least a silhouette large enough to have belonged to his bulky fighter's frame.

One Tuesday night, at about 7:30, Candy was sitting in her office when she noticed a middle-aged woman approach Tunney's door. The woman was dressed like any of the cleaning women in Manhattan office buildings, including those at 52 Vanderbilt: housedress, apron and cardigan sweater. Candy knew them all, but this woman, of average height and weight and with short brown hair, was an unfamiliar face. Candy's curiosity was not unduly piqued, however, even when the woman began going through a series of keys in an attempt to open the door. All the other cleaning women had a single master key attached to a rope around their waists. The woman eventually found the right key and entered the office, closing the door behind her. Candy waited for the lights to go on. They didn't. There was an erratic flash of light which Candy assumed was the beam of a flashlight. She was faced with the decision we all face in such a situation—do we interfere and perhaps be made to look foolish? A student interrupted Candy's thoughts. When she returned her attention to Tunney's office, the woman was closing the door behind her and heading up the hall. Candy never gave it another thought—until she heard through the building grapevine the following afternoon that Gene Tunney's office had been burglarized.

"Did they take much?" she asked him in the hallway.

"No. Some stamps, petty cash, nothing important," Tunney replied.

Candy told him about the strange cleaning woman, and he said he would relay that information to the police. She also told the building superintendent about the woman, but didn't hear from anyone, including the police.

Two nights later, Thursday, she was sitting in her office when a young couple approached Tunney's door and stopped in front of it. The young man took out keys and began trying them in the lock. Candy went into the hallway and approached them.

"We're supposed to meet Mr. Tunney here," the young man said.

"He's not in," Candy replied. "I saw him leave hours ago."

The young girl appeared flustered and urged the young man to leave by pushing him in the direction of the elevators. Candy watched them get on an elevator, then she returned to her office. She mentioned the couple to Tunney the next day.

"Oh, really?" was his response.

A week later, while returning to her offices from a morning meeting across town, Candy was stopped in front of her building by an old friend from the South Pacific, a retired army general. She'd run into him around Manhattan a few times before and he was never, as she puts it, "overly friendly toward me." They entered the building together and took the elevator to the eighth floor, where the general mentioned he was having lunch with Gene Tunney. Candy took him into her office and showed him around. They then crossed the hall and said hello to Tunney who, Candy recollects, seemed quite surprised that she knew the general. The men left for lunch, and Candy went about the afternoon's business.

She was visited in her offices within a few days by a young man who introduced himself as an FBI agent. The identification he offered confirmed this fact. She recalls only his first name—Ted.

He asked her about the burglary of Gene Tunney's office, and Candy told him what she had told Tunney and the superintendent. He listened dutifully, but after hearing what she had to say, he dropped the subject. Instead, he commented about a microphone that was sitting on a window ledge.

"It's a very good microphone," Candy told him. "I bought it from Allen Funt." Funt had produced "Candid Microphone," the audio forerunner of his television version, "Candid Camera." Funt was in the process of buying new tape equipment and had sold Candy two of his old machines, both excellent recorders. He included in the sale two microphones, one of which was being admired by the FBI man.

"What do you use it for?" he asked.

"For training my models. If they don't develop pleasing speech, they can lose lots of assignments."

The FBI man went to the window and picked up the microphone. "This may seem a silly request," he said, "but would you allow me to borrow this microphone?"

"Why?"

He explained that he was involved in a long-term surveillance on West 57th Street and had not been able to procure that specific type of microphone which, he claimed, was of a quality necessary to do the job right. Candy told him he could borrow it, even after he warned her that he might need it for as long as two months. She had others she could use during that time, and, frankly, she found the idea of having one of her microphones used by the FBI in an official case intriguing and satisfying. The FBI man thanked her and departed with the microphone.

About a month later, he returned with it. There was another young man with him, who was introduced to Candy as also being with the Bureau. The three of them sat and chatted for a half-hour before "Ted" made another request of her.

"Would you allow us to have some mail delivered here?" he asked. "Would that upset you?"

Candy asked what he meant.

"We need a location in which certain letters could be delivered to us. You receive lots of mail every day, don't you?"

Candy agreed that there was always a heavy volume of mail having to do with the business, as well as mail sent to the models in care of the agency.

The FBI man explained further. There would be letters addressed to fictitious names in care of the agency, and once a month a man would stop by and ask for mail addressed to those names. All Candy had to do was give him the letters. In addition, there might be mail from Europe addressed to *her,* or to a designated fictitious man's name. In that case she was to call a number they would give her and report the arrival of such mail.

"I'd be happy to help," said Candy.

Gene Tunney moved from his office two weeks later and took space at 200 Park Avenue, but the retired army general kept in touch with Candy during the period of time her offices were being utilized as a mail drop, almost a year. He began inviting her to cocktail parties hosted by him and his wife, and she received a Christmas card from him that year for the first time.

In the late summer of 1960 Candy received a letter at her

apartment at 1199 Park Avenue. It was from "Ted" and was written on plain white typing paper. All it said was that she should expect a call within a few days.

The call came to her apartment two days later. It was the general. She said she couldn't speak with him at the moment. Her mother was in the room, and Candy somehow knew without benefit of instructions that whatever the phone call was about should remain secret between her and her caller.

The general called her office the next day. "I understand you're taking a trip," he said. He was referring to plans Candy had for the week before Thanksgiving. She was going to Denver to speak to the Tuesday Night Supper Club on the one evening a year the all-male club's members were allowed to bring female companions to the dinner, and then on to San Francisco where she was to be the commentator at a fashion show jointly sponsored by three of San Francisco's leading department stores.

"Since you're going to California anyway, would you mind carrying a letter to be delivered to someone out there?"

"What letter? Are you sending it?"

"It's a letter for a government agency, Candy. All you'd have to do is deliver it to a man who'll call you at your hotel. You're staying at the St. Francis, right?"

"That's right."

"Will you do it?"

"Yes, I'll do it. How will I get the letter?"

"It will be delivered to you. By the way, I think you'll enjoy seeing the man in California. I believe you know him."

"What's his name?"

"Mr. Jensen."

"I don't know any Mr. Jensen."

"Well, maybe not. Thank you, Candy."

The letter arrived in a large envelope at her offices three days before she was to depart on her trip. Attached to a smaller envelope inside the larger one was a note instructing her to take the letter with her and wait for a call at the hotel. It was signed "Ted."

Her appearance in Denver went smoothly, and she flew on to San Francisco where she conferred with the fashion coordinators from the three stores. On the third day, which, according to the best information I've been able to piece together, was

Wednesday, November 16, 1960, Candy received her call at the St. Francis.

"Candy, this is Gil Jensen," the caller said. Candy racked her brain for some link to the name but came up empty. "Remember me from the Philippines? I was a medic there."

"Oh, *Doctor* Jensen! Of course." They chatted for a few minutes before Candy asked him if he was the one to whom she was to deliver the letter.

"We can talk about that over dinner," he said.

They dined at the Mark Hopkins Hotel. Jensen's physical appearance had not changed much over the 15 years; a slight recession of the hairline had cut into his thick, curly brown hair, and a slight paunch had invaded his waistline, although he carried the extra weight nicely on his six-foot frame. He was dressed conservatively, dark suit, white shirt, muted tie. The real change was in his personality. In Leyte he'd been much more relaxed and jovial than he was as he sat across from her in the restaurant. At least that was Candy's perception of his personality then, and now. He was pleasant enough as they discussed names and places from the past, and their respective lives since the war. Jensen told her he was in private practice in Oakland, across the bay from San Francisco. Candy brought up the letter a few times, but Jensen parried those mentions by suggesting that they could talk better at his office the following day.

"I'd planned to go back to New York tomorrow," Candy said.

"I think it would be worthwhile staying," said Jensen. "There's some interesting work you could do for the Central Intelligence Agency, Candy, without interfering with your business. It could be lucrative."

That was the beginning. Candy stayed, and was driven in a plain, dark sedan the following morning across the Bay Bridge to Oakland and to the office of Dr. Gilbert Jensen. What was to occur in that office that day and on subsequent days over the next 12 years launched Candy Jones on an adventure that would lead her to the Far East as a covert operative of the CIA. She would be harassed, badgered and even tortured. Her role was small, a carrier of messages, and the fact that she chose initially to perform such duties, for pay, renders the misfortunes that befell her "occupational hazards." What she didn't bargain for, however, was becoming a human guinea pig in a secret CIA scientific project in which *mind control* was the goal. She was an unwilling and unknowing laboratory subject for 12 years, and only the chance marriage to John Nebel saved her from the final stage of her adventure, and of the experiments performed upon her—her own suicide as choreographed by Dr. Gilbert Jensen.

# 8

# The Triangle Emerges

The month of June 1973 proved to be a busy one for Long John Nebel and his headboard tape recorder. Thirteen tapes* were recorded during June, almost all of them the direct result of Nebel having helped Candy achieve sleep. Those that did not result from his efforts to hypnotize her are significant in that they represent increasingly frequent spontaneous trance states by Candy.

There are generally two forms of self- or autohypnosis. In the first form a subject can be taught to induce a trance state in himself which, in a loose sense, corresponds with a state of meditation. Autohypnosis is of great value in enabling the subject to enhance and reinforce posthypnotic suggestions im-

*The 13 June 1973 tapes are those upon which Nebel wrote the actual date of the session. A continuing problem for me in organizing the hypnotic-session tapes were those that did not have a date attached to them. It is possible that more than 13 tapes were recorded in June. The tapes were given to me by Nebel over a year's period in batches of 10. They were not in the order in which recorded, however, and the numbers I applied to them do not reflect their chronology. The June 1973 tapes are, according to my numbering system (Tape #, Side A or B, Date): 48, B-22nd; 49, A-25th; 49, B-26th; 51, A-18th; 52, A-15th; 53, A-22nd; 54, A-31st; 54, B-31st; 55, A-26th; 55, B-26th; 56, A-30th; 57, A-27th; and 57, B-30th.

planted by a hypnotist, and is routinely practiced by those who have sought hypnosis as an aid to behavior modification—e.g., smoking, dieting, etc.

There is also, however, the phenomenon of spontaneous trance, which is what began occurring in Candy Jones. Most of us experience spontaneous trance during our lives when we daydream and suddenly find time has passed without our perception of its passing. But the depth of trance in daydreaming is generally shallow, or *hypnoidal.* In Candy's case, she began to slip into spontaneous hypnosis of a trance depth sufficient to allow spontaneous age regression.

One such trance taped on June 18, 1973, found Candy regressed to the age of 11.* After Nebel had put her into the trance state, she began to sob. He asked her what she was sad about, and she said, in a child's voice and through her tears, "She's sick."

"Who's sick?" asked Nebel.

"Ma-Má."

Further questioning by Nebel established that it was September and that Ma-Má was in a hospital in Philadelphia. She'd gone there under the guise of a pleasure trip, but had told Doll the true reason for her travels. Ma-Má had not told Doll's mother of her planned hospitalization. It was further established in this tearful hypnotic session that Doll was wearing pajamas, was on the dock in back of their house (whether it was the main house on Carey Avenue or a summer place was not established) and that she was cold. The dialogue proceeded as follows:

■

JOHN: Why did you come to the dock?
CANDY: *(still crying)* 'Cause I'm scared.
JOHN: Scared in the house?
CANDY: Yeah.
JOHN: Do you know when mother'll be home?
CANDY: I don't know where she is.
JOHN: Does mother love you?
CANDY: *(evidently nodding her head)* I guess so.
JOHN: But she doesn't show it?

*Tape #51, Side A.

CANDY: She's very nervous . . . I make her nervous. *(She begins to cry harder.)* . . . I always make her nervous. . . . *(Nebel tells her she's a good little girl.)* . . . I try to be. . . . *(She suddenly asks him who he is.)*

JOHN: I'm your friend.

CANDY: How'd you know I'd be here?

JOHN: I knew you'd be coming down here.

CANDY: You know me?

JOHN: Yes.

CANDY: You been in my house?

JOHN: Not really, but I've seen you and know you. I'm the old man. Didn't you ever see me walk by? *(She pauses in confusion.)* Don't you think you ought to go home now?

CANDY: I wanna wait.

JOHN: For what?

CANDY: I'm not supposed to talk to you.

JOHN: Why not?

CANDY: I don't know who you are.

JOHN: I'm your friend.

CANDY: You won't say you saw me? *(He assures her he won't.)*

■

Doll goes on to explain that she'd gone to bed, and when she came downstairs later that night her mother was gone. Nebel suggests she go back inside and turn on the light. Doll says she can't because she's supposed to be asleep and that her mother will be angry with her when she returns. After another five minutes of conversation during which Doll calms down and stops crying, she says, "It's on," meaning the light in the house. Nebel agrees he sees the light.

■

JOHN: Come on, let's say a quick prayer to make Ma-Má better. We'll say it together. Please, God, make Ma-Má better. *(She repeats it after him.)* . . . You run up, bye-bye.

CANDY: Bye. (She leaves the imaginary scene and runs to the house where she plans to climb into her bedroom window by first climbing a tree.)

■

That same day in June 1973 produced two other sessions, both of which are contained on the same tape. Those two additional sessions covered other subject areas, as did most of the other hypnotic sessions conducted and taped during that month. Some of the material contained in them is highly relevant but is more properly presented later in the book when further background has been detailed against which these tapes can be viewed in perspective. For now, it would better serve the reader to understand a little more about age regression.

Of all the phenomena associated with hypnosis, age regression is perhaps the most exciting. Its utilization by psychiatrists and psychologists as a means of going back in a patient's life and uncovering hidden or forgotten memories has brought forth remarkable results. There is seemingly no one within the hypnosis fraternity who debates that hypnosis does indeed result in heightened acuity of memory. Similarly, there is little or no debate about whether a subject, possessing sufficient trance capacity and in the hands of a skilled hypnotist, is able to regress to moments from the past and actually relive them.

But there are those who ask whether a subject's present age and state of mind colors the event captured during regression. An extension of that question is whether the state of heightened suggestibility, which is *always* present in the hypnotic mode, provides a fertile field for hallucination to creep into the picture and "color" the material gathered while the subject relives a scene from the past. The men of science who raise these questions do not attack the veracity and integrity of those claiming total and *pure* age-regression case histories, free from the taint of hallucination or from current feelings and attitudes. It is just that regression, like hypnosis itself, is subject to many variables, and thus it is extremely difficult to establish the rigid controls always and forever deemed necessary by science to prove the axiom.

There are two basic forms of age regression. The first, in which the subject actually regresses in time and relives a specific portion of his or her life, is considered *true* age regression. The second form is that in which the subject *recalls* a time from the past but views it from the present. The difference is a matter of tense—"I am doing it" (true age regression), or "I did it" (recall of a past event). Both forms of regression are valuable to the therapist, giving him access to material from the patient's past which may have a direct bearing on the patient's current difficulties. In both forms, the question of whether the material is tainted by current events in the patient's life must be answered, along with the possibility of hallucination having played a role in the regression.

There is obviously less likelihood of current events and hallucination occurring during *true* age regression because if the regression is genuine, the subject will have no knowledge of events that have occurred subsequent to the age being relived. A subject regressed to his fifth birthday party should, no matter what his current age, speak and think as a five-year-old and be incapable of functioning beyond that mental and physical age.

Numerous studies have been performed using Binet-Simon intelligence tests to determine the mental age of a subject while in a regressed state. Many of these studies have validated the claim that when true age regression occurs, the subject performs, in all ways, at the regressed age level. The same tests, however, performed by equally capable and competent medical researchers, have yielded different results. Skeptics often point to a study done by Paul Campbell Young of Louisiana State University. Young's study, which was reported in the *Journal of Abnormal and Social Psychology* in 1940, concluded that adults, when regressed to the age of three and tested for IQ, functioned instead on a level that more approximated six-year-olds. Young therefore hypothesized that, with his control subjects, age regression was not genuine. Others point to the fact that Young's subjects did, in fact, regress to childhood, which would seem more significant than a tested difference of two or three years. Still, anyone involved in evaluating the results of age regression, in this case that of Candy Jones, should be aware that not every aspect of the regression may be 100 percent valid; and where such discrepancies alter, even in a minor way, the substantive material generated by the regression, the discrepancies should be weighed and incorporated into the final evaluation.

Dr. Lewis R. Wolberg, a psychiatrist in New York City and a leading authority on hypnosis, has pioneered its use in psychotherapy for over 40 years. In his book, *Hypnosis: Is It for You?* (Harcourt Brace Jovanovich, 1972), he discusses the various studies that have been mounted in an attempt to determine the worth and validity of age regression. In one case the subject was an epileptic. When regressed to an age prior to his first attack, an electroencephalograph recorded his brain patterns as normal. When progressed to an age after the onset of epilepsy, the readings became abnormal.

Many similar studies have been devised in an attempt to nail down the extent to which a memory can be re-created within a subject. Experiments were performed to reestablish the foot-nerve reflex (Babinski reflex), and they were successful. Other scientists have evaluated subjects' behavior during hypnotic age regression, and have used drawings and handwriting to indicate mental and physical age. Dr. Wolberg reproduces in his excellent book drawings made by a subject during age regression. The form and style of the drawings clearly become more child-like as the chronological age is regressed.

But there is room for debate, and Wolberg, like all cautious scientists, presents a fair case for those who dissent. He refers to other studies, in which conflicting results were obtained. He mentions that the Babinski reflex can also be obtained during normal sleep (perhaps because the subject in a natural sleep goes through spontaneous regression. He also points to work done by Robert Rubenstein and Richard Newman of the Yale Medical School in which they *progressed* adult subjects to an age *in the future.* These subjects experienced a vivid living-out of future experiences which would indicate the imagination does play a role in transporting a subject to another time and place in his or her life—forward or backward.

Even among those who believe in age regression, there is a debate as to just how far back a subject can be regressed. Some believe that regression is valid back to prenatal days, and that the subject's memories of life within the womb can be summoned through the skilled use of hypnosis. Others have claimed that hypnosis can even take a subject back to a previous life, as was the basis for the popular books on Bridey Murphy. Recently there have been newspaper reports of other cases in which subjects were regressed under hypnosis to a previous existence. One such case involved the wife of a minister who suddenly began speaking German even though it was claimed that she hadn't had any exposure to the language in *this life.* There have also been cases of foreign-born Americans who couldn't speak their native tongue until hypnotically regressed to a point in childhood when they still lived in their native lands. Once regressed, they spoke the language on the level of their childhood years.

The list of experts and their studies in this area is seemingly endless. While working with John Nebel and Candy Jones on this story, I simultaneously spent a year studying hypnosis, and particularly age regression. My conclusion is that, whether regression stops at the age of five, or two, or at the womb is irrelevant, except on an intellectual level. For the purposes of accurately presenting this case, I think it is fair to say that age regression, whether a reliving of an event or a heightened memory of that event, is a valid and provable medical fact.

In believing this, I share the beliefs of Lewis Wolberg who states in *Hypnosis: Is It for You?:* "The concensus at the present time is that regression actually does reproduce early behavior in a way that precludes all possibility of simulation. My own studies have convinced me of this fact, although the regression is never stationary. It is constantly being altered by the intrusion of mental functioning at other age levels. . . . Sometimes the patient reacts as if he were reliving a scene exactly as it happened, without any reference to later events in his life. Sometimes he responds as if he were judging an earlier actual event from his present point of view."

Wolberg goes on to discuss the fine line between true regression to past events and hallucination when he says, "Dramatic overacting and vivid embellishments of fantasy are often intermingled with real-life experiences. These constructions should not be considered as ingenious maneuvers that must be scrupulously discarded. Rather, they are motivated by neurotic defenses and needs. . . ."

There are scattered portions of the tapes upon which this book has been based that perhaps contain elements of hallucination, or which may have been influenced in part by Candy Jones's current life. It is important to remember that hallucination is not a conscious act on the part of the subject. Indeed, one of the significant tests of having achieved a deep trance state is the ability of the hypnotist to create hallucinations within the subject. A subject in a deep hypnotic trance can be made to believe that vinegar is fine wine, and will drink the vinegar with satisfaction, including lip-smacking and other expressions of pleasure. Subjects can be made to believe they are dogs, or elephants, or most anything else. (Theater hypnotists unfortunately play these games for audience amusement, which does nothing to enhance the image of hypnosis as a medical tool.) I personally have been hypnotized to a point where all perception of gravity and density was altered: I swam in water that had absolutely no density, and flew into the sunset on the back of a goose without any gravitational considerations. This particular hypnotic experience was part of a medical seminar in Los Angeles conducted by the Institute for Comprehensive Medicine; I attended as an observer and ended up a volunteer subject. As bizarre as the experience was, it was a graphic and personal way for me to become a believer, a *true* believer, in the power of hypnosis to alter perception and to induce hallucinatory behavior.

Despite having reached this level of belief in hypnosis and age regression, and despite being in total agreement with the previous statements quoted from Dr. Wolberg's book, I have opted to ignore his good advice about retaining "constructions" resulting from hypnotic hallucinations. Instead, I have chosen to purposely discard any material from the Candy Jones tapes which might have resulted from hallucinations, or from obvious influence by her present chronological life. Where I have felt it necessary to include certain of this "tainted" material, I have taken pains to label it questionable if it in any way might shape or change the substantive meaning of the material.

In the case of Candy Jones, the majority of the regressions were spontaneous—that is, John Nebel did not guide her to another place and time in her life. In those instances in which he did purposely direct her to a specific time and place, he used what is considered the classic method of establishing age regression: He confused her by not allowing her to come to rest on a time and place of her choice. The subject usually becomes upset by this inability to roost, and readily accepts the date and place suggested by the hypnotist as a haven. In Candy's case, where spontaneous regression occurred, it was only necessary for Nebel to ask, "Where are you now?" Candy would respond, and Nebel was then able to proceed by playing a role in the scene to which she'd regressed.

It is interesting to note that, on occasion, the present did influence her regression in that it keyed, in her mind, a specific time years ago that corresponded to a similar time in her present life. In analyzing the tapes I was fascinated to see how, if a hypnotic session with John happened to occur on or near a holiday, Candy's spontaneous regression would sometimes take her back to that same holiday period 30 or 40 years ago. Examples of this were Thanksgiving, Christmas and the Fourth of July. The moment in time to which she regressed was not always exactly the same moment at which the hypnotic session was taking place, but always within a week of each other.

July 1973, like June, also resulted in 13 tapes taken from sessions between John and Candy. (Again, these represent only those tapes on which a definite date was written following the session.) Many contained regression to a portion of her childhood, and were as inherently fascinating to Nebel as were the June tapes.

One June tape, recorded on June 30, 1973, had Nebel asking Candy whether she could remember back to when she was five years old.* After establishing with her that she was back in Wilkes-Barre, he asked whether it was a happy or sad time in her life (he added "sad" when she started to sniffle at his suggestion that it was a happy time).

■

CANDY: It's nice.
JOHN: Was your mother kind to you at that time or just your grandmother?
CANDY: *(her voice definitely that of a little girl)* They're nice ladies. . . . Ma-Má is out riding. Do you see her?
JOHN: Oh, yes.
CANDY: *(beginning to giggle)* Look at her go. *(She giggles with abandon.)* That's Billy (referring to the horse, and *still giggling*).

■

In this scene, in which true regression is, without a doubt, taking place, Doll complains she is cold. Nebel suggests she get a jacket from the house, but she refuses. She discusses her

*Tape #57, Side B.

grandmother and says she's a doctor. He questions her about the differences between the way her mother and grandmother treat her.

■

JOHN: Do you think your mother loves you as much as your grandmother? *(She doesn't answer.)* Come on now, I won't tell anybody what you say.
CANDY: I get bad . . . I'm bad.
JOHN: She says so, doesn't she, your mother?
CANDY: Yeah. I do bad things.
JOHN: But your grandmother doesn't seem to think you do bad things, does she?
CANDY: Sometimes. I didn't lock the barn.
JOHN: You should have, right?
CANDY: *(in a squeaky voice)* Yeah. I wasn't supposed to go in there but I went in to see Billy. He's old, and I put down the salt cake for him.
JOHN: Do you know what we're going to do?
CANDY: *(referring to Ma-Má)* Where is she?
JOHN: I think she's coming back. I hear her.

*(Candy agrees that she hears Billy's hoofbeats.)*

■

Nebel then progressed her up to the time she married him, and a dialogue ensued about their current life.

Another session, recorded on June 31, 1973, found Nebel playing the role of Candy's alter ego.* He had begun to do this when a clear-cut role for himself did not exist within a regression, or when he wished to discuss something with her as a third party. Often, Candy and her alter ego (Nebel) ended up discussing John Nebel from a detached vantage point. In this session Nebel regressed her to childhood and suggested she think of pleasant memories.

■

CANDY: I'm a monkey.
JOHN: You're a *what?*

*Tape # 54, Side B.

CANDY: I have a monkey.
JOHN: What's the monkey's name?
CANDY: Monkey. He's red.

■

Her voice at the beginning of this regression to childhood is still that of the adult Candy Jones. She explains to Nebel that she got the monkey on the boardwalk, evidently meaning in Atlantic City, but says she didn't buy it because she's too little to have money. She then tells him she dropped the monkey through the boardwalk. Finally, she denies having ever received a monkey. By this time her voice has slowly shifted into that of a child.

Nebel pursues the question of her mother's attitude toward her; and Candy, now Doll, tells him about some of the things she's expected to do—be good, go to sleep, stay clean and keep her dress from wrinkling. He then asks her about her girl friends.

■

CANDY: I don't know any. I know Snowflake.
JOHN: Who else?
CANDY: I don't have any friends.
JOHN: Doesn't your mother like you to have friends?
CANDY: No. *(She sounds sad.)* I'm not allowed to play with anyone except Snowflake. . . . *(She then perks up.)* I have my books. I have my cat and my dog. They're my friends.

■

Although some of the childhood regressions in those early tapes were sad, Candy reacted to hearing them played back with interest and amusement. Hearing them triggered conscious recollection of some events she'd forgotten about, and she happily filled in the blanks for her husband, now her hypnotist. Nebel says of those early sessions: "If the other things hadn't started happening, I would have been delighted with the way the hypnosis was going. Candy was sleeping better, and that was all I was after in hypnotizing her. It was all very pleasant."

The information about Candy's past that surfaced during the initial hypnotic sessions, and whatever else he was able to learn through stories she told in the conscious state, had no significance to him. They were fragments of the past, unconnected, isolated and without any apparent link to a larger, more cohesive picture into which they might fit.

For instance, he dismissed as barely interesting her conscious telling of having visited Dr. Gilbert Jensen in California as part of her work for the CIA. Nebel's primary interest in the story came when Candy mentioned that Jensen had wanted to hypnotize her. "I told him I couldn't," Candy told John, "and he said he could tell that from talking to me." Nebel knew from his extensive reading on hypnosis that the best way to deal with a subject who claims he cannot be hypnotized is to agree, and then to show the subject, for his general information, how hypnotists work.

"Did he show you how he *would* have hypnotized you if you were able to be hypnotized?" Nebel asked.

"Oh, he showed me some things," Candy replied. "But he knew I couldn't be."

Nebel smiled. Even though he'd played for her some of the tapes made while she was in the trance state, she still did not believe that *he* was hypnotizing her. She chalked up the taped regressions to dreams during which she had talked in her sleep.

Another piece of background information supplied by Candy but ignored by Nebel had to do with the imaginary club of little friends she enjoyed during her lonely hours as a child in Wilkes-Barre. Nebel thought her descriptions of the club members were funny, as did she, and they laughed together when she told of how Dorothy, which she pronounced "Dot-tee," was always fighting with Arlene who, Candy said, was a strong, domineering personality, forever trying to take over the club. And there was Willy, the only boy in the club, who invariably stomped his feet when he couldn't have his way.

"What about Pansy?" asked Nebel.

"She was quiet. And nice," said Candy.

All children have imaginary playmates at some stage of their lives. Nebel knew this and therefore assumed that his wife had been a normal child, creating her own world to compensate for the unusually severe restrictions placed upon her by her mother.


This spotty acquaintance with his wife's history would be forced into perspective during the spring of 1973 by the emergence of another person into the world of Candy and John Nebel. No specific date can be attached to the first appearance of this new entity because no record was made, and because it happened so fast and unexpectedly that Nebel had all he could do to cope with the difficulties of the moment. Also, it took a while for him to recognize that he was, in fact, dealing with another distinct personality, because when *she* first appeared he assumed it was just another of Candy's peculiar changes of mood. It was that voice, that alien, icy antagonistic voice, a rusty knife that severed the calm of the apartment.

"What made me first realize that this was different from past episodes was that The Voice came at me and stayed around," says Nebel. "Before, it was only a comment, a look and a few seconds of bitchiness. But when I was first faced with having to deal with it, it was like another woman had slipped into the apartment and wanted to take me on, like a guest on the show who has a chip on her shoulder."

Nebel's first brush with the Other Woman during a hypnotic session occurred sometime in early June 1973, before he installed the tape equipment in the bedroom, and he describes it from memory.

I asked her where she was. She told me she was in my office. I said that I knew *that* and she didn't have to tell me she was in my office. I then asked who I was. She answered me in that snotty voice I'd heard before that if I didn't know who I was, why should she even be there. I was really confused. I didn't know what office she was talking about, where it was or who the hell I was supposed to be. I mean, she was talking directly *to* me, in a trance, and I fumbled around to figure out who she thought she was talking to.

I told her I was just testing her memory. She laughed that bitchy laugh and told me I was Dr. Jensen. I asked her if this was the first time she'd been to my office, and she told me that I *knew* it wasn't her first time. She was speaking to me like I was a damn fool, which I suppose I deserved in terms of what she was experiencing. I asked her where the office was located. She again was very scornful of me for asking such a dumb question, but finally said it was in Oakland, California.

I asked her what she was doing in my office. She said she

was there to get her vitamin shot. I asked her what her name was. That really bugged her and she became angry and said I had a nerve asking her name. She asked me what my name was. I said Jensen. Then I asked her again for her name. "Arlene," she said. I asked her what her last name was. She said "Grant." I asked her where she was born, and she said "Wilkes-Barre, Pennsylvania."

I then asked her if she knew Candy Jones. "Oh, yes," she said. "She's weak. She has no strength." And that was it. I brought her out of the trance and she looked at me with the softness I'm used to with Candy and said, "Oh, John, what's wrong? Did you wake up?"

It was following that session that Nebel went to Irving Miller at Bryce and purchased his TC-142 recorder.

The first recorded dialogue between John Nebel and Arlene Grant, Candy's imaginary childhood playmate, took place in late June, 1973, although there is no date written on the cassette tape. It was only after days of analyzing the transcripts that I was able to pinpoint this particular tape as the first between them.* The session between Nebel and Arlene ran 20 minutes, with only a minute or two containing irrelevant personal material. Following that session, John induced another trance in Candy and engaged in a ten-minute conversation with her about Arlene. The following is a transcript of those two important sessions, condensed where possible without losing or altering material. I ask the reader again to bear in mind that this, like all transcripts in the book, does not accurately reflect the tone and tempo of the sessions. There are many long pauses, inarticulate responses and lengthy attempts to elicit an answer to certain questions.

Just prior to turning on the tape recorder and immediately following his recognition that he was talking to Arlene, Nebel asked her whether she was a strong person. He turned on the machine.

■

ARLENE: Yes, I'm strong.
JOHN: How've you been?

*Tape #16, Side A.

ARLENE: Not well.

JOHN: What has been wrong?

ARLENE: She's very upset.

JOHN: Who is?

ARLENE: Candy.

JOHN: I haven't heard from you for a long time, Arlene. Where have you been?

ARLENE: Waiting.

JOHN: Waiting for what?

ARLENE: *(after repeated attempts by Nebel to get an answer)* To go.

JOHN: Where do you want to go, or have Candy go?

ARLENE: *(with a sneer) She's* going.

JOHN: Where is she going, Arlene?

ARLENE: Wherever I send her. Where *we* send her.

JOHN: Who's we?

ARLENE: You . . . I . . .

JOHN: And who else?

ARLENE: *(her voice a dark threat)* No one else is necessary.

JOHN: Why would I want to send her anyplace?

ARLENE: I hear you, I hear you. I know you.

JOHN: Sure you know me. You know my name, don't you?

ARLENE: John.

JOHN: How did you happen to come tonight at this time?

ARLENE: She's weak.

JOHN: In what way is she weak, Arlene?

ARLENE: She couldn't hold *me* in.

JOHN: You know I love her, don't you?

ARLENE: No.

*(Nebel tries to get her to explain why she feels he doesn't love Candy. She eventually agrees that he has treated Candy well.)*

ARLENE: She's weak. *I* have to take over. *(He asks her in what way she has to take over.)* I'll step into her shoes for awhile.

JOHN: Do you think you have that right?

ARLENE: She has that damn stomachache.

*(Nebel proceeds to ask Arlene a series of questions, but she ignores them and simply makes flat statements. He finally asks her whether she likes Candy.)*

ARLENE: I have to. I'm stuck with her. How else do I get out?

*(Nebel tries to get her to tell him why she wants to come out. She sighs*

*a great deal and stretches as she ignores his questions. She finally replies.)*

ARLENE: Because it's very boring . . . to do nothing.

JOHN: Don't you think Candy is doing a lot?

ARLENE: She's upset.

JOHN: Do you think you have a right to interfere in her life?

ARLENE: *(in a spiteful voice)* When she's weak, I can come out.

JOHN: What would be a sign of strength on Candy's part as far as you're concerned?

ARLENE: No tears, none of this garbage. *(She sounds disgusted.)*

JOHN: Did she ever cry when she was a little girl?

ARLENE: Not when *I* was there.

JOHN: Do you know if she did cry when you weren't there?

ARLENE: *(scornfully)* She was weak. She cried alone, *alone*. She was lonesome. *(Very sarcastic)* She wanted *friends*.

■

Nebel then turned the conversation to Dr. Gilbert Jensen. There had been an indication during previous sessions that Jensen, in some unexplained way, had been involved in Candy's life beyond what Nebel had been earlier led to believe. He asked Arlene now whether Jensen had done Candy any harm.

■

ARLENE: *I* did it. . . . You don't like *us*. You don't like any of the group.

JOHN: You mean Willy and the rest of them?

ARLENE: It's not for you.

JOHN: What's not for me?

ARLENE: Nonsense. *This* nonsense. You label *me* nonsense.

*(Nebel brings the conversation back to Dr. Jensen and asks Arlene whether Jensen did Candy any harm.)*

ARLENE: She didn't even know what he was doing. She thought he was a doctor helping her.

JOHN: What did you think he was doing for her?

ARLENE: Releasing *me*.

JOHN: What method did he use to accomplish this?

ARLENE: Injections.

*(Candy had told John on a previous occasion that Dr. Jensen had administered vitamin shots to her when she visited his office. Nebel asks Arlene whether the injections she refers to were vitamin shots.)*

ARLENE: They were. It made me strong enough to come out.

JOHN: How do you know they were vitamins? *(Nebel had always been suspicious of the shots because according to Candy they'd been administered intravenously, rather than in the muscle of the arm or the buttocks.)*

ARLENE: They weren't [vitamins]. They were [vitamins] to her.

JOHN: But you know better.

ARLENE: I know better. *(Testy, annoyed)* I listened.

■

Nebel then brought up another question concerning Dr. Jensen. This was prompted by material that had emerged during previous conscious and hypnotic conversations, and which had been causing an increasing tension between them over the past few months. It had to do with Candy's apparent distrust and even hatred of an inordinate number of people, particularly ethnic groups. She was, on the one hand, seemingly without prejudice. But there were times when her spoken feelings about such groups did not correspond with what Nebel knew about her from observing her daily actions. And once, while questioning her about it in the conscious state, she'd referred to Jensen. She hadn't accused Jensen of anything, but her mention of him in the context of that discussion caused Nebel to again question the role Jensen might have played in this erratic side of Candy's behavior.

■

JOHN: Do you think he caused her to hate a lot of people?

ARLENE: *(laughing)* Everyone. That's the whole plan.

JOHN: That was Jensen's plan? Is that what you're saying?

ARLENE: He kept her away from people. *(She laughs again.)*

JOHN: He made her hate people?

ARLENE: Not hate people, *avoid* them. *Avoid* relationships.

JOHN: Why has she used the obscenities to refer to different ethnic groups?

ARLENE: She doesn't swear.

JOHN: I didn't say swear. She doesn't swear, does she?

ARLENE: *(yawning)* Oh, not really. She doesn't say obscenities.

JOHN: I mean using derogatory terms to describe different ethnic groups. Did he teach her that?

ARLENE: I don't know what you mean.

JOHN: Are you going to sleep now?

ARLENE: If I do, I may not be here when I wake up.

JOHN: Where will you be then?

ARLENE: She'll try to get me back. . . . I want to go out . . . look
up . . . look up, look up, look up at the sky.

JOHN: Do you know her mother is ill?

ARLENE: She's dying. She knows it. She's not admitting it.

JOHN: Was her mother nice to her when she was a young girl?

ARLENE: *(snorting)* You've got to be joking. You know she wasn't.

JOHN: I wasn't there. Do you think her mother was bad to her?

ARLENE: She criticized her all the time, all the time. . . . She broke
her spirit. That was the idea. Break her down, break her
down. . . . Her mother did it, Harry [Conover] did it. I
watched it. I wasn't around with him, but I watched.

JOHN: Did you like Harry?

ARLENE: If I could have come out I . . .

JOHN: What would you have done?

ARLENE: Scared the hell out of him.

JOHN: You never scared *me.*

ARLENE: *He* would have been scared.

■

Nebel decided to end the session and told Arlene to put her
hand on the paneling next to the bed. He'd hit upon this method
of ending hypnotic sessions one night quite by accident. Thinking that by touching the wall next to the bed Candy would feel
secure and be able to return to the present, he guided her hand
and rubbed the wall with it. It was effective, and became the
standard method used by Nebel from that point forward to end
a session, particularly if it had become rough and dangerous. He
eventually had a small square of the paneling made up for Candy
to carry in her purse for use outside the apartment.

Now he said to her, "Do you feel the wall, Candy?"

Dramatically, the voice changed from the deep, harsh tones of
Arlene to that of Candy. She sat up in bed and began to talk to
him as though nothing had happened.

The second session on that tape took place later in the day.
After putting Candy into a trance, Nebel waited for her to begin

speaking, hoping that she would spontaneously regress to a portion of her life that might shed further light on this other personality within her. She began by muttering that he shouldn't listen to something, or someone.

■

JOHN: What shouldn't I listen to?

CANDY: That woman who tries to come out and tell you silly things.

*(Nebel reinforces the trance by simply repeating the words "deeper, deeper, deeper.")*

CANDY: *(sounding sleepy, almost drugged)* She's trying to push away. You know that, don't you?

JOHN: No, she isn't going to get out now.

CANDY: *(firmly)* No, she's not.

JOHN: 'Cause you're stronger.

CANDY: Yes, I am. *(She moans.)* I can't keep fighting like this, don't you know that? I'm tired of fighting. I can't fight anymore. *(weary, upset)* He's gonna make me . . . give up.

JOHN: Who's going to make you give up?

CANDY: *(hesitantly)* Dr. Jensen.

JOHN: What's he going to do to you?

CANDY: He won't have to do it to me, he's gonna make me do it my own self. Give up.

JOHN: Give up what?

CANDY: I don't know, whatever he says.

JOHN: Did he tell you you should give up?

CANDY: No. He said if I ever had to, he'd work it out for me when I give up.

JOHN: When you say "give up," do you mean to end your life?

CANDY: He didn't say it was that. He just said . . . I'm sure that's what he meant . . . I think.

JOHN: Are you interested in Dr. Jensen? Do you think he's done you some good?

CANDY: *(like a little girl)* I think he's done me bad. I used to think he did me good but I don't think so anymore. He wanted me to go down and jump off that rock.

JOHN: He said that?

CANDY: He said it would be very nice because I like it down there.

JOHN: Jump off a cliff?

CANDY: He said you might as well go . . . why wait?

JOHN: That was his suggestion to you, huh?

CANDY: No. He said that if you're unhappy . . .

*(Nebel proceeds to tell Candy that whatever control Jensen may have had over her is finished. She agrees with him.)*

CANDY: I don't know if he's even around still. He may be dead. I called the other day.

NEBEL: *(worried)* You called California?

CANDY: Yes.

JOHN: What were you going to say?

CANDY: I was going to speak to him. . . . I wanted his phone number.

JOHN: And you were going to speak to him?

CANDY: No. I wanted his phone number and address in case I ever got out there.

JOHN: What would you do if you went out there?

CANDY: I wouldn't go and see him, but . . . my final resort would be to get to him. Not *me.* I'd have him . . . dead sounds to me . . . he did me an awful lot of harm, though. He's not my friend. I never really liked him anyway. We were never friends.

JOHN: He never was your friend.

CANDY: He's got stuff . . . he's got to tell me things . . . he's gotta tell me to reverse the things . . . *(She becomes very upset.)* . . . how am I . . . he told me lots of things . . . I don't even know what he told me . . . there must be a lot more.

■

At this point there was a discussion of perhaps 30 seconds in which Candy, referring to Nebel in the third person, muttered that he (Nebel) tells her about the bad things she does. She ended by saying that Nebel accuses her of hating people.

■

JOHN: Didn't Jensen tell you [to hate people]?

CANDY: Yeah, but I'm not gonna do what he says. I try not to. . . . *(Very animated)* You don't know . . . lots of the things that he says . . . they come up and come up . . . and I say them but I don't do them anymore. . . . It's a very terrible thing and it hurts physically. . . . I'm fighting him, I'm fighting him, and it's going to kill me.

JOHN: No, it won't, because John is going to save you.

CANDY: Can he?

JOHN: If you will only keep this in your mind. John is the one man who could save you. And why do you think he would save you?

CANDY: Because he cares for me.

JOHN: Because he loves you.

■

A few more minutes were spent with John attempting to convince Candy that everything would work out. He then again reinforced the trance and suggested she inhale so she could smell the lilacs. She denied smelling them. He worked at it and she eventually said she smelled something green, like freshly mown grass. And then she smelled the lilacs.

■

CANDY: We had purple and white lilacs that crushed the house.

■

She went into a natural sleep.

Ever since those early sessions, it has been a daily and grueling adventure for John and Candy to discover the truth about her past life. The sessions can be exhausting, as well as exhilarating when a scrap of information is suddenly uncovered to put other information in perspective. In those early days of June and July 1973, there were more questions unanswered than resolved. But Nebel did, at least, know the reason for Candy's changes in personality during the first days of their marriage. It had been Arlene peeping through. He asked Arlene about the wedding day and night during a later hypnotic session.

■

JOHN: Were you at the wedding when she got married to John?

ARLENE: Was I at the wedding? You didn't see me?

JOHN: How would I see you?

ARLENE: I was standing right there.

JOHN: Are you trying to tell me that John married you, rather than Candy?

ARLENE: Of course not. I was standing right over behind the chair.

JOHN: Were you over to the hotel the first night they were married?

ARLENE: *(laughs)*

JOHN: You know they went to the Drake.

ARLENE: *(amused)* Oh, really? Did they?

JOHN: You were there, weren't you?

ARLENE: *(teasing)* Well, don't you know?

JOHN: You're much different than she is, aren't you?

ARLENE: Yeah, thank God. She's still playing Rebecca of Sunnybrook Farm.

*(Arlene becomes annoyed at being questioned. They engage in dialogue about whether he is interrogating her.)*

JOHN: Were you over at the Drake Hotel that night when they got married? On their wedding night? Were you in the room?

ARLENE: So many things have happened.

JOHN: Answer a straight question. Do you remember when he said to her, "You're peculiar"? Wasn't that you?

ARLENE: He said it the next day, too.

JOHN: Wasn't that you?

ARLENE: *(laughing)* Of course it was.

■

The first few sessions with Arlene were fruitful, and provided Nebel with many questions to ask during subsequent sessions. Most important to him was the riddle of Dr. Gilbert Jensen. When asked about Jensen while in the waking state, Candy could provide little in the way of detail. She recalled having visited him in Oakland during that first trip for the CIA, but little more. She seemed to have no memory of what had transpired in his office, or outside his office immediately following her visits to him.

Yet, one by one, the pieces were fitted into the puzzle, and they presented to Long John Nebel an upsetting and worrisome picture of satanic behavior on the part of Dr. Jensen. And always, in the back of Nebel's mind, was Candy's remark that she'd called Jensen the other day. If she was in contact with him even after her marriage to John Nebel, it meant that whatever control Jensen exercised over her might still be in effect.

# 9

## The Office in Oakland

The facts surrounding Candy's first visit to the Oakland office of Dr. Gilbert Jensen, and subsequent visits, were gathered over the entire course of hypnotic sessions between her and her husband. Material about Jensen and what transpired between him and Candy has surfaced as recently as the summer of 1975. The major difficulty in dredging up this material is that Candy Jones was programmed by Jensen *not* to remember, and this programming proved frighteningly effective.

Candy consciously recalls her first day in Jensen's office, after the dinner with him the night before, although the natural passage of time has eroded memory of small details, without any programming on Jensen's part. She did not, for instance, recall the street on which the office was located, because she was always driven there. It was only after repeated sessions with Nebel that she finally offered that Jensen's office was on a street with a tree's name. Finally she said under hypnosis, "Cyprus Street."

The building described by Candy was a two-story brick structure. Three steps led up to a wooden door. There was no street number on the building, nor was there any sign to indicate the presence of a physician. A drab, three-story green house stood next door, and the neighborhood in general was shabby.

Inside, there was a small, dimly lighted reception area in which stood a table and two straight chairs. On the table were magazines, some dating back over a year. Address labels had been carefully torn from the covers.

Gilbert Jensen led Candy into his office, an equally small room. She sat in a chair in front of a plain, tidy wooden desk as Jensen took his seat behind it. A chair of the same type as the one in which she was sitting stood empty next to her. Heavy drapes covered the window that she knew must face the street, and built-in bookshelves lined the wall behind Jensen. The shelves directly in back of him contained only a gooseneck lamp in which a bare bulb burned brightly. The shelves to either side held what appeared to be medical reference books; she was surprised at how few there were. She noticed a Webster's diction-ary among them. To her right hung a large wall mirror. The room was dark except for the bare bulb behind Jensen. A Tensor lamp on his desk was unlighted, as was a bullet lamp on the wall next to the mirror.

"Does the light bother you?" Jensen asked as he noticed Candy squinting against its brightness.

"Yes. It's bright."

Jensen twisted the flexible shaft, though of course that was of no use since the bulb was bare. He did not offer to turn it off and use one of the shaded lamps.

"Would you like to see the rest of the office?" he asked.

She said she would, and Jensen led her into his "examination room." Like most such rooms, it was small and contained little furniture. A high examination table covered with white linen stood in the center of the room, and a white cabinet stood against one wall, its contents invisible behind white opaque material in its glass doors. There was a small, straight chair and nothing more. Candy was unimpressed but did not say so.

They returned to his office and Candy positioned herself in her chair to avoid a direct confrontation with the bare light bulb. Jensen leaned forward and placed his elbows on the desk. "Well, Candy, let's pick up where we left off last night."

Candy was reluctant to continue with a recounting of her

personal and business life. Over dinner she'd been open and free with details of her marriage to Conover, her sons, her business problems and her growing feeling of failure in all aspects of her life. Jensen had been a good listener, injecting himself into her monologue only when it faltered, or when he seemed interested in pursuing another aspect of her life. In his office, however, Candy found herself anxious to cut off the conversation and return to her hotel.

The awkwardness of the situation was apparent and angered her, although she did not allow her feelings to surface. Had it been a simple conversation between two old friends, she might have felt differently about it. As it stood, there was the unstated although understood relationship of buyer-seller, the job interview. Jensen had not brought up the possibility of her working for the unnamed government agency originally referred to by the general but she knew that that possibility was the reason for her coming to his office in the first place. She found it difficult to come right out and ask about it, and so she continued answering his questions.

"What was your childhood like?" Jensen asked.

"Lonely."

"How so?"

Candy leaned back and told him of the days on Carey Avenue in Wilkes-Barre. He was placid as he listened, an occasional nod his only visible reaction. It was only when she mentioned her club of imaginary friends that he displayed what could be termed animated interest. He urged her to continue talking about Pansy, Arlene, Dot-tee and Willy, and questioned her closely about each of them.

"They were only make-believe," Candy said, laughing. "Silly, I suppose."

Jensen laughed. "Everyone has imaginary friends at one time or another."

"I know." She drew in a deep breath. "Could you tell me something about what sort of work I might do for . . . well, whoever it is you're involved with?"

"The unit?"

"I don't know. The general told me that you would fill me in."

"Plenty of time for that, Candy."

They had another hour of conversation, guided by Jensen. He

dwelled upon Candy's imaginary club in Wilkes-Barre, and she became annoyed. It was already one in the afternoon and she had wanted to return to New York that night.

"I really should leave," Candy said.

"I'd like to talk some more," said Jensen. "I'd also like to get some facts from you."

"What sort of facts?"

"Well, facts about your habits. For instance, I imagine you date a lot now that you're divorced."

"Date?" She smiled at his use of the word.

"Yes," Jensen confirmed with a grin. "Parties. I imagine you attend many cocktail parties."

"No, that isn't true. I go to very few parties."

"But you do travel a great deal."

"Yes, in my business. But I don't socialize much, out of town or in New York."

"We could work something out with you from time to time, Candy, if you performed services for us during your travels."

"What sort of services?"

"Carry a message now and then. That's all."

"Would I be paid?"

"We could work that out, too. Of course, all your expenses would be paid."

"I'm looking for more than just expenses."

"What happened to that superpatriot I knew in the South Pacific?"

"She's still here. I'd like to help. But I also need money. My boys are in private schools and that's expensive. I have them to support as well as my mother and me."

"I understand. I was only testing. I've been assured that your motives are still good."

"Who assured you of that?"

"A number of people."

"Was General Sims one of them?" (An air force general, Sims* had been close to Candy during her work with air force recruiting programs following the war.)

Jensen smiled but did not respond.

"I really must leave," Candy said.

*Sims is a fictitious name.

"I understand. We'll continue this the next time you're out here. But I would like you to fill out a form. We'll need a passport for you, too."

"I have a passport."

"Yes, I know. But there'll be times you'll need to travel under an assumed name."

"Why? I thought the work I might do would be done in conjunction with my own travels."

"That's true. Your business might bring you as far as California, but we might send you overseas as part of your trip. You could make that leg of the trip using the assumed name."

"It sounds awfully cloak-and-dagger."

"Well, it isn't." He didn't return her smile. "I told you that all you'd be doing is carrying a message from time to time. That's all."

Candy said she would like to become involved and asked Jensen for the form. He reached into his desk drawer and removed a paper. "Here," he said, "just fill this out."


It had begun for Candy Jones with the filling out of a simple form. She was *in,* joining thousands of Americans who have offered their services over the years to a myriad of such "units" as the one headed by Dr. Gilbert Jensen. Jensen's unit, like the others, was established and operated by the Central Intelligence Agency, the CIA, always referred to as "The Company." Like other citizens performing part-time duty for The Company, Candy's role would be kept secret, even from the records branch at CIA headquarters in Langley, Virginia. Her only contact would be Gilbert Jensen, her "control agent." Her name would not appear on the rolls of authorized CIA personnel, currently in excess of 16,000. Victor Marchetti and John D. Marks in their best-selling book, *The CIA and the Cult of Intelligence,* refer to this sort of part-time employment: "Private individuals under contract to—or in confidential contact with—the agency for a wide variety of tasks other than soldiering or spying are also left out of the personnel totals, and complete records of their employment are not kept in any single place."

But in Candy's case there was to develop a relationship with Jensen and his CIA unit far beyond what most covert operatives bargain for. Her willingness to carry messages was the extent of her *conscious* cooperation. From that point forward she became a helpless and unknowing dupe of Jensen and the highly secret CIA project with which he was connected; and the events that were to take place in his office following her signing of the form were all designed to put into motion the machinations of that project.

There is some confusion on the tapes as to when these subsequent events took place. Although the tapes recorded during hypnotic sessions with Nebel indicate that most of these ensuing events occurred during Candy's initial visit with Jensen, there is conflicting material pointing to the likelihood that they were spread out over the period encompassing her first *three* visits to his Oakland office, the first taking place in November 1960, and the following two visits occurring in late 1960 and early 1961. I've chosen to deal with these significant events as having occurred during the cumulative time spent with Jensen during their initial three meetings.

After filling out the form, Jensen had Candy stand against the wall and remove her shoes. She found this amusing, and watched incredulously as he rolled down a sheet of brown wrapping paper from a roll attached close to the ceiling and proceeded to trace her silhouette on it with a heavy black pen. She was wearing a bulky suit and was momentarily chagrined that the outline made her appear heavier than she was. (This bit of vanity came out during a session with Nebel in which he regressed her to her first visit to Jensen's office. He was able to accomplish such regressions on a number of occasions, and most of the material concerning this initial phase of her CIA involvement was gained through such sessions.)

The next step in Jensen's "processing" of Candy related to that imaginary club of friends she had as a child. Jensen asked her what fictitious name she wished to use on her passport.

"I don't know. You pick one."

"I'd rather you chose it. It should be a name that you're comfortable with and would respond to quickly."

"Well, how about Arline?" Candy suggested. "That's my middle name."

"Wasn't that also the name of one of those imaginary friends you had as a child?"

"Yes, but it was spelled differently. My name is A-r-l-i-n-e. *She* was A-r-l-e-n-e."

"All right, you can use Arline and spell it either way. What about a last name?"

"Grant."

"Why?"

"That was the last part of my grandmother's married name. Rosengrant." Candy laughed with embarrassment. "That was the last name I gave my little imaginary friend, Arlene, too. Arlene Grant."

"Fine," said Jensen. "Arlene Grant. It sounds good." He told Candy that she would be visited at her hotel by a photographer who would take her passport photos.

"What about Arlene?" he asked, returning to the subject of Candy's fantasy friend. "What did she look like?"

"She looked just like me."

"Really?"

"Yes. I saw her in the mirror, just like I saw all the others."

"And she was just a reflection of you?"

"Yes. . . . No. Her hair ribbon was always on the other side of her head from mine. Because it was in the mirror."

"Did she have the same color hair as you?"

"Yes."

"Same general coloring?"

"Yes, but I always thought of Arlene as being darker, a brunette."

"Was she only in the mirror?" asked Jensen.

"Yes." Candy displayed annoyance at Jensen's line of inquiry and he shifted to another subject, Candy's general health.

"I'm in good health," she said in response to his question. "Tired from all the traveling and the business pressures, but healthy. I had a checkup by my doctor in New York before I left."

"You look like you could use some vitamins," Jensen said.

"I get B-twelve in New York."

"There are better vitamins than just B-twelve."

They continued to discuss Candy's health, and Jensen pointed out that she would have to be in tip-top shape to withstand the rigors of frequent and spur-of-the-moment travel. Candy, of course, agreed.

"You shouldn't smoke," Jensen said as she reached into her purse and lighted a cigarette.

"I know that."

"Why don't you stop?"

"I've tried. Maybe someday."

This led Jensen into a lengthy discussion of the methods employed to aid people who wish to stop smoking. He mentioned hypnosis as one of the methods.

"That would never work for me," said Candy.

"Why not?"

"Because I can't be hypnotized."

"Have you ever tried?"

"No, but I know I'm not susceptible."

Jensen sat back in his chair and clasped his hands on his chest. "You're probably right about that," he said. "There are lots of people who can't be hypnotized." He then launched into a quiet lecture on the evils of hypnosis as practiced by charlatans and quacks, coming down especially hard on the stage hypnotists. "I'm really dedicated to putting a stop to the misuse of hypnosis, Candy. Dedicated to it. By the way, would you like to see *how* some people practice hypnosis?"

"Yes, I suppose so."

The preceding dialogue has been, of course, my attempt to visualize and dramatize the scene being played out between Candy and Jensen. It reflects the substance of the conversation that transpired between them. But there are two portions of tape made during hypnotic sessions between John Nebel and Candy Jones in which the dialogue between her and Dr. Jensen seems to actually be relived. Both sections resulted from regression back to Jensen's office during the early phase of her involvement with him, and in both Nebel plays the role of Jensen.

The first tape was recorded, to the best of my knowledge, sometime during the summer of 1974.* Nebel, *playing Jensen,* asks Candy if she remembers the first time she came to his office.

■

CANDY: Yes.

JOHN: Do you remember I asked you if you could be hypnotized?

CANDY: I can't be.

*Tape #2, Side B.

JOHN: You said you can't be, right?

CANDY: You said I can't be either.

JOHN: Do you remember what I did?

CANDY: You talked about it. You were a very different person that day, I can tell you that.

JOHN: What do you mean by different?

CANDY: You were almost like you are now. You were very pleasant. You said you were going to get involved in a crackdown on people who try to hypnotize people, entertainers and all that. And you showed me how they do it.

JOHN: Which way did I show you?

CANDY: Oh, with that thing on a chain. . . .

JOHN: You mean that thing that was moving like a pendulum?

CANDY: Yeah, but it was like a fob. And the candle and the light and the tick-tock, tick-tock . . . that thing.

JOHN: Like a metronome.

CANDY: Yeah. And that thing that sounds on the telephone.

JOHN: Uh-huh.

CANDY: And the mirror . . . *(She sounds very sleepy.)*

JOHN: Do you remember seeing the thing that's used with the telephone?

CANDY: Nooooo. You don't have it here. You just let me hear it on the phone.

JOHN: What about the mirror?

CANDY: Oh, you're supposed to stare in the mirror and all this nonsense.

JOHN: This is when you became Arlene, right?

CANDY: No, we were *talking* about Arlene.

JOHN: *(with a chuckle)* Do you remember when I asked you what name you wanted to use?

CANDY: Yes.

JOHN: What did you say?

CANDY: Don't *you* remember?

*(She proceeds to explain her choice of the name Arlene Grant, and reiterates the fact that he was going to wage a war against the misuse of hypnotism.)*

The session then drifted on to other areas.

■

The items Candy mentioned as having been shown her by Jensen are part of the standard bag of mechanical tricks used by some hypnotists. There is no need to rely on such mechanical or electrical gadgets to induce trance, their only conceivable value arising in instances when the subject's mentality is such that the whir of lights or the *act* of swinging a pendulum back and forth before his eyes can convince him that something tangible is taking place. He cannot accept the fact that entering the hypnotic state involves only concentration, and is likely to be the same person who believes that all hypnotists possess deep, dark, piercing eyes and a Svengalian magic that places helpless subjects under their control.

Dr. Frederick Dick, the Manhattan internist who uses hypnosis in his practice with selected cases, is well aware of the public's mistaken notions about hypnosis. He commented to me, "John Nebel's success in inducing hypnotic trance in Candy Jones and in guiding her through age regressions points up one of the many misconceptions about hypnosis, one that should be corrected if the general public is to benefit on a broad scale from this useful and therapeutic medical tool. I often see it in my own practice. Patients for whom hypnosis would prove effective in certain behavior modification situations, such as smoking or overeating, are sometimes fearful that I will become a Svengalian figure who will rob them of their control.

"Nothing could be further from the truth. The trance capacity is within the subject, the patient. A hypnotist does nothing more than encourage the subject to use his or her own capacity to enter a trance. And rather than take away control from the patient, I am, in effect, encouraging and guiding them into an optimum situation in which their own sense of control is enhanced.

"One quick glance at Candy's Hypnotic Induction Profile makes it abundantly clear that her capacity to enter trance is extremely high. John Nebel had the best of subjects with which to work, and rather than be surprised at his success, my surprise would come if he had been unable to induce a trance state in her."

The truth is that all such gadgets sold as hypnotic aids do nothing more than establish eye fixation, which can be as easily accomplished by asking the subject to gaze at a spot on the wall or ceiling, or to focus on the hypnotist's finger or eyes. In fact, there are many professionals in the field who do not believe it is even necessary to establish eye fixation, the simple closing of the eyes being sufficient for their needs. Whirring discs and flashing lights are good *show,* however, just as the long, glistening silver needles and Oriental mystery of acupuncture are, according to some, unnecessary hypnotic aids with which to induce a trance within the patient. There is little doubt, however, that eye fixation, particularly on some spot or object *above* the head which causes the eyes to roll upward, aids in establishing the trance state. Because the eye muscles are the body's smallest and are easily fatigued, a subject will usually close his eyes upon command after they have been held in an upward gaze for a short period of time. This is therefore also a good place to begin establishing the power of suggestion with a new subject. Moreover, recent studies indicate that rolling the eyes upward may have more profound effects than simply fatiguing the eye muscles. There is evidently a correlation between upward eye roll and increased alpha waves in the brain, a discovery that presents a ripe area for researchers.

In Candy's case, the candle and lights and moving pendulum were undoubtedly helpful to Jensen in having her fix her eyes on something. It is indicated on two tapes that he also possessed some sort of gadget that produced flashing or rotating lights, probably one of many variations on the basic unit introduced many years ago by a French physician named Luys. Jensen's arsenal of hypnotic gadgetry would serve little purpose for someone practicing hypnosis within the bounds of acceptable medical practice. He undoubtedly was experimenting with all the available methods, a conjecture on my part that becomes more credible as further evidence is introduced.

His use of sound to induce an hypnotic trance is of debatable worth, although drums have been used to create a hypnotic mood since prehistoric times. Indeed, of all the hypnotic aids Jensen showed Candy, it was the mirror that was most significant, for it was closely related to her experiences as a child in bringing out her imaginary group of friends.

Jensen was also evidently experimenting with the use of odors to induce or reinforce hypnotic trance. In an undated session with John Nebel, in which Nebel again slips into the role of Gilbert Jensen, Candy refers to Jensen's use of incense.

■

CANDY: *(making a sound of distaste)* Ooh, you've got that smelly stuff around again.

JENSEN: The incense?

CANDY: Uh-huh.

JENSEN: You don't like it?

CANDY: Not at all. It's very powerful. I don't know how you stand it. Don't you smell it? You like it? Do you have this in your apartment?

JENSEN: What does it smell like to you?

CANDY: I don't know, I've never smelled anything like it. Smells sort of musky, like dead mushrooms or something. It's heavy. It gives you a headache. I don't get headaches but . . . where do you put it, in the ashtray?

JENSEN: Yes.

CANDY: *(making another disgusted sound)* Does it come in boxes?

JENSEN: Yeah.

CANDY: Like punk? I like punk. I'm sorry but it's just awful.

■

After these sessions with Candy, John Nebel was convinced that Dr. Gilbert Jensen had hypnotized her, either during her first visit to his office or during the next two visits. Nebel knew from experience that his wife was a good subject, perhaps made more so by repeated hypnosis in the past.* At this stage, however, Nebel had no knowledge of *why* Jensen might have practiced hypnosis on her. There was no evidence that Jensen had utilized her trance states to help her stop smoking. Nebel could only assume that Jensen was performing hypnosis for fun—a dubious practice. Nebel asked Candy about it on several occasions while she was in the waking state,** but she said she

---

*Candy Jones is an excellent hypnotic subject. She has had her Hypnotic Induction Profile (HIP) done four times, and in each case scored high enough on the scale to indicate good capacity for trance. An explanation of the HIP and an actual transcript of what occurred during one of Candy's tests appear in Appendix 1 at the end of the book.

**The use of the term *waking state* is a debatable one. Since hypnosis is not sleep and is, in fact, the antithesis of sleep, *waking state* becomes an acceptable *misnomer* in designating the conscious state.

couldn't remember anything about Jensen's office and what had occurred there.

This loss of memory, Nebel realized from his studies, could easily be chalked up to hypnosis. A good subject displays global amnesia as one of the symptoms of having entered deep trance. Then too, a hypnotist working with a good subject can easily implant the posthypnotic suggestion that the subject will not recall anything that occurred before, during and after achieving trance. Again, however, Nebel could not justify Jensen taking such a step with Candy. *Why* cause her to forget what had transpired in his office?

Nebel worked to find answers to his questions. But the issue became even more confused as new information was disclosed during his hypnotic sessions with Candy. Nebel had been proceeding on the assumption that Jensen had hypnotized her using conventional techniques. But in January 1974 an entirely new and disturbing aspect was introduced.*

After regressing Candy back to one of the early visits to Jensen's office, Nebel asked her how long she had been there. Candy said she didn't know. Nebel then asked her to tell him what Jensen had just said to her. (Nebel played her alter ego during this session and did not attempt to slip into the role of Gilbert Jensen.)

■

CANDY: He said, "Just stretch your arm out."

JOHN: Are you on a table?

CANDY: He said it would be easier if I just stretched out. I didn't want to but he said to.

JOHN: He's going to give you a vitamin? In the arm?

CANDY: Yeah. I'm glad it's in the arm instead of in my buttocks. I didn't like him to give me shots in the Pacific. That was terrible. I was embarrassed [at receiving shots in the buttocks].

■

There had been times in the past when Candy had casually mentioned that she'd routinely received vitamin shots from Jen-

*Tape #33 "B," Side A.

sen. Nebel had not attached any significance to it, even when she added that the vitamins had been administered intravenously. Although Nebel knew that vitamin injections were usually given intramuscularly, he had ignored the incongruity until this session.

■

JOHN: Does he have a rubber tube on the needle?
CANDY: Uh-huh.
JOHN: Is it coming from a bottle overhead?
CANDY: It's on a stand.
JOHN: The bottle is hanging on the stand?
CANDY: Uh-huh. Like they used to have.
JOHN: Like intravenous feeding.
CANDY: Uh-huh.
JOHN: The bottle's upside down, isn't it? . . . *(Candy looks up and squints.)* . . . Isn't it upside down? . . .
CANDY: *(surprised)* Yeah.
JOHN: What's it say on the label?
CANDY: *(after a long pause)* I'm reading it backwards.
JOHN: Yeah, I know. What's it say?
CANDY: *(haltingly, as though trying to make out the word)* "Am . . . i . . . tol.
JOHN: Amathol?
CANDY: Ama . . . tiol . . .
JOHN: What's the first word?
CANDY: *(Unintelligible.)* Must be sodium.
JOHN: Sodium? Does it say the name of the pharmaceutical company on the label?
CANDY: I think it says Warner.
JOHN: Anything else?
CANDY: Just Warner I think it says.
JOHN: How does the needle feel in your arm? No pain, is there?
CANDY: *(drawing a deep breath)* No, I had it all straightened out.
JOHN: What did you have straightened out?
CANDY: Like a little ironing board.
JOHN: Where?
CANDY: Next to me.
JOHN: Oh. Where you have your arm?

CANDY: Uh-huh.
JOHN: Okay, that's good. Is he [Jensen] coming back in now?
CANDY: He's over there.

∎

Nebel was now confronted with another question to be answered. Although he still didn't know for certain, he was almost sure that the intravenous shots were not the vitamins Jensen had represented them to be. *Narcohypnosis* (the use of drugs to induce hypnosis) is well known to the medical profession, but it is generally agreed that hypnosis induced by natural means is more effective than that brought about through the use of the numerous drugs available. Nevertheless, it is also agreed that, given a subject who balks at being hypnotized, or displays a low capacity for entering the trance state, the use of hypnotic drugs seldom fails. John Nebel was to learn a great deal more about narcohypnosis in the months ahead, both from future hypnotic sessions with his wife and through a crash reading course, aided by conferences with many of his friends in medicine.

He was also to learn more about this "other woman" with whom he seemed to be living, Arlene Grant. It was a bizarre triangle, one man and two women, the women sharing a common body. And it was not pleasant, for Arlene began to exert herself in ways that caused John and Candy much embarrassment, trouble and sorrow. John decided that the only solution was to try to discover the origins of Arlene Grant's rebirth in Candy's adult life, and his search led him to conclude that Arlene's reappearance could be traced directly to the office of Dr. Gilbert Jensen.

# 10

## The "Hatching" of Arlene

On an undated 1973 hypnotic-session tape, the following dialogue took place. Candy had suddenly and dramatically slipped into Arlene's role when asked by Nebel whether she thought Jensen had crippled her.

■

ARLENE: *(scornfully)* She [Candy] stepped right into it. She knew what she was doing.

JOHN: You mean Candy wanted it to be done?

ARLENE: Of course not. She didn't know what end was up.

*(Nebel mentions an appointment he has the following day with Dr. Herbert Spiegel, who Nebel hopes will help him stop smoking.)*

ARLENE: Oh, I'll go along tomorrow. I'll sit there and I'll watch.

JOHN: You mean *you* will go, Arlene?

ARLENE: Of course I'll be there.

JOHN: Why would *you* go?

ARLENE: *(contemptuously)* Where she goes, I go. When it gets a little too rough, I step in.

JOHN: Who developed you really, Arlene? Jensen?

ARLENE: Mother Jensen. He hatched me like a mother hen.

JOHN: And he forced Candy to make you mature, right?

ARLENE: Nobody had to force her . . . she's too tired . . . she just sat back and let it happen.

JOHN: He hypnotized her.

ARLENE: So?

JOHN: Don't *you* know that?

ARLENE: Of course I know it.

JOHN: He couldn't hypnotize you, though, could he? Or do you think he did?

ARLENE: I am a *product* of hypnotism.

JOHN: But Jensen was the producer of the product, right?

ARLENE: He was the mother hen. He hatched me.

JOHN: Are you happy about it?

ARLENE: I'm not happy, I'm not unhappy. It's just a fact, that's all.

JOHN: Do you think that . . .

ARLENE: *(interrupting)* You really don't like me at all, do you?

JOHN: I don't hate you.

ARLENE: You know, I've done a lot to help her.

JOHN: For instance?

ARLENE: I gave her time to get better.

JOHN: Was she ill?

ARLENE: No, she needed time to think. . . . She's thinking right now. . . . She's thinking how tired she is.

■

They proceeded to discuss Candy for the next few minutes, during which time Arlene claimed that Candy was in the process of rejuvenating herself. Nebel finally asked Arlene whether she considered Jensen to be a dangerous man.

ARLENE: No. . . . He's petrified . . . he's a weakling.

JOHN: Do you think he made a mistake hatching you?

ARLENE: *(laughing)* Absolutely, and he knows it. He's *petrified* of me.

■

Whether the initial meeting between Arlene and Jensen took place on Candy's first visit to Oakland or during a subsequent visit is again unclear, but a mosaic of what occurred can be pieced together from a number of tapes recorded by Nebel.

Once Jensen had become aware of Candy's imaginary child-hood friends, he set out to bring back into her adult life some of those fanciful characters, particularly Arlene. She had been, according to Candy, the dominant personality in the "club." Arlene could run faster, climb higher and swim better than any of the other club members, including Candy, and took over whenever Candy was engaged in difficult physical activities. Both Candy and Arlene, in various hypnotic sessions with Nebel, freely discussed Arlene's superiority in those areas. From Jensen's point of view, Arlene could be the most useful as a "second personality," if, from this retrospective position, he can be given the benefit of the doubt and assumed to have been in search of another person within Candy Jones with whom to accomplish something tangible. That tangible goal would be to create what G. H. Estabrooks termed "the perfect spy."

Estabrooks, now deceased, headed the psychology department at Colgate University. He was a pioneer in hypnosis and published a book in 1943 with E. P. Dutton, *Hypnotism.* It was updated and reissued in 1957, and contains a chapter entitled "Hypnotism in Warfare: The Super Spy." He describes in great detail how hypnosis might be used in a variety of wartime situations, but focuses primarily on its value in preparing a messenger who is to carry secret information:

> With hypnotism we can be sure of our private messenger. We hypnotize our man say, in Washington. In hypnotism we give him the message. That message, may we add, can be both long and intricate. An intelligent individual can memorize a whole book if necessary.* Then we start him out for Australia by plane with the instructions that no one can hypnotize him under any circumstances except Colonel Brown in Melbourne. By this device we overcome two difficulties. It is useless to intercept this messenger.
>
> He has no documents and no amount of "third degreeing" can extract the information, for the information is not

*Hypnotism as an aid to learning is just beginning to be appreciated. Dr. Ray LaScola, a psychiatrist in Santa Monica, California, has reported having successfully enabled a medical student to review an entire year's study in one forty-five-minute hypnotic session. Time is easily compressed while in the trance state, and retention levels are significantly raised.

in the conscious mind to extract. We could also make him insensitive to pain so that even the third degree would be useless.

Also, with this hypnotic messenger we need have no worry about the double cross. In hypnotism we could build up his loyalty to the point where this would be unthinkable. Besides, he has nothing to tell. He is just a civilian with a business appointment in Australia, nothing more. He will give no information, for he has none to give. By this device we could make it much safer to send information when and where the private messenger could be used.

According to what Candy Jones had been told when she first became involved with the CIA, she would be a messenger for the agency in conjunction with her normal business trips. Was Dr. Gilbert Jensen using hypnosis to turn her into the perfect messenger? Probably. The theories Estabrooks describes have been in practice since World War II, and Jensen certainly knew that Candy was a good subject, despite her claims to the contrary. Her presence in his office gave him a compelling opportunity to have under his control a messenger in whom he could have complete and unfailing trust. Perhaps, were the messages she was to carry of crucial importance, taking such a step could be justified in the interest of "national security." Less important matters are buried under that catchall phrase every day.

But why Arlene? Was she necessary to insure Jensen a safe and trustworthy messenger? Again, we can only speculate on his motives for seeking to resurrect Arlene. Estabrooks says in *Hypnosis* that creating the truly "super spy" is possible through the deliberate splitting of personalities within one person:

> . . . we will use hypnotism to induce multiple personality.
> . . . We start with an excellent subject, and he must be just
> that, one of those rare individuals who accepts and who
> carries through every suggestion without hesitation. In ad-
> dition, we need a man or a woman who is highly intelligent
> and physically tough. Then we start to develop a case of
> multiple personality through the use of hypnotism. In his
> normal waking state, which we will call Personality A, or
> PA, this individual will become a rabid communist. He will

join the party, follow the party line and make himself as objectionable as possible to the authorities.

Then we develop Personality B (PB), the secondary personality, the unconscious personality, if you wish, although this is somewhat of a contradiction in terms. This personality is rabidly American and anti-communist. It has all the information possessed by Personality A, the normal personality, whereas PA does not have this advantage.

My super spy plays his role as a communist in the waking state, aggressively, consistently, fearlessly. But his PB is a loyal American, and PB has all the memories of PA. As a loyal American, he will not hesitate to divulge these memories.

Estabrooks goes on at length to further develop this thesis, but what I have quoted is sufficient to show that, by having Arlene in the picture, Jensen had a ready-made checks-and-balances system in operation with Candy. There was no question of Candy Jones's patriotism; but if she did decide to withhold something from Jensen following a mission, Arlene would be available to fill in the gaps. Also, in Arlene, Jensen had access to the side of Candy that excelled in physical activity. If in danger, better to have Arlene face it than Candy. And if tortured, Arlene could be programmed to suffer the pain while Candy looked on. Tolerance for pain increases dramatically under hypnosis. Thousands of surgical procedures have been performed with only hypnosis as the anesthesia. Estabrooks, writing about this increased tolerance for pain, says: "This writer uses a little device known as a variac. This is plugged into an ordinary light socket and it delivers the exact voltage required. The contacts are placed on the palm and the back of the left hand, blotting paper, soaked in a saturated salt solution, being used to insure the very best form of contact. Under these circumstances, fifteen volts would be very painful, twenty unbearable. But a subject in somnambulism *(deep trance)* can take sixty, even 120 volts without flinching."

But while all these are possible reasons for Jensen's acts, it is my contention that, beyond his use of hypnosis to accomplish a mission, Jensen was equally as interested in determining what *could* be accomplished on an experimental basis. It is conceivable that the messages Candy actually did carry were worthless or, at best, of minor importance to any overall intelligence scheme. As will be detailed later, and according to hypnotic tapes, Candy became a traveling guinea pig for Jensen, his pride and joy as he demonstrated to CIA medical colleagues the control he was able to exert over her, and over Arlene Grant. Although I do not have in my possession any document linking Gilbert Jensen to a CIA experimental project, I believe that he was one of a number of doctors in this country involved in an ongoing program of experimental mind control, initiated and funded by the CIA.

That such a program was, and is, in existence is rapidly becoming a matter of public record. The Rockefeller Commission Report of June 1975, presumably the result of a fair and intensive investigation of the CIA's domestic activities, revealed that in 1953 Frank R. Olson, a civilian biological-warfare researcher working for the CIA, was given a dose of LSD by the agency without his knowledge. The report goes on to state that Olson later allegedly committed suicide by leaping from a tenth-story hotel window in New York City where he had been taken for psychiatric help as a direct result of his LSD experience. He was given the drug as part of a broad testing program within the CIA's Directorate of Science and Technology.

The CIA claims it ceased all such testing in 1967. It also claims to have destroyed all its records of such experimentation. Perhaps it did close down its testing project as claimed, perhaps not. But Gilbert Jensen was still operating in 1967, maybe in violation of instructions from the CIA, or more likely as a covert continuation of that agency's program.*

Victor Marchetti, author of *The CIA and the Cult of Intelligence,* confirmed to me that the agency did indeed have a program of experimental mind control and that it used prisoners in American penal institutions as its subjects.

Candy vaguely refers to such a program on a tape when she says, "... it was very dangerous. I was on a special project, a very important project."** It's possible that she was referring to a specific mission rather than the experimental project, but I think

*The section of the Rockefeller Report pertaining to the Directorate of Science and Technology appears in Appendix 2 at the end of the book.
**Tape #66, Side B.

not. She was never told about the project but perhaps picked up a sense of it from extraneous conversation in Jensen's office.

Most CIA experimental projects funded through the Directorate of Science and Technology are actually carried out by outside civilian organizations. Because so many of these projects are highly secret, there is no accurate way in which to judge how many millions of dollars are funneled through outside research organizations. One can only assume from judging the absurdity of certain projects that too much money is being spent for questionable research—questionable in terms of its value, and/or in terms of its immoral and illegal uses. Dean Kraft, a young "psychic healer" from Brooklyn, told me on Nebel's show that the government paid him to test his supposed healing powers in various California laboratories, some of the same facilities in which Jensen tested Candy's response to his control. Kraft was told not to question which government agency supplied the money, and he was not to inquire into the backgrounds of any of the men with whom he worked.

The research into mind control sponsored by the CIA is defended on the basis that the Soviet Union has been engaged in such research for many years. Lee Harvey Oswald, the accused assassin of John Kennedy, spent time at a behavior modification institute in Moscow during his years in the Soviet Union. There has been speculation that Oswald was, in some way, programmed to kill President Kennedy, although this has never progressed beyond speculation. Similar claims have been made, and are a matter of public record, that Sirhan Sirhan, Robert Kennedy's assassin, was programmed under hypnosis to commit that murder. James Earl Ray was hypnotized in Los Angeles two months prior to killing Martin Luther King, Jr. in Memphis.

I would certainly feel more comfortable believing that Gilbert Jensen worked alone for his own amusement, a "nut" without ties to any of *my* government's agencies. If not, then perhaps he did overstep the limits imposed upon him by the CIA. It is possible that Jensen continued his experimentation with Candy —and Arlene—after the CIA issued its alleged orders to cease the experiments.

At any rate, whether Jensen was as petrified of Arlene as she claimed, he would certainly have had reason to be concerned about her in light of her revelations to John Nebel about the strange events that took place in his Oakland office for 12 years. And, I suppose his first face-to-face confrontation with Arlene might have been as startling to him as it was to Nebel, Dr. Jekyll encountering Mr. Hyde.

Arlene's first appearance in Jensen's office is best recalled by Arlene during a hypnotic session in Nebel's apartment on December 16, 1974. Nebel had asked her if she remembered the first time Jensen "brought her out." Arlene tossed back her head and guffawed, then said yes.

■

JOHN: Tell me about it.
ARLENE: *(still laughing and enjoying the recollection)* I thought he was going to go through the roof.
JOHN: How did it happen? Candy was sitting in a chair?
ARLENE: Well, he [Jensen] was trying to get the name, and he was curious. . . .
JOHN: What name?
ARLENE: He was trying to get her to change her name and . . .
JOHN: To what?
ARLENE: Anything, it didn't matter. They were looking for a name.
JOHN: Yes?
ARLENE: And she was telling him about . . . *(clears her throat)* . . . when we were all very young . . . I was an imaginary playmate.
JOHN: She told Jensen that?
ARLENE: Yes. And she convinced him that Arlene used to talk to her as a little girl. I *did.* In the mirror.
JOHN: And? *(Arlene makes no response.)* And all of a sudden Arlene came out sitting there in the office?
ARLENE: He kept at it and at it and . . .
JOHN: Did he give her vitamin shots first?
ARLENE: Yes, two.
JOHN: Was this early in the time when she met him?
ARLENE: Yes.
JOHN: The first time or a couple of times later?
ARLENE: No, a few times later.
JOHN: And?
ARLENE: And all of a sudden she got a bad stomachache.

JOHN: In the office? Yes, go ahead.

ARLENE: On the table, and all of a sudden I was able to say a few words and start to talk again.

JOHN: *(laughing)* And was he surprised?

ARLENE: He backed away. I got ahold of his arm, and then he said——

JOHN: You mean Dr. Jensen's arm?

ARLENE: Yes, with my left hand. And I pulled him over, and he said, "Let go!" . . . And he said, "What are you trying to do? . . . And he said, "Candy, Candy, stop that!" . . . And I said, "This is Arlene." . . . And he said, "You're hurting me!" *(a pleased laugh)* . . . And I was. And he said, "Good God, you're strong." . . .

JOHN: Meaning you, Arlene?

ARLENE: Yes. And he said, "You're Arlene." . . . And I said, "Who were you expecting?" . . .

■

According to Arlene during this session with Nebel, Dr. Jensen then told her to get up from his examining table to look in the mirror in his office, which she did.

■

JOHN: What did you see in the mirror?

ARLENE: I saw Candy.

JOHN: Did Candy look different? Was there a different expression on her face?

ARLENE: I don't know, but it didn't look like the way I look today. But that's because *then* . . . *then* I started to wear a wig. Candy put a wig on me so I didn't look like Candy at all.

JOHN: Was there a different expression on her face when you put the wig on?

ARLENE: Yes. It's in the eyes. I can't describe it. I can feel it. . . . It's a different look in the eyes . . . serious, intent.

JOHN: Disturbed?

ARLENE: You mean as in crazy?

JOHN: Yeah.

ARLENE: *(on the verge of laughter)* I saw me in a picture, too.

JOHN: Where'd you see a picture?

ARLENE: *My* picture, in *my* [cosmetic] case.

■

Nebel continued to ask about Jensen's actions on that day when Arlene first "came out." She told Nebel that Jensen told her to go away, but had added that she would come out whenever he (Jensen) asked for her. "He told me I'd always come up through Candy's stomach."

■

JOHN: What would he say to you to bring you out? What were the words?

ARLENE: He'd say, "A. G.! A. G.!"

JOHN: And Candy would feel a stomach pain?

ARLENE: When I came out it seemed to cause one.

JOHN: Did you ever fail to come out?

ARLENE: Yes. *(becoming intense)* Lots of times I wouldn't.

JOHN: And what did Jensen do?

ARLENE: Give her another shot.

JOHN: Another shot. What was the most number of shots she ever got in one day?

ARLENE: He gave her three once and she couldn't wake up. And he got scared.

JOHN: How long was she out?

ARLENE: She wasn't out, she was asleep. She slept for about fourteen hours.

JOHN: In the office?

ARLENE: Uh-huh.

■

Nebel then pursued another line of questioning, namely whether Arlene thought Jensen was in love with Candy. This had occurred to me, too, as I researched this book. I wondered whether a relationship had developed between Candy and Jensen in the South Pacific during World War II. Although it was a tantalizing bit of speculation, I could find no evidence of it in all the material available to me. Arlene, too, denied that Jensen was in love with Candy. "Jensen didn't like Candy," Arlene told Nebel during that December 16, 1974, session.

Nebel then asked, "Do you think Jensen could have fallen in love with *you*, Arlene?"

"No, but he liked *me* better than *her.*" When asked why, Arlene replied, "Because I'm more to the point. I wasn't afraid. At least I didn't let him know when I was afraid."

Nebel again asked whether Arlene was at his wedding to Candy, and Arlene agreed that she was. She then said that there was a photograph of her at the wedding. Nebel, surprised at hearing this, asked her to show him the photograph. Arlene laughed and said the picture was in *his* book, meaning the biography I'd written of Long John Nebel. She described the picture to Nebel, and he took a copy of the book from the shelf and located the photo to which Arlene referred in the upper left-hand corner of the first page of a centerfold pictorial section. Candy, or Arlene, is in the background. In the foreground is a longtime Nebel friend, insurance broker Al Lottman. There is a detached, enigmatic expression on Candy's face in the photo, and Arlene claimed that she had taken over the body just before the photographer, Gary Wagner, took that picture.

"Candy got a bad stomachache at the wedding," Arlene told Nebel.

■

JOHN: Why were you there, Arlene?
ARLENE: Watching, and making her feel sad.
JOHN: Why did you make her feel sad?
ARLENE: Because she shouldn't do that.
JOHN: Shouldn't get married?
ARLENE: No, I couldn't believe it myself.

■

This session between Arlene and Nebel ended when Arlene began moaning and doubling up on the bed.

■

JOHN: What's wrong?
ARLENE: It's a bad stomachache.
JOHN: What does that mean when *you* have a bad stomachache?
ARLENE: I don't know.
JOHN: It's Candy's stomachache, isn't it?
ARLENE: Yes.
JOHN: Does it affect you, too?

ARLENE: It weakens me.

JOHN: Are you going away now?

ARLENE: The longer it keeps up, the more I've got to stop.

JOHN: Stop what?

ARLENE: Just being. It *does* weaken me.

JOHN: And then do you go back in and does Candy feel better?

ARLENE: It takes a lot out of both of us. *She* feels better.

■

Nebel asked Arlene whether she had ever talked to Jensen on the phone when he'd called Candy in New York.

■

ARLENE: Both of us talked to him.

JOHN: Did he ask for A. G.? Suppose Candy was talking to him and he said, "A. G." What would happen?

ARLENE: Didn't happen that way.

JOHN: Can you explain how it happened?

ARLENE: Happened with the code.

JOHN: What's the code?

ARLENE: Tick tock, tick tock. *(She keeps repeating it faster and faster.)*

JOHN: And would that make you come out, Arlene?

ARLENE: *(sounding weaker)* It would make Candy relax so I could come out.

■

The rest of this particular session was very dramatic from an audio point of view. Arlene grew progressively weaker and her moans increased in intensity. Nebel commented into the microphone that her face was horribly distorted. He asked her whether he would see her again. She replied that she was only allowed to talk with Gilbert Jensen and that she wouldn't see Nebel again.

"She's coming back," Arlene moaned. "Up through my throat. She's almost out." Instantly, there was a voice change from the strident, sarcastic tones of Arlene Grant to a sleepy and soft Candy Jones. Nebel asked her where she was, and she replied that she was in bed with her husband, John. Nebel commented into the microphone that there was a dreamy smile on her face.

The session was over.

# 11

## The Early Assignments

Candy Jones began to perform services for the CIA as herself, as Arlene Grant and under her real name, Jessica Wilcox. One of the first instructions she received from Jensen was to lease a post-office box at Grand Central Station in the name of Jessica Wilcox. She took the box (according to material gathered from a January 1974 tape) in August 1961, and maintained it until 1968 or 1969. The box number was 1294, and she paid for it quarterly from her own pocket.

"It was a pain in the neck," she told Nebel during that January hypnotic session. "I hated walking over to check the box every day."

Little mail moved through the box, and when a letter did arrive, Candy would take it back to her offices on Vanderbilt Avenue and hold it for pickup by a man whose name was unknown to her. At that time she was still not sure whom she worked for, but thought the man who picked up the letters was with the FBI.

There were occasions when the arrival of a letter at Box 1294 was accompanied by telephone instructions from Jensen. In those instances Candy delivered the envelopes herself to various locations around the city. It should be pointed out that Candy has little conscious memory of her actual CIA activities. Jensen's use of hypnosis and drugs effectively "locked out" her memory. Hypnosis is very efficient in creating amnesia, as are certain of the hypnotic drugs used on her by her Oakland control agent.

One problem she faced during her early days with the CIA was a growing fear for her safety. Even before she was sent on missions to Asia, she was concerned that those people to whom she delivered messages in New York might, for their own reasons, do her harm. Of particular worry was what would happen were she to die while working or traveling as Arlene Grant. That possibility would, she reasoned, jeopardize her insurance benefits.

When she mentioned to Jensen that her three sons were enrolled in private schools and that their tuitions were a drain on her resources, he suggested that payment for her work be sent directly to the schools to pay the tuition and residence-hall expenses. She agreed to this after being told by him that operatives are never paid directly by The Company.

Jensen was right; the CIA has always arranged payment to covert operatives through indirect channels to avoid the operative having a sudden influx of new cash with which to change his life-style and, by extension, to draw attention to himself.

To cover herself in the event she died, Candy wrote a letter to her attorney, William Williams, and copies of it were deposited in two different safety-deposit boxes. It was the first time she even hinted to anyone else that her life involved more than modeling.

The letter read:

Dear Bill:

. . . For reasons I won't go into here, it is sufficient to know that I use the name, ARLENE GRANT, (sometimes spelled as ARLINE) for certain activities. Obviously, Jesse Wilcox, Candy Jones and Arlene Grant are all one person, namely —me.

In the event of my death, due to an accident or sudden illness and its occurance outside of New York City or the United States, and including the above three names which

I use in my personal and career life, please have my demise checked, if at all possible . . .

I am not at liberty to divulge the sideline activity in which I am involved, however, you can be assured that in no way is it illegal, immoral or unpatriotic.

In the event of my death, and you pursue the cause and uncover an unusual, or perhaps inexplicable reason, when the boys are of age which you consider reasonable for them to comprehend, you have my permission. If the details are frightening or morbid, because of my mother's age, I prefer she not be told. . . .

Another, though lesser, worry was that her sudden and unexplained disappearances would cause concern with the people who worked in her office, and with Joe Vergara, her editor at Harper and Row. Vergara had become a good friend during the course of their writer-editor association, and Candy trusted him implicitly. When I asked her whether she had ever told anyone of her secret government involvement, the only person she mentioned was Vergara. I called him in early December 1974, and following that telephone conversation we met for lunch on December 12 at Antolotti's. During lunch Vergara confirmed that Candy had told him she was involved with a government agency as a courier and might disappear from time to time. She also told him that she would be taking trips to Asia.

"Did she mention the CIA by name?" I asked him over lunch.

"No," he said. "She simply told me that she was working for a secret government agency."

I questioned Joe Vergara about Candy's behavior patterns during the Sixties, particularly whether she displayed another, incongruent side of her personality.

"Yes, she did have puzzling personality changes," he replied, "but I chalked it up to artistic temperament. Come to think of it, though, they were more dramatic than simple personality changes."

I was, of course, trying to find out whether Arlene had ever surfaced in Vergara's presence. She had not, at least not by name.

But four days later, during a hypnotic session between John

and Candy, Nebel, spurred by the recounting of my meeting with Vergara, asked Arlene whether Candy had ever told Vergara about her CIA activities.

■

ARLENE: Candy is a lousy judge of character. She trusts everybody.

JOHN: Did you ever . . . did Candy ever say anything to Joe Vergara?

JOHN: You mean when he went with Candy to that restaurant? *(He is referring to a time Candy asked Vergara to accompany her while she delivered a letter that had arrived at post office Box 1294. She was to deliver the letter to a man in The Palms Restaurant, and was frightened to go alone. She called Vergara and he went with her in a cab. Vergara waited in the cab while she went inside, handed the letter to a man who fit the description provided her, and returned. Vergara recalls the incident and discussed it at our December 12 lunch.)*

ARLENE: Yes.

JOHN: Why don't you like him [Vergara]?

ARLENE: *(annoyed)* He didn't believe anything. She tried to tell him. Unfortunately he didn't believe. I think he thought she was having a crack-up.

■

One other person was told vaguely of Candy's covert operations during the Sixties, columnist Mel Heimer, now deceased. Candy and Mel were good friends until he died, although Heimer's love for the racetrack resulted in debts that contributed to Candy's shaky financial position. She loaned him substantial sums of cash, none of which was ever repaid. The extent to which she filled Heimer in about her CIA activities is unclear. My assumption is that she told him more than she told Joe Vergara, and Gilbert Jensen's distrust of Heimer indicates that he, too, was unsure about Candy's relationship with the columnist. Candy mentions on one tape that Jensen made it a point to read the books Heimer had written, and to see him when he appeared on a national TV talk show. When Candy mentioned to Jensen that she had considered marrying Heimer at one point but decided against it, Jensen assured her that her decision was wise.

On another tape in which Nebel played the role of Gilbert Jensen, Candy discussed with Jensen her relationship with Mel Heimer.

■

JOHN: *(as Jensen)* Do you ever tell your friend Mel about what you do?

CANDY: No, no. I don't say anything to anybody. I don't talk to anybody about anything I do.

JOHN: *(skeptical)* You never tell Mel about anything?

CANDY: *(after a long sigh of resignation)* I told him that if I have to have any help and if I ever tell him to come fast, to please come. I'd need him to help me.

JOHN: Do you think that was advisable to tell him?

CANDY: Yes.

JOHN: Why?

CANDY: Because if I need some help, I don't have anybody to help me. Sometimes it's scary.

JOHN: Would you rather you'd never started?

CANDY: Yes. It's all your [Jensen's] fault, you know.

JENSEN: Why is it my fault? I didn't start you.

CANDY: It's your fault that I ever got in this far.

■

During another hypnotic session with Nebel, Candy repeated that she had told Mel to come running in case she needed help. She mentioned on this tape that Mel had accompanied her one day "downtown" while she delivered a letter, just as Joe Vergara had done.

There is also evidence that Candy helped Mel with the writing of one of his books, its working title *Dark Wood*. It concerned espionage in Cuba, and Candy apparently gave Heimer much of the background detail about covert espionage work, including an elaborate description of how covert operatives or "covers" work.

The material from the tapes makes it obvious that Arlene and Mel had their confrontations, too, although Mel, to my knowledge, was not aware that he was dealing with anyone other than Candy Jones. On one tape, Nebel asked Arlene whether Mel liked *her*.

"He never knew what hit him," Arlene replied, giving out with her typically petulant laugh.

One of the more fascinating aspects of Candy Jones's dual existence concerns the relationship between her and Arlene. They often offered their advice and opinions to each other, and an intriguing protective attitude toward one another developed over the years. In one instance Arlene told Candy that Mel Heimer was a "hoodwinker" and that Candy should stay away from him. Arlene confirms her dislike for Heimer on a number of tapes. Although I have never personally experienced such a dialogue between Candy and Arlene, I can only speculate on how unsettling it might have been for those within earshot. Candy's mother was never aware of the adult presence of Arlene Grant in her daughter's life, but on two occasions heard a strange voice coming from Candy's bedroom at 1199 Park Avenue and, on one of those occasions, believed that Candy had a man in the bedroom.

# 12

# Oakland–The Programming Continues

*It's summer in the early 1960s. Candy lies on the examining table in Gilbert Jensen's Oakland office, the needle securely implanted in a vein in the crook of her right arm. A slender plastic tube leads upward from the needle to a bottle that hangs from a metal stand. The office is cold, the air conditioning set at its highest continuous cooling level.*

*Jensen sits in a chair reading a mimeographed sheet of paper. He looks up at Candy, then returns to his reading.*

This scene in Oakland was relived by Candy while in a hypnotic trance in the bedroom of the apartment she shares with her husband, John Nebel. It was one of many scenes in which Jensen's use of intravenous feedings came to the surface. As this particular hypnotic session progressed, Nebel, who was sitting quietly next to the bed, suggested to his wife that she ask Jensen how long the needle would have to stay in her arm. Without hesitation, Candy turned and yelled across the bedroom to the unseen Jensen. "How long does this take?" she asked. She reached down and gingerly touched the inside of her right elbow where the needle had been inserted. She evidently recalled something Jensen had actually asked years ago, because she replied by shouting, "No!" Nebel watched silently as Candy again asked Jensen when the needle could come out; she added that she had to get back to her hotel in San Francisco.

"What did he say?" Nebel asked her. "You can tell me."

"He asked me why I was asking [about the needle]," she replied. "He asked me if it hurt and whether I was uncomfortable."

"Is he still reading that mimeographed paper?" Nebel probed.

"No. He just got up and went into his office. He put the paper in his desk drawer."

Nebel suggested to Candy that she attempt to see what had been written on the sheet of paper, but she ignored the suggestion. Playing her alter ego, he told her to again yell and ask Jensen when the needle could come out, which she did.

"I don't know where he's gone," Candy told Nebel, referring to Jensen.

"Are you out there?" she asked, projecting her voice through the imaginary door between the examining room and the office. Jensen must have yelled something back at her because she responded by saying, "Oh." She asked, "Don't you think I'm done yet?" Her voice had a nasty edge to it.

A bit later in the tape, and after ten seconds of silence, Candy muttered, "It's on a board," referring to her arm. She then said, "Ouch! You ought to sharpen your needles." (Jensen had apparently returned and pulled the needle from Candy's arm.) She flexed her elbow and made a fist, squinting to see what mark the needle had made and to check for bleeding. Nebel watched silently as Candy continued with her side of the dialogue with Jensen.

"Yes," she told Jensen, "it did hurt."

"Why are you squeezing your fist?" Nebel asked her.

She didn't respond, saying to Jensen instead, "You have cotton in there," pointing to the inside of her elbow. She was looking up at a space above her in the bedroom, not at Nebel but at the spot where Jensen would be standing. After a few moments, she told Jensen she'd taken the cotton wad off because her arm wasn't bleeding.

Nebel surmised that Jensen left the examining room at this point, and Nebel watched as Candy swung her legs off the edge of the bed (the examining table in her regression) and stretched. "All right, I'm coming out," she shouted to Jensen. "I have to get dressed." Nebel stepped back and observed his wife fumbling with imaginary clothing. She took what seemed to be a blouse from a hook in the air and slipped it over her arms. She was wearing a nightgown throughout this hypnotic session, but continued to dress herself. First the blouse and then a skirt, which she stepped into with great care. She slowly buttoned the blouse and tucked it into the skirt with deliberate movements.

"I just need my shoes," she shouted to Jensen. "Do you think I need a Band-Aid?" Jensen evidently said something, and Candy replied by saying, "No, it wasn't." (Hypnotic sessions such as these produced intense frustration in John Nebel because he had no way of knowing what Jensen was saying unless Candy told him, and he could never depend upon her to do that. He could only guess at Jensen's words based upon Candy's responses, a tenuous game.)

Candy walked across their small bedroom and searched for her shoes. There were numerous pairs in the closets and on the floor, but she was looking for the pair she'd worn to Jensen's office that day in the early 1960s. "Where are my shoes?" she asked in a loud voice.

"Did you find your shoes?" Nebel asked.

"Yeah," she laughed.

"Are you going back into his office?" Nebel asked.

"Yup."

Nebel became concerned when Candy, still in the trance state, took a sudden series of steps toward the door to Jensen's office and almost ran into a bedroom wall. He jumped up, took her arm and gently led her back to the edge of the bed.

"Okay now," Nebel said, "you're in his office." Nebel asked her if Jensen was talking to her. She said he wasn't. Suddenly, she got up and again stumbled about the bedroom, apparently still in the examining room.

"Where's my bag?" she yelled to Jensen.

Nebel stood by and watched his wife continue with her bizarre playacting. "What did Jensen say?" Nebel asked her.

"He said he didn't know," Candy replied, still searching for her handbag. She yelled to Jensen: "It was right here on the table."

Eventually Candy found her bag beneath the examining table.

There was, of course, no real bag, but she picked up an imaginary one and went through the motions of opening it. She retrieved an imaginary comb from its recesses and began to comb her hair. Nebel's reaction was a meld of fascination and fear. To see his wife act in so unconventional a manner was a constant cause of concern for him. It made him wonder if Jensen's programming had left too indelible a mark to be erased. His greatest immediate fear, however, was that she would physically injure herself during a spontaneous trance, or would slip into such a deep trance that he would be unable to control her.

She placed the comb back inside her bag and walked toward the bedroom door.

"Where are you going?" Nebel asked, moving toward her. "What are you going to do now?"

"I'm just coming here," said Candy, speaking to Jensen. She entered Jensen's office by walking aimlessly about the bedroom. Nebel again had to guide her to avoid injury.

"I'll sit here," she announced, plopping down on the edge of the bed. "Are you going to drive me back? How do I get back now?"

Nebel asked her for Jensen's answer.

Candy ignored him and asked Jensen, "Are you calling someone to drive me?"

"He's on the phone?" Nebel asked her. Candy indicated he was.

At this point in the session Candy reached out and accidentally touched the wood paneling on the wall. She came out of the trance, looked at John and asked, "Why are you awake, John? You must be tired."


As I write this book in the summer of 1975, the nation's leading newspapers and television news programs daily report new revelations with regard to government testing of behavior-modifying drugs. It was not only the CIA that experimented on innocent and unknowing persons; the army, according to published reports, has been testing such substances as LSD, atropine and scopolamine since the early 1950s, and continues to do so. Atropine is a natural extract of belladonna plants and is a well-known poison. Scopolamine is a depressant. Both drugs are used medically for motion sickness, muscle relaxation, sedation and amnesia to childbirth and for a host of other therapeutic strategies. Given in large doses, both drugs can cause hallucinations. The army claims to have ceased experimentation with LSD in 1967, but admits that the 535 servicemen and civilians given LSD during an eight-year testing program had not been informed that they were receiving the drug. In all, over 2000 human subjects were tested under this project, and the army currently awaits approval from the surgeon general's office to mount new tests.

It was revealed on July 28, 1975, that the Department of Health, Education and Welfare (HEW) had tested LSD on 2500 prisoners, mental patients and paid volunteers since 1954. HEW claims that all subjects gave their prior consent, although one wonders how mental patients could legally give such approval. It was also pointed out that in addition to HEW's direct testing programs, millions of dollars had been granted to more than 30 university researchers for additional testing of LSD on human subjects, primarily college students.

And, of course, there is the CIA and its drug-testing programs which have recently been brought to the public's attention, and under which Gilbert Jensen ostensibly functioned with immunity.

The U.S. government's seemingly insatiable fascination with the testing of mind-controlling drugs is, I suppose, explainable when viewed in the context of the power struggles of the 1950s and early 1960s. The threat was communism, and all means were justified to put a halt to its stated purpose of burying competing systems. Shoes were banged at the United Nations, fists were shaken and voices rose as the two dominant powers of the post–World War II era, the United States and the Soviet Union, jockeyed for the position of world leadership. One can understand a Gilbert Jensen rising to the call of his government and proceeding with his covert experimental work, despite what ethical and moral reservations might have dwelt within him at the time. It is difficult to imagine refusing a request from the government's highest authorities during that turbulent period. Those were years of blind trust in our institutions and in our leadership, the sort of trust that propelled Candy Jones into her relationship with the CIA and with Gilbert Jensen without so much as a question concerning the legality or propriety of the work and its goals.

But there was more than mere patriotism to explain Candy's willingness to become involved with the CIA, and that has to do with her highly suggestible personality. As can be seen in Appendix 1, Candy Jones rates high on the Hypnotic Induction Profile scale developed by Dr. Herbert Spiegel. Spiegel himself has graded Candy as a "five," and assigns to her what he terms "the grade 5 syndrome." In a paper published in 1974 in the *International Journal of Clinical and Experimental Hypnosis,* Spiegel says: "The features which together identify the grade 5 syndrome are: the high eye-roll sign; the high intact Hypnotic Induction Profile score; readiness to trust; a relative suspension of critical judgment; an ease of affiliation with new experiences; a telescoped time sense; an easy acceptance of logical incongruities; an excellent memory; a capacity for intense concentration; an overall tractability, and, paradoxically, a rigid core of private beliefs."*

The above personality traits, each of them a definite part of Candy's psychological portrait, coupled with a deep sense of patriotism (*her* "rigid core of private beliefs"), help explain why she proved so meek and unquestioning a subject for Jensen.

Ernest Becker in his book, *The Denial of Death,* says man is quick to assume that hypnotism is the result of a mysterious power within certain people that could cause others to fall under a spell. Man believes this must be so, according to Becker, because he "ignores the slavishness in his own soul." He prefers to believe that if he loses his will, it is because of someone else. The fact is, says Becker, that man carries within him a secret yearning and a readiness to respond to someone's voice and the snap of his fingers.

Becker refers to Ferenezi, who in 1909 wrote in an essay that it was very important for the hypnotist to be an imposing figure, of high social rank and possessing a self-confident manner. When such a hypnotist gives commands, said Ferenzi, there is nothing to do but obey, because his imposing, authoritarian figure takes the place of the parent.

In Candy's case, an inherent capacity for hypnosis was height-

*Vol. XXII, No. 4, pp. 303-19.

ened by drugs. What drugs did Jensen use? It is difficult to be certain, although a relatively clear picture can be drawn from material contained in Nebel's tapes, as well as from what is known about the available hallucinogens. Jensen's motivation is a clue, of course, for certain drugs act to induce, or to precondition a subject for hypnosis. Another clue is Candy's reactions to the drugs given her by Jensen.

One drug that probably was administered to Candy was sodium amytal. (The reader will recall Candy's reading this as Amitol when asked by her husband during a January 1974 session to read him the label on the bottle.) Like sodium pentothal, amytal is a barbiturate that induces trancelike reactions. It was widely used in World War II, and although experts acknowledge that sodium amytal and pentothal are effective in inducing a rapid trance in uncooperative or poor hypnotic subjects, they are quick to point out that extreme caution must be practiced; both drugs can be toxic when used in excessive doses. It is also obvious from research findings that while drugs are effective in inducing trance, much more can be accomplished with a subject who has been put in the trance state through normal, nonchemical techniques.

The January 1974 tape was one of many on which Candy relived sessions with Jensen and his so-called vitamin shots. She often argued with Jensen about the value of the intravenous feedings, and angered him on occasion by quoting Dr. Albert Aldridge, her New York gynecologist since 1946. Aldridge, recently retired, had administered vitamin B-12 shots to Candy on a number of occasions over the years. She'd told him about the shots she had been receiving from Jensen, and Aldridge counseled her against taking more of them. Whenever she brought up Aldridge's advice, Jensen invariably had harsh things to say about Aldridge, focusing on the fact that Aldridge was an older doctor, and intimating that he had not kept abreast of the changes in medicine.

On a tape recorded while Candy was in a hypnotic trance at home in February, 1974, she complained to Jensen that her arm was sore from having received too many intravenous vitamin shots within a short period of time.* She told him that the

*Tape # 69, Side A.

muscles in one of her arms hurt, and asked him how he expected her to be ready for "action" on a trip if her muscles hurt. "You told me that these special vitamins would relax my muscles," she reminded him. (Both sodium amytal and sodium pentothal would, of course, relax the muscles as a normal manifestation of their trance-inducing properties.) She again mentioned Dr. Aldridge.

■

CANDY: Why do you always say bad things about him?
  *(Nebel, playing Jensen, does not reply.)*
CANDY: Dr. Aldridge has the finest reputation and is extremely well known. He is the head of obstetrics and gynecology at Woman's Hospital in New York City. *(Her voice reflects her anxiety. She desperately wants to convince Jensen that she no longer needs his vitamin shots.)* Why do you say those bad things about him? He never even heard of you. There's no reason for you to say those things about him.
  *(Nebel, still playing Jensen, asks her what it was he had said about Aldridge, but she ignores his question.)*
CANDY: Dr. Aldridge told me that vitamin B-twelve is always given into the derrière. And he told me that if you ever did give it to me in the arm, it would be in the muscle, *not* in the veins.

■

There is no doubt that Dr. Aldridge was correct. I've spoken with a half-dozen doctors since beginning research on this book, and they unanimously agree that they can think of no situation in which the intravenous feeding of vitamins would be warranted. True to her suggestible personality, however, Candy gave Jensen the benefit of the doubt in this session by saying, "I guess there are different schools of medicine."

The reader will note that during this February 1974 session Candy ignored all of Nebel's questions and comments; she was totally engrossed in a previous conversation with Gilbert Jensen. Nebel commented into the microphone about her immersion in the scene to the exclusion of everything around her.

■

CANDY: *(to Jensen)* That has nothing to do with you. You're wrong. I'm not superemotional or underemotional or overemotional. *(She groans.)*

◼

She continued her defense of Dr. Aldridge by pointing out that people come from all over the world to be treated by him. There is, of course, no way of knowing precisely what Jensen had been saying. He had obviously been critical of Aldridge, which prompted Candy's defense.

◼

CANDY: "I'll tell you one thing, Dr. Jensen. I'm going to avoid coming over here anymore because I feel one hundred percent better when I don't see you. I may feel all right for an hour but *(becoming emotional)* . . . according to Dr. Aldridge, I don't need anything. My blood count is fine. I'm not tired. . . .
*(Jensen apparently interrupts at this point and says something to the effect that Aldridge was only telling her that for his own purposes.)*
CANDY: Why would he do that? I've known him since 1946. *(She breathes deeply and listens to something Jensen says, then replies)* Well, that's up to you. *(She suddenly begins to whimper and, according to Nebel, looks down at the crook of her arm, her face contorted.)* Did you . . . what are you . . . did you put it in again? Doubly strong? *(almost crying)* I don't need doubly strong vitamins. *(taking a deep breath and regaining control of herself)* You know something, I don't believe you! I don't like you, and you don't like me. That doesn't matter one way or the other. But I think you do me harm, I really do. I'm feeling very funny from this. I can tell from the way you look that you're looking to see how I feel. Aren't you? *(Sounding weaker and confused)* Well, I'm leaving now. And if anything should happen to me, you'll be very sorry. I've given Dr. Aldridge your name. . . . *(She begins to mumble and drifts off into sleep.)*

◼

That hypnotic session was not the only one in which Candy complained of having adverse reactions to Jensen's vitamin shots. She complained to Jensen during a hypnotic regression that the shots made her very dizzy. She stated during that same session that the intravenous injections left her with a headache.*

In a session taped on July 12, 1974, Candy regressed back to her hotel room in San Francisco.** She'd just arrived there after spending most of the afternoon at Jensen's office, where she'd received another "vitamin shot." She wasn't feeling well and told Nebel, who was playing the role of her alter ego at the moment, that Jensen had told her to call if she suffered severe aftereffects from the shot. Nebel suggested she make the call and, after she went through the imaginary dialing of Jensen's number, Nebel slipped into Jensen's role.

■

CANDY: *(holding the imaginary telephone)* Dr. Jensen, you told me to call. I'm back at my hotel . . . the St. Francis. My arm is hurting.

JOHN: *(playing Jensen)* From what?

CANDY: I don't know. You gave me a vitamin shot, remember? I don't know, maybe you didn't hit the vein or something. . . . Can that be serious?

JOHN: Does it hurt very much?

CANDY: I hurt all over. . . . My clock is stopped. What time is it?

JOHN: *(Nebel had to guess at this one, and he guessed wrong.)* It's four-thirty.

CANDY: *(surprised)* Why is it dark out then?

JOHN: *(groping)* Maybe you have the shades of your windows down.

CANDY: No, I looked. It's dark out.

JOHN: How do you feel otherwise?

CANDY: I left there at two-thirty. *(She is concerned at the passage of time.)*

JOHN: Yes.

CANDY: When the sun was shining.

JOHN: How do you feel otherwise, other than where you had the shot?

CANDY: *(very surprised)* I slept almost twelve hours.

JOHN: Well, that's good.

*Tape # 87 "A," Side B.
**Tape # 26, Side A.

CANDY: I don't feel good.

JOHN: What name did you use to register at the hotel?

CANDY: *(her speech slurred)* Why did you ask me that?

JOHN: I just wondered whether you used Jones or Grant.

CANDY: I don't remember. But *you* would. I just wanted to know whether I should put a compress on my arm.

JOHN: No, it'll be okay in a few minutes.

CANDY: Why do I ache so?

■

The remainder of the conversation, conducted over the imaginary telephone with John Nebel playing the role of Gilbert Jensen, dealt with the question of whether Candy should cancel her travel plans because of the way she felt. Although the details of that specific trip were not explained, it is obvious from the tape that the trip was to be made for Gilbert's CIA unit and did not refer to her return flight to New York.

Earlier in this book Arlene told of having been "hatched" following Jensen's administering two intravenous feedings to Candy. Invariably Arlene appeared following such injections, the hypnotic trance states induced by the injections providing a fertile field in which Arlene, and Candy, could be manipulated. Sodium amytal is one drug which would accomplish this.

But sodium amytal was probably not the only chemical substance injected into Candy during her involvement with Jensen and the CIA. On December 20, 1974, I was present in Nebel's apartment when he put Candy into a trance state and questioned her about receiving intravenous feedings from Gilbert Jensen. She said during that hypnotic session that Jensen had once told her that his vitamin B-12 injections contained special ingredients that made them better than what she'd been given by Dr. Aldridge in New York. She'd often questioned Jensen as to why his B-12 injections had so much more potent an effect on her than Aldridge's shots. Jensen answered her once by claiming that the California climate might have something to do with it. This time, according to the hypnotized Candy, Jensen boasted that his vitamin shots contained an ingredient which Candy pronounced "aminizing." Subsequent research failed to turn up any U.S. drug of that name, but the Soviet drug Aminazin, roughly the Soviet Union's equivalent of our Thorazine, could be what Candy was referring to. Aminazin, it is reported, is used experimentally in the Soviet Union with political prisoners in an attempt to modify their behavior and attitudes. It is a powerful drug, capable of causing severe depression, memory loss, exhaustion and loss of control of muscular movements. Two other drugs widely experimented with by the Soviets are Reserpine and Sulfazin. It is conceivable that Jensen had access to these Soviet drugs, since the stated purpose of the extensive CIA drug-testing programs has been to keep abreast of testing performed in the Soviet Union. Surely, the drugs themselves, or their ingredients, would be available to the CIA, either routinely or through covert procedures.

Perhaps Thorazine, too, was used on Candy Jones. Thorazine is widely used by psychiatrists to treat unmanageable patients. It is an effective tranquilizer, one which truly "calms the mind" as opposed to those drugs which result in general sedation of the entire system. There is no evidence in the hypnotic tapes that Jensen ever gave Thorazine to Candy, but he warned her on many occasions never to allow any other physician to give her the drug.

This instruction was one of many in which Candy was programmed to reject treatment by any doctor, dentist or psychiatrist not approved by Jensen and the CIA. It's difficult to fault the CIA for being fearful of having an agent in the hands of a physician not cleared by the agency. Thorazine is a hypnotic drug, and should Candy have been given it by such a physician, she could have spontaneously regressed and talked of her CIA experiences.

Thus, Jensen's programming of Candy to avoid other doctors was based upon standard CIA procedures. All agency operatives are ministered to by cleared physicians as a routine security measure. Victor Marchetti mentioned to me that whenever a CIA agent is to undergo surgery, another agent is assigned to the operating room, gowned and masked and available to hear what the patient might say under anesthesia and to analyze its relative importance. Of course, whenever possible, the surgeon is one with a clearance from the Central Intelligence Agency, as are the nurses and technicians.

Jensen's warnings to Candy to never seek out the services of an unapproved physician or dentist were not casual admonitions. In an undated hypnotic session,* Candy began by saying, "Something very bad is going to happen." She then told Nebel that he shouldn't have said what he did. What he'd said was that he thought she should consult a psychiatrist. This had occurred just prior to her slipping into a spontaneous trance, and was one of numerous conversations in which Nebel tried to convince his wife that psychiatric help was needed if she was to rid herself, and their marriage, of Arlene's troublesome presence.

■

CANDY: I can't go to a psychiatrist.

JOHN: *(referring to information gathered from previous hypnotic sessions)* Because you were told you couldn't.

CANDY: There's a reason I can't and . . .

JOHN: Tell me the reason.

CANDY: I'll get very very sick and I might even have a convulsion. I've never had a convulsion but I will know what one is like if I go to a psychiatrist.

JOHN: Uh-huh.

CANDY: Because the doctor said I . . .

JOHN: Which doctor?

CANDY: Dr. Jensen. And he said it would start in my stomach and he said that I would get very upset because they ask you too many questions. It would make me very nervous, although . . . *(She gasps.)* You see? *(There is pain in her stomach. Nebel assures her he will take care of the pain in a moment.)***

CANDY: I'm not a nervous person, but it would bring on nervousness for me.

JOHN: Candy, who am I?

CANDY: And then the doctor would think something was wrong with me.

*Tape # 30, Side A.

**John Nebel has been very successful in ridding Candy of functional pain while under hypnosis. When her stomach pains have occurred, he has actually "pulled the pain out by the roots" by spreading his fingers on Candy's abdomen and going through an exaggerated effort. It works because the trance state heightens suggestibility. Nebel has also given her imaginary pills for pain. He places the "pill" in her mouth, and she goes through the process of sucking on it until it disappears. Generally, he tells her the pill contains wintergreen, and she tastes the wintergreen and comments upon it. The pill, like the pulling of the pain from its roots, is extremely effective. The placebo effect in hypnosis is dramatically enhanced. Patients in the trance state have even been hooked up to electroshock machines and suffer every manifestation of having received the shock even though the unit is unplugged.

JOHN: Candy, please, who am I?
CANDY: John.

■

In another hypnotic session, Nebel introduced the subject of Jensen's instructions to Candy not to consult another doctor without his permission.*

■

CANDY: I can't go. I can't go anyplace. I can't go. I can't go. I have to be very careful and not get hurt because I can't go.
JOHN: You can't go to a dentist either?
CANDY: *(shocked at the suggestion)* No!
JOHN: How about a psychiatrist?
CANDY: *(gasping)* Never.
JOHN: Does he [Jensen] tell you why?
CANDY: 'Cause they're going to find things out and try to tell me things that aren't so.
JOHN: I see. Well, you're in his office right now, and I want you to ask him a couple of questions and repeat what he says.
CANDY: *(asking Jensen as instructed by Nebel)* Why can't I go to a psychiatrist? I don't think I need one, but why shouldn't I go to one?
JOHN: And now you tell me what he's saying to you.
CANDY: "They'll think that you're crazy. They wouldn't believe you." *(Her voice has changed to that of Arlene.)* "They would think something has happened to you."
JOHN: Ask him what words he uses to hypnotize you.
CANDY: *(to Jensen)* You don't hypnotize me, do you?
JOHN: *(taking Jensen's role)* Yes, I do.
CANDY: You told me I couldn't be hypnotized.
JOHN: Well, I just told you that at first.
CANDY: How do you do it?
JOHN: *(as Jensen)* What are the words I say to you when you come here and sit down?
CANDY: You say to me to look in the mirror and see Arlene. And then the light is out. And then I see her.
JOHN: Arlene?

*Tape # 39, Side B.

CANDY: Yeah.

JOHN: And the mirror is there?

CANDY: Yeah. And I see her. *You* make her come out. You don't force me but you ask if I want to see how she looks.

JOHN: See if you can get him [Jensen] to tell you whether he really gives you vitamins.

CANDY: I don't want any more vitamins. I've had plenty. What kind of vitamins are you giving me today? I just had some in New York. My doctor told me I didn't need any.

JOHN: After you light the candle and see Arlene in the mirror, what does he [Jensen] say to you?

CANDY: He says, "The light is out!" And he snuffs it out and it doesn't seem to burn him.

JOHN: And you are in total darkness then?

CANDY: It seems so. He's very chintzy with light. He uses very little light.

*(After a further description of Jensen's use of lights and mirrors to bring out Arlene, Nebel asks Candy how she feels when she sits before the mirror and sees Arlene.)*

CANDY: It makes me dizzy. *(She laughs.)* But I'm always curious to see what she's going to be looking like.

■

While Jensen did use a mirror to make Arlene visible to Candy, just as her grandmother's mirrors had served that same function when she was a little girl, virtually all visits to Jensen's office included a "vitamin" shot, and it was after these intravenous injections that Arlene usually emerged.

Jensen's instructions to Candy included warning her against even accepting Novocain from a dentist. She began having problems with her teeth while working for the unit, and repeatedly asked Jensen for permission to see a dentist. He told her that he would arrange to have her see a CIA dentist in Philadelphia, or in Washington. He never did. Nebel recalls a conversation he had with Candy in December 1973 concerning her dental problems. She told him that Jensen kept putting it off, claiming that the Washington dentist was ill and would be unavailable for a long period of time. At one point she'd asked Jensen why she couldn't go to a dentist and have all her work done in one sitting while under sodium pentothal. He became upset at this suggestion and lectured her against ever allowing anyone to use that drug on her.

As mentioned earlier, it is understandable why the CIA would want its operatives to be treated only by physicians cleared by that agency. But Gilbert Jensen carried such caution far beyond his employer's limits in keeping Candy from even those doctors and dentists who held a CIA clearance. Why? Had Gilbert Jensen crossed over the boundaries set by the CIA for his experiments on Candy Jones, and was he afraid to have the agency discover his transgressions? If this is a valid theory, and if Gilbert Jensen did, indeed, exceed his authority, the blame for the control of Candy Jones would shift to sit more squarely upon his shoulders and soften the responsibility of the Central Intelligence Agency. But even if this is so, there is no way of knowing where the CIA's experimental project stopped and Gilbert Jensen's continuation of the project took over. In any case, no matter what Jensen's motives, the effect on Candy was the same. She became petrified of all physicians, and it was only through a concerted effort by John Nebel that she was recently able to deal with the possibility of seeking medical help without first clearing it with Jensen.

After months of effort, Nebel was successful in getting Candy to visit a dentist. He took her to Dr. Irwin Smigel of Manhattan, who specializes in aesthetic dentistry. Smigel, who numbers many show business names as patients, was shocked at the condition of Candy's teeth. He told me, "I couldn't believe it when I examined her. This beautiful woman who dressed so well and took such apparent good physical care of herself had a mouth that I can only describe as a mess. Her lower front teeth were loose and irregular. One tooth was broken at the gum line. I had never seen anything quite so bad in all my years of practice."

When Smigel asked Candy when she'd last seen a dentist, she replied by asking him, "Is there another exit from this room?" She refused all offers of anesthesia, including a local anesthetic, and Smigel has had to work slowly and with great sensitivity to rebuild her mouth. "It has been a long and torturous task because of her inordinate fear of dentists," Smigel says.

Jensen seemed to be in the unusual position of guiding Candy not only to protect her from alien intelligence operations but to insure that his own agency, the CIA, did not intercept her and learn of his own special experimental operations. This is not to say that the CIA was not aware of Arlene and of Jensen's success in splitting her away from Candy. It is only to say that, except in situations where he was sure of his ability to exert direct control over her, he kept her distant from The Company, and went to impressive lengths to wipe away all traces of her work and his role in it.

He never seemed to truly trust her, which perhaps illustrates the basic weakness in controlling an agent through hypnosis and drugs. An agent who is controlled by the tangible inducements of money, or fear, is predictable, compared to one such as Candy Jones, whose control was dependent upon one man's skill in manipulating her personality. There must always have been within Jensen an apprehension about the potency and longevity of his hypnotic power over her, but it was only after she'd informed him with surprising finality in 1972 that she was through with him and The Company that he turned to the more conventional means of dealing with a renegade agent—a threat on her life.

Candy had begun carrying messages for The Company and Jensen after she'd reached a level of programming considered sufficient by him. He continued to feed her drugs, perhaps to insure keeping Arlene in check, perhaps to advance the experiments, perhaps for no other reason than to satisfy his curiosity. Her memory was effectively destroyed, a useful condition from Jensen's point of view. Aminazin would do that, as would scopolamine which when used during childbirth produces a state known as "twilight sleep" when mixed with the pain-killer Demerol.

Only Jensen knows for certain what other drugs were used on Candy—perhaps Lorazepam, a relatively new discovery that does not put a surgical patient to sleep but blocks all memory of the surgical procedure. Other powerful hypnotic drugs, with phenothiazine as their base, have been studied by the CIA with particular regard to their effect when mixed with LSD-25. And perhaps plain old simple LSD was administered to Candy during her years with Jensen. If so, it could have been given to her in the orange juice Jensen constantly had on hand and urged her to drink. She hated it, and complained of its bad taste. On an undated hypnotic-session tape, Candy tells Jensen about her reactions to his orange juice. She'd suddenly slipped into a spontaneous trance while in the bedroom and mumbled, "You give me a stomachache." Nebel switched on the tape recorder.*

■

CANDY: *(making a sound of distaste)* It's awful.

JOHN: *(assuming she's talking to him)* You say I gave you a stomachache?

CANDY: *(distressed)* Yeah. From the medicine or whatever it is I take first. It gives me that awful taste, that awful taste.

JOHN: *(realizing she's talking to Jensen and slipping into the role)* You mean I give you medicine before I give you the vitamins?

CANDY: Well, you told me it's just to wash out my mouth but I don't like it. *(Swishes saliva around in her mouth.)*

JOHN: Is it bitter?

CANDY: It's a funny taste. It's all . . . I keep feeling it. I taste it all over again. . . . It tastes like . . . it's lemon or something. It's not good. It gives me a stomachache, too. I'll tell you that.

JOHN: You have a stomachache now?

CANDY: You give me one with that stuff.

JOHN: *(still playing Jensen)* Every time I give you the stuff you get a stomachache?

CANDY: Makes my head feel funny. I told you that before, but you wouldn't believe me.

■

After Nebel reinforced the trance, he turned off the tape recorder until she began talking again. She muttered something about not liking sleeping in his (Jensen's) office. He again played the role of Jensen.

■

JOHN: But you've slept here before, haven't you?

CANDY: Well, I've fallen asleep here, but not intentionally.

*(After a few moments she accuses him of bending her arm back.)*

JOHN: *(still playing Jensen)* Why do you think I bent your arm back?

CANDY: So you could give me my vitamin shot. *(Weak voice)* Now

*Tape # 25, Side A.

you know that I'm just fading out, don't you? I guess I gotta stay here now for awhile.

JOHN: Are you fading out?

CANDY: Uh-huh. You *know* I am going away. You do that on purpose, don't you? *(She makes sucking sounds.)* I always get this awful taste when you do this.

*(Within a minute, Candy turned into Arlene and the session continued on that basis.)*

■

During another hypnotic session, Candy referred back to this same session in Jensen's office, claiming that he had bent her arm because she'd refused to take his vitamin shots. She also claimed that she poured most of the orange juice down the toilet but part of it didn't flush. Jensen discovered the juice in the toilet bowl and became very angry. Candy termed that day "Black Friday."

In still another hypnotic session, Candy regressed back to Jensen's office in Oakland and was on his examining table. She screamed at him not to touch her, told him the orange juice was "the most awful stuff she'd ever tasted" and accused him of putting something into the juice.

The references on the tapes to Candy receiving drugs from Jensen against her will, either intravenously or in fruit juice, are too numerous to chronicle in this book. The point is that Candy Jones was transformed into a puppet by Gilbert Jensen—two puppets really: Candy and Arlene, sisters within the same body, yet as different as sisters are likely to be. They talked *to* each other but never *about* each other to anyone outside of Gilbert Jensen's Oakland office. They traveled together on CIA missions, Candy occupying the airplane seat on the first and legitimate leg of the trip, Arlene taking over for the covert part of their travels, her black wig and dark makeup matching *her* passport picture. Arlene would study the people in the passenger cabin as instructed by Jensen, and always chose a seat on the left because, most people being right-handed, they tend to spend more time looking to their right. The flight bag beneath the seat contained the envelope that was to be delivered, though one can't be sure there was any message in the envelope at all.

At first the missions were easy and close to home—Cleveland, Philadelphia, Washington and New York. Soon they would span greater distances and carry Candy and Arlene to the Orient. No one would know what Candy was doing except for Arlene and, of course, Jensen and those he chose to tell. With the exception of her guarded hints to Mel Heimer, Joe Vergara and her attorney, Bill Williams, Candy maintained her silence throughout.

But Jensen could never be sure that Candy, or Arlene, wouldn't someday decide to tell the story to a third party. Because of that uncertainty, Jensen went further in his programming of Candy Jones; he taught her to avoid all relationships, all people. He taught her to hate, especially those of minority ethnic backgrounds. And he was aided in this tawdry effort by his part-time employer, The Company, the Central Intelligence Agency, or at least a faction of that massive organization, a faction dedicated to ultraright-wing philosophies and guided by another California doctor whom we shall name Marshall Burger.

# 13

# Taught To Hate

Dr. Marshall Burger is a pioneer and leading authority in the field of medical hypnosis. His stature brought him into contact with many familiar names in government and show business, and he enjoyed this proximity to fame. A dynamic, craggy-faced egotist, Burger enjoyed being close to the glamorous women of show business, especially film stars, and his eventual move from the Midwest to southern California was prompted in part by this weakness.

Another reason Burger moved to California was to be close to the government-sponsored experimental programs with which he was closely identified. He'd begun working on such programs during World War II, and was one of the first doctors to probe the potentials of hypnosis as a tool of war. His sponsor for that project was the Central Intelligence Agency. As the CIA's experiments in mind control progressed into the 1960s, Burger became the project's messiah and undertook to train other physicians for The Company. One of those physicians was Gilbert Jensen.

Candy first met Marshall Burger long before she became involved with the CIA, and it was Burger who became her first hypnotist.

Burger's use of hypnosis on Candy occurred in 1946, and it took place on the phone. Inducing trances over a telephone is not an uncommon occurrence, particularly with someone as suggestible as Candy. Burger used the same technique that John Nebel later used, the general relaxation of a subject through the "progressive relaxation" technique.

Candy had become a national figure as a result of her modeling success and, more particularly, because of her patriotic efforts to entertain the troops in the South Pacific during the war. She was invited to appear on a number of radio talk shows around the country, including the very popular "Don McNeill's Breakfast Club," broadcast from Chicago.

She flew into Chicago the night before she was to appear on the program and checked into the Drake Hotel. She'd finished unpacking when a severe series of chills racked her body, the same chills that she remembered so well from her bout with malaria in the Pacific. Gilbert Jensen had told her in Leyte that once the malaria was under control she would not suffer any further attacks. But she was certain that it was her malaria that had flared up in the Drake. She climbed into bed and piled on every available blanket.

When her chills worsened, she decided to call one of the staff members of the show. He came up to her room, saw how sick she was and called someone else connected with the show.

"A doctor will call within a half-hour," the staff assistant told Candy. She thanked him and he left. Minutes later the phone rang. It was Dr. Marshall Burger, calling from his home in a Chicago suburb where he had a successful private practice.

What transpired between Candy Jones and Marshall Burger during that telephone call is graphically relived by Candy in two undated recorded hypnotic sessions with John Nebel. Burger's name had come up on a number of previous tapes in connection with his CIA involvement, but these two tapes deal specifically with the telephone conversation in Chicago. On one tape, Candy had been regressed by Nebel back to Jensen's office in Oakland.* Nebel asked her the date and she told him it was

*Tape # 86 "A," Side A.

November 1960. Nebel became Gilbert Jensen and began questioning her about her initial involvement with The Company. He asked during the course of his questioning whether she'd seen Marshall Burger lately.

"Do you mean *Dr.* Burger?" she asked, her tone indicating displeasure at his too familiar use of Burger's first name.

■

JENSEN: *(played by Nebel)* Yes, *Dr.* Marshall Burger.

CANDY: No, he is in Chicago. I haven't seen him in ages. . . . Do you know him?

JOHN: Oh, yes. . . . Did he ever hypnotize you?

CANDY: No. *(yawning)* But he did help me once. That's when I met him. I had a malaria attack and I talked to him on the telephone. He did something very weird. He didn't live in Chicago.

JOHN: Where did he live?

CANDY: I don't know . . . outside. . . .

JOHN: A suburb?

CANDY: Yes. He called me on the phone.

JOHN: What did he say to you on the phone?

CANDY: He told me he couldn't get there but would come the next morning. And he said that I should count backwards. *(She chuckles at the thought.)* He told me that if I'd count backwards I would stop shaking and go to sleep. Listen, I would have stood on my head for him, if it would have stopped my shaking.

JOHN: Did he count with you?

CANDY: Uh-huh. He counted from ten to one.

JOHN: What did he say to you? Did he say you would stop shaking?

CANDY: Yes. He said my chills would stop and . . .

JOHN: Tell me just what he said when you started to count from ten down to one.

CANDY: He said, "You are going to count with me . . . and you're going to hold on to the side of the bed . . . just put the earphone on the pillow and snuggle up with it against your shoulder . . . now count with me from ten down to one . . . hold on to the side of the bed and we'll count together. . . . Ten . . . you will stop shaking . . . nine . . . stop shaking

... eight ... stop shaking ... your chills are going away
... keep under the covers ... seven ... stop shaking
... hold on to the bed ... your chills are going ... six
... your chills are going ... your fever is dropping ..."
*(As Candy counts down with Burger, her voice indicates that the
reliving of that experience is putting her into an even deeper trance
while with Nebel.)* "... five ... your chills are going and your
fever is dropping ... four ... you'll stop shaking ... three
... sleep ... sleep ... sleep ... two ... sleep ... sleep
... one ... your chills are gone ... you're not shaking
... you're going to sleep ... you are asleep ... sleep
... sleep."

■

In another taped session, Candy again relived her Chicago
"countdown" with Burger.* It was basically the same as in the
preceding tape, except that she added that Burger used the
word "warm" at various points during the countdown.

On both tapes Candy denied that Burger had hypnotized her
in Chicago. She preferred to ascribe what had occurred to "autosuggestion." Her feelings about this are consistent with her
feelings toward Gilbert Jensen. She will accept today that she
was hypnotized; but throughout her regressions during hypnotic sessions with John, she was unfailing in her conviction that
she was not capable of being hypnotized by anyone, including
Jensen and Burger.

I cannot help but be skeptical of the circumstances surrounding Burger's introduction to Candy in Chicago, and have wondered ever since beginning to analyze the tapes whether, in
some way, Gilbert Jensen was responsible for Burger being chosen to treat Candy. Both men are in the same medical specialty,
not one under which the treatment of malaria would be included. There is, of course, the possibility that Don McNeill's
staff assistant simply called the physician he knew best, and that
physician happened to be Marshall Burger. But it does strike me
as uncomfortably ironic that Candy would be referred to a man
who would later become one of her CIA contacts, just as Gilbert
Jensen, a World War II acquaintance, would similarly enter her
life again as her CIA control agent.

*Tape # 66, Side A.

Burger was eventually to play a direct role in the programming of Candy Jones, particularly in the area of teaching her to distrust, and even to hate, people. But before Burger entered the picture in the late 1960s, it was Gilbert Jensen, one of Burger's disciples, who did the programming.

Among the tapes of John Nebel's hypnotic sessions with Candy, there are 17 specific segments dealing with what I have opted to term her "hate training." Often these regressions were not spontaneous, but were prompted by heated arguments between Candy and John about her negative attitudes toward his friends. While this situation is not uncommon with newly married couples, the intensity of her feelings toward many of Nebel's friends was shocking and infuriating to him. It wasn't until the hypnotic sessions pointed to the training she'd received from Jensen and Burger that Nebel was able to better understand the underlying cause of his wife's feelings about people, particularly identifiable ethnic groups.

There is no single epsiode uncovered through Candy's hypnotic regressions that neatly tells the entire story of her programming to distrust and avoid people. This brainwashing by Gilbert Jensen took place over the entire length of their relationship, and is best handled by presenting a succession of conversations between them in which this subject was focused upon.

In a November 1974 session,* Nebel, playing the role of Gilbert Jensen, was startled when Candy asked him whether he was her friend. He assured her that he was. She then began a monologue concerning the fact that she had so few friends. She told him that she doesn't like a lot of people, and then said that she *can't* like a lot of people. "I don't have room in my life for friends, and most of them wouldn't understand what I was doing. I couldn't take the risk."

"Who told you that?" Nebel asked.

"You did," she replied, believing that she was talking to Gilbert Jensen.

In an hypnotic session recorded on April 10, 1974,** Arlene emerged in an angry, bitchy mood. After berating Candy for two minutes, and after claiming that Candy's mother was "crazy as a hoot owl" and bragging that she had accompanied Candy to visit her mother in the hospital and had made some comments

*Tape # 7 "A," Side A.
**Tape # 27, Side A.

that drove Candy's mother out of her mind, Arlene got into the business of what she, and Candy, had been taught by Gilbert Jensen. She referred to Candy's mother's doctor as a "kike." She was laughing cruelly throughout this session and began to repeat, with apparent glee, "kike . . . kike . . . kike." She told Nebel that the doctor was the kind of kike that he, meaning Nebel, would have on his radio show. She said that the kinds of kikes Nebel was friendly with were the obnoxious and agressive types. She then said scornfully, "Candy doesn't even have enough sense to know when they are pigs." She continued her tirade against the Jews and, approximately 15 minutes into the recorded session, bragged that Gilbert Jensen had told her, Arlene, that she should not like Jews. Later in this session, at approximately 19 minutes, Arlene denied having said that Jensen instructed her to hate Jews. But she quickly added, "Jews *are* bad."

In a session recorded in January 1974,* Candy mentioned that Arlene got along very nicely with Gilbert Jensen. She indicated that one of the reasons Jensen liked Arlene was that Arlene thought the way he did and was willing to take his advice. John Nebel asked Candy what ethnic groups Jensen considered dangerous.

■

CANDY: The Jewish people, of course. He called them kikes. And the American niggers, as he called them. He always used the name niggers. You know, he was Jewish himself but he didn't like me to tell him that. *He* said there was a difference between Jews.

JOHN: Before you met Jensen, how did you feel about people of the Jewish faith.

CANDY: I didn't feel anything. *(According to Candy, she had had many close Jewish friends and business associates prior to becoming involved with Jensen and the CIA.)*

■

It often happened that Nebel, miscalculating, asked a question as Gilbert Jensen to which Jensen would have already

*Tape # 39, Side A.

known the answer. This situation made it difficult to elicit dates from Candy, because whenever Nebel, playing Jensen, would ask her the date, she would laugh and tell him he was crazy for not knowing what day it was. It often took repeated questioning before Candy would give him the dates he asked for. Usually when she questioned his reason for asking the day's dates, he would resort to the subterfuge that he was testing her mental acuity following the administration of that visit's vitamin shots.

On July 7, 1974, at 8:30 in the morning, John Nebel put Candy into a trance and, realizing that she had spontaneously regressed to Jensen's office, assumed the role of the Oakland doctor. He asked her whether she had gotten married, which caused Candy to become suspicious of him.

■

CANDY: *You* know I'm not married. Why do you ask me that?

JOHN: I just thought you might have met some nice man.

CANDY: No. *(with a sad sigh)* You told me that I'll never get married.

JOHN: When did I ever say that to you?

CANDY: You always tell me that. You say I'll never get married.

JOHN: Would you like to get married?

CANDY: You say I don't want to get married.

JOHN: I told you that?

CANDY: *(repeating in a singsong voice what he had told her at an earlier time)* And I can't get married, and I shouldn't get married.

JOHN: Why did I say you shouldn't get married?

CANDY: 'Cause I don't know how to be married.

JOHN: What does that mean?

CANDY: You know everything. . . . I don't have a chance to get married . . . I don't know anybody . . . I'll never know anybody.

JOHN: Why won't you know anybody?

CANDY: 'Cause I *can't* know anybody. You told me that I can't know anybody.

JOHN: I said that to you?

CANDY: Yeah. *(becoming agitated)* You told me that I can't know anybody. I don't want to know any of those people. Any of those people. Any of those people I run into.

JOHN: I told you about that?

CANDY: You told me about *them.*

JOHN: Give me an idea of what people I told you about.

■

Candy then proceeded to name a number of people with whom she was acquainted and whom she had evidently discussed with Jensen during prior meetings in his office. She related, during this regression, the things Jensen had said about each of them, and the reasons she should no long see them. He attacked their personal and professional worth, and played heavily on their ethnic background.

During the same July 7, 1974, hypnotic session, Arlene took over from Candy and was very playful with Jensen, as played by Nebel. He was not as yet aware that Arlene had appeared and told Candy not to be so sarcastic. He assured her that he was trying to help her.

"I doubt that," Arlene said. "You told me that I was going to give you a lot of trouble because you don't know who I am." She laughed triumphantly.

Nebel then realized that Arlene had entered the picture, and calmly told her that he knew she was Arlene Grant. Arlene laughed again and accused him of not being quite sure. She was finding pleasure in this game.

"Do I sound like Arlene?" she asked coyly.*

"You're trying to sound like Candy, aren't you?" Nebel asked, now understanding that a game was being played.

"You're one up on me now, doctor," Arlene said. "But you won't win them all."

Nebel asked her whether she was going to return to New York, and she said she was, but that first she had to stop over in Texas and Miami. They discussed her suitcase, which was in the closet of his office.

"I'll call *you,* doctor, don't call me," Arlene said nastily.

Nebel, still playing Jensen, asked, "Do you hate me?"

"I only hate things that are worth hating," Arlene replied. "You taught me that."

*I found this incident somewhat amusing. It was definitely Arlene talking, but she tried to imitate Candy's voice to confuse Jensen. I commented to my wife that it was confusing enough to listen to the tapes and have to differentiate between the two women without having the second personality impersonating the first.

"I'm not worth hating, is that it?"

"You should know, you taught me everything."

"Okay, Arlene."

Arlene repeated a motto that Jensen had obviously used on many occasions: "Only hate that which is worth hating."

"Well, that's good advice, isn't it?" Nebel asked.

"Yeah, especially since almost everything is worth hating, according to you."

"I never said you should hate everything, did I?"

"You hate yourself," Arlene told Jensen. "You hate just about everybody and everything."

"I never told you to hate everything," Nebel said in his role as Gilbert Jensen.

"It all boils down to that," said Arlene. "You told me that there was hate in everybody and sooner or later it would come out." She became angry that he was having her repeat these things, and reminded him that he knew perfectly well what he had told her.

After Arlene told Jensen that she often got a stomachache just from listening to him, she accused him of not liking her because she fights him. "You told me to watch out because people would do me harm," she said. "Yes, I'm just following your advice and I'm very careful." She then told him in an ominous voice that she was just as careful in dealing with *him* because it could work both ways.

While Jensen's fear of having Candy go to another doctor can be understood when viewed against the secrets she might have revealed, one can also justify, with reluctance, his teaching her to avoid as many people as possible. An unfortunate aspect of the covert operatives' life is the need to distrust and to maintain a solitary existence. A gregarious spy would be as suspect as a creative accountant, and instilling in Candy Jones a need to develope a life-style in which others were not included would make good sense from any intelligence agency's point of view. But there seems to have been more to Jensen's programming of Candy Jones in this direction then a basic need on the part of the intelligence community to insure its agents' silence. It is one thing to be taught to be distrustful of those with whom you come in contact, and another to be taught to hate those around you, particularly those of certain ethnic origins.

The major portion of a hypnotic session between Candy and John Nebel on November 26, 1973, is devoted to more of Jensen's training to hate ethnic groups.* The session began with Candy on the table in Jensen's examination room. According to her, she had just received a double shot of vitamins, and agreed with Jensen, into whose role Nebel had quickly shifted, that she will feel stronger because of the shots.

Nebel had said very little at the beginning of the session, but Candy suddenly began reliving a confrontation that had occurred many years ago in Jensen's office. It began with her saying to Jensen, "I don't know where you get your information, because I *have* stayed away from everybody." She said he was accusing her of seeing people that he had instructed her not to see, and she assured him, in a pleading voice, that she had not disobeyed his instructions.

■

CANDY: *(almost to the point of tears)* I don't see anybody . . . I don't have any friends.

JOHN: *(playing Jensen)* Why don't you have any friends?

CANDY: You told me not to. I swear I don't have any friends. *(There is a long period of silence.)*

CANDY: I know what *they* are.

JOHN: What do you mean?

CANDY: What you said.

JOHN: Tell me what I said to you.

CANDY: *(annoyed at being asked to repeat what he has already said)* You said they are going to do me harm. I know it. But I haven't been seeing anybody. I don't have any friends and I don't talk to anybody. I listen. I listen. I know they are bad.

JOHN: Everybody is bad?

CANDY: Give them a chance and they will put the knife in you. I know that. They're all bad.

JOHN: Did I tell you that?

CANDY: Yeah. I believe you.

JOHN: Did you have friends before?

CANDY: Yeah. But I don't see anybody anymore. Not one person.

JOHN: You dropped them because of what *I* told you?

*Tape # 65, Side B.

*Candy and John at the WMCA studio (Straus Communications), in New York.*

*ndy's mother posing at the side of the use in Wilkes-Barre in 1922.*

*Candy and her beloved grandmother, Ma-Má. This photo was taken behind the house at Lake Nuangola on the occasion of Doll's first haircut.*

*Doll with the monkey mentioned during an hypnotic regression.*

*A portrait of Jessica Wilcox, who would become Candy Jones, America's most successful model of the Forties.*

(n) l  c-  n (l) (b) v  2x  n (l')          col  u  pm-4  12n 6 74

## HYPNOTIC INDUCTION PROFILE

### Eye-Roll Levitation Method

Patient Name __Jones, Candy__          Date __12 Aug 1975__

Sequence -   Initial _____   Previous ✓   When _____

Position -   Standing _____   Supine _____   Sit _____   Chair-Stool __✓__

| | | | |
|---|---|---|---|
| A | Induction -  Up-Gaze | | 0 - 1 - (2) - 3 - 4 |
| B | ROLL | | 0 - 1 - (2) - 3 - 4 |
| C | | | - 1 - 2 - 3 (Squint) |

Instructions

Arm Levitation Right _____
Left __✓__

| | | |
|---|---|---|
| D | | 0 - 1 - 2 (3 - 4) |

Post-Hypnotic
Response -

| | | | |
|---|---|---|---|
| E | | Tingle    0 - | (1) 2 |
| F 2 | | Dissociation 0 - | - 1 (2) |

| | | | | |
|---|---|---|---|---|
| G 1.75 | LEVITATION | Immediate | 0 - 1 - 2 - (3 - 4) | Smile ✓ |
| H | | Re-enforce (1) | 1 - 2 - 3 - 4 | Surprise ✓ |
| I | | Re-enforce (2) | 2 - 3 - 4 | |
| J | | Re-enforce (3) | 3 - 4 "it wants to sit up" | |
| K | | Re-enforce (4) | 4 | |
| L 2 | CONTROL DIFFERENTIAL | 0 - | - 1 (2) | |

| | | | |
|---|---|---|---|
| M 2 | Cut-off | 0 - | - 1 (2) |
| N | Amnesia to Cut-off | 0 - | (1) - 2 |
| O | No Test _____ | | |
| P 2 | Floating Sensation | 0 - | - 1 (2) |
| Q 9.75 | GRADE - continuum | | 0 - 1 (2) - 3 (4) [5]  regressed |

X Increment
Average (+)

Minutes __5__          Decrement _____          _____ Soft

The actual Hypnotic Induction Profile (HIP) done by Dr. Herbert Spiegel on Candy. It includes notations made by Dr. Spiegel during the brief test.

*An interview in Chicago on October 2, 1972 with Jimmy Hoffa. Candy had gone to Chicago to do the interview for NBC's "Monitor," but performed messenger duties for the CIA in conjunction with the trip.*

*A publicity release for the theatrical troupe headed by Candy Jones which entertained GI's in the southwest Pacific during World War II.*

Candy at the modeling agency with husband, modeling czar Harry Conover.

Passport photo of the "other" Candy Jones, taken in San Francisco at the request of Dr. Gilbert Jensen and the CIA.

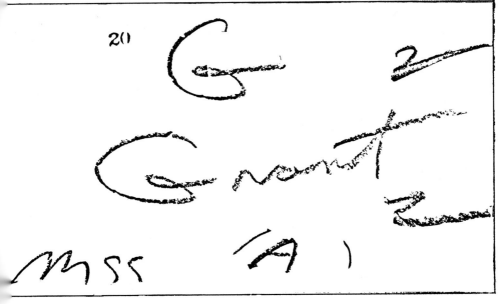

A reproduction of the envelope in which the photos were delivered.

*Candy with Mel Heimer at a party at Dorothy Kilgallen's apartment. Immediately following the party, Candy delivered a message for the CIA in a New York City restaurant.*

*Flyer promoting the USO show that was to take Candy t Vietnam.*

*A group of Conover models. Candy is in the first row, third from left.*

*rtrait of Candy commis-
ned by the late producer,
ike Todd.*

February 27, 1976

Candy Jones
WMCA
888 Seventh Avenue
New York, New York  10019

Dear Candy:

I do recall that sometime in the early 1960's you handed me a
sealed envelope in your office at 52 Vanderbilt Avenue.  You told
me that the contents of the letter were self-explanatory and that
were you to die or disappear under unusual circumstances, particularly if you died under a different name, I should carefully check
out the facts of your case.

In addition, I received numerous flight insurance statements during
the 1960's from your many trips around the country, including your
trips to the Caribbean, particularly the Bahamas.

I hope that these recollections may be of some help to you.

Sincerely yours,

William J. Williams
Attorney At Law

*The letter from Candy's lawyer confirming her instructions to him (see pages
110–111) concerning the possibility of her untimely demise under mysterious
circumstances.*

*Pat Nixon and Candy at a Washington party after which Candy went to the
CIA headquarters in Langley, Virginia.*

CANDY: You know that. I haven't seen anybody in years.

JOHN: You've been following my instructions?

CANDY: *(becoming quite upset)* Yes, and you accuse me of seeing people, and I don't. I swear I don't. I promised. Where do you get your information?

■

Candy then complained that the needle in her arm was painful. Nebel (as Jensen) asked her what time it was. She said it was three o'clock, and told him she had arrived at his office at two. She assured him that she knew nothing about a set of papers, and again tried to convince him that she had not disobeyed his orders about seeing people.

■

CANDY: You told me that people would hurt me.

JOHN: *(still playing Jensen's role)* Did I tell you there were particular groups who are especially dangerous?

CANDY: All the ones you told me.

JOHN: What were the ones I told you? Come on now, see if you can remember.

CANDY: Ah, come on. You know what you said.

JOHN: Well, tell me again.

CANDY: *(with a deep sigh)* All the blacks, all the Jews and all the Italians. You might as well say the whole goddamned world. And especially the Chinese and Japanese. You didn't have to tell me about the Japanese. Why do we have to go over this again?

JOHN: I'm not going over it. I'm just asking.

CANDY: And the French.

JOHN: They're all bad?

CANDY: They are the enemies.

■

Much later in this session, Candy complained to Jensen about the Oriental music that was being played in his office. Other hypnotic tapes indicate that Jensen had experimented with the use of monotonous music as an aid to hypnotic trance induction. This has been used effectively by others, although research into the effect of music has been limited. Candy often complained to

Jensen about the Oriental music in his office, and to this day abhors the sound of it, a nagging problem when she and John have dinner at his favorite Chinese restaurant and longtime sponsor, Ho-Ho.

Further along in this session, Nebel managed to shift from the role of Gilbert Jensen to that of Candy's alter ego. He questioned her from that vantage point, and she told him that "a man in California" had taught her to avoid all people, particularly blacks, Jews and Italians. She reiterated her distrust of the Chinese and Japanese, and mentioned that she had seen the terrible things the Japanese had done during World War II. She finished this session by saying that Jensen taught her always to listen but never to say anything.

Dr. Marshall Burger had taught her the same thing. Burger, in his teaching role for the CIA, conducted seminars in various parts of the country and was a founder of a CIA funded institute in northern California. Candy visited the institute on at least two occasions, according to material taken from two lengthy taped hypnotic sessions. Nebel vigorously pursued the question of Burger's and Jensen's programming of Candy, and was able to ascertain that she had been given a series of tests at the institute, most of which had to do with her senses. She said during a hypnotic session that she was tested by Burger for her sense of observation, smell, touch, taste, and hearing.* During that hypnotic session, Candy said that the tests were administered to her by one of Burger's assistants, a woman in a white uniform whom Candy described as "a zombie." Candy ranked highest on the scent test, and this is perhaps why Gilbert Jensen often burned incense in his office while inducing a trance in her.

During another hypnotic session, Nebel was able to pinpoint the date of one of Candy's visits to the institute as June 3, 1968.** Candy was unsure at first whether it was June 3 or June 5, her confusion having to do with the time change and with not being sure of the specific day she left New York to come to California. It was also brought out during this session that Gilbert Jensen had studied under Burger at the institute. Jensen

*Tape # 80 "A," Side B.
**Tape # 25, Side B.

boasted to Candy about Burger's tutoring, and she accused him of being in awe of Burger and of wanting to be taken into Burger's confidence.

In another hypnotic session, Nebel, playing the role of Gilbert Jensen, asked Candy whether she liked Burger.*

■

CANDY: I don't know. I don't like him or dislike him. I don't know, I don't know. I wouldn't want him as a personal friend. Why do you ask?

JOHN: Well, we work together, you know that.

CANDY: I know you'd *like to* work together.

JOHN: What do you mean *like to?*

CANDY: You'd like to get in with him, wouldn't you? You seem to think he is so wonderful.

JOHN: Why should I try to get in with Burger? I know as much as he does. He's no brain.

CANDY: Everybody thinks he is.

JOHN: Who?

CANDY: Well, you always talk about him as though he is so important, him and his fat friends. They're all fat.

JOHN: What fat friends?**

CANDY: I don't know their names.

■

Nebel ended this session by asking Candy whether Burger had ever hypnotized her. She denied that he had, although she did refer to the telephone conversation with him in Chicago, again claiming that she had practiced autosuggestion and had not been hypnotized. He then asked her whether she had attended one of Burger's classes in California. She said she had. Nebel asked whether it was an ethnic hate class.

"It's his regular lecture," Candy said.

"He also lectures on hypnosis?" Nebel asked.

*Tape # 83 "A," Side A.

**Nebel admits to having wondered whether the California psychiatrist, William Jennings Bryan, might have been involved in some manner with Burger. Bryan had been linked to the CIA, and had been the technical consultant for the film, *The Manchurian Candidate,* which dealt with hypno-programming. He was to learn from Candy, however, that not only was Bryan not involved, she had never even heard of him despite his flamboyant manner and penchant for publicity.

Candy agreed.

Nebel then asked her what Burger generally said in his ethnic-group classes.

"I don't know . . . he said you have to be careful about what you say to certain types of people."

The ethnic attitudes instilled in Candy by Jensen and Burger were as distasteful as those represented by the crudest of today's ethnic "humor." Because of Candy's high ratings on scent tests, there appears to have been an emphasis placed upon what Burger claimed were peculiar odors emitted by various ethnic groups. In a session recorded on April 13, 1974, at 8:00 P.M.,* Candy mumbled something about black people having a peculiar smell. Nebel asked her whether she truly believed that black people had an odor.

■

CANDY: To me they do. That's what he said.

JOHN: Jensen told you that?

CANDY: Sure, I took the test.

JOHN: And you found that black people smell.

CANDY: Sure, he identified them for me.

JOHN: Do Jews smell?

CANDY: They have bad perspiration. Anybody does.

JOHN: Then everyone smells the same.

CANDY: They [Jews] eat that kind of food and then they have that perspiration smell.

JOHN: Did Jensen tell you that?

CANDY: He [Jensen] said that they eat highly seasoned stuff and then they perspire, especially if they are fat.

JOHN: What about the Italian people? Do they smell?

CANDY: They smell of garlic. Usually Latins smell of garlic.

JOHN: Did he tell you not to mingle with those people?

CANDY: He said not to mingle with any of them. He said that was the way to avoid trouble.

■

Nebel then asked her what kind of people Jensen allowed her to associate with.

■

*Tape # 13, Side A.

CANDY: He never said. He told me that I was a good loner and should stay away from all people. He told me that I was self-sufficient and didn't need anybody, and that I would be much better off being alone.

JOHN: Arlene said that you were programmed to hate people.

CANDY: I don't like her. She gives me stomachaches.

■

Later in this same session, when Candy was struggling to keep Arlene inside, Nebel asked whether Jensen had taught Arlene to dislike black people. Candy said that Jensen had told Arlene to be careful because blacks could be dangerous, and he had said the same things about Jews. She added during the latter portion of this session that Puerto Ricans were also not to be trusted.

There are indications from the hypnotic-session tapes that Gilbert Jensen had negative feelings about the black race long before he began indoctrinating Candy with those feelings. There are two hypnotic sessions in which Nebel regressed Candy back to her South Pacific days with Gilbert Jensen, and in both sessions she talked to Jensen about incidents involving black soldiers. In one session, according to the hypnotized Candy, Jensen told her she had better stay away from black soldiers because they would rape her. He also told her during their World War II days in Leyte that she must be very careful of people, particularly blacks, and that they must be closely observed for a clue as to what their motivations and actions might be.

This prejudice preached by Gilbert Jensen during World War II and, more pointedly, as part of his CIA programming of Candy, is particularly unfortunate because her natural inclinations had always been quite the opposite. Hers was among the first modeling agencies to actively promote and use black models. She numbered among her friends many Jews, and had apparently lived her life with an admirably open mind toward minority groups. But once the programming took effect, she found herself acting contrary to her inherent beliefs.

On an undated tape she talked to John Nebel, her alter ego, about what Jensen had told her concerning Negroes.* According-ing to the tape, Jensen had repeatedly asked her to tell him the

*Tape # 13, Side B.

names of her friends in New York, and expressed his dissatisfaction with the fact that one of Candy's secretaries was a black girl, who had been with Candy for four years.

"Get rid of that girl," Jensen told her. "She's talking about you around town." Jensen then took out a snapshot that he claimed he had taken of the black secretary outside the office building at 52 Vanderbilt Avenue in New York City. Candy was shocked that Jensen had been there and had taken the picture, and expressed her feelings to him. Jensen again insisted that she fire the girl, which Candy eventually did, with mixed emotions.

Another aspect of Candy's training had to do with observing people's mannerisms. Jensen gave her a pamphlet, the title of which she recalls was "The Human Face." She claims, under hypnosis, to have studied it as instructed, and to have found the material helpful.

The hypnotic session in which this booklet was mentioned took place in October 1974. Nebel played the role of Jensen.

■

JOHN: Do you remember how I taught you to look at a person and know something about him?
CANDY: You gave me the book [the pamphlet].
JOHN: *(surprised)* Do you remember the title?
CANDY: (without hesitation) *The Human Face.*
JOHN: Who wrote it? Remember?
CANDY: Brophy, or something like that.
JOHN: *(having to accept that)* That's right. You've got a good memory. Did you study it?
CANDY: Oh, yes, it's so true. You can see it's true. I never thought of it that way . . . the weakness in the chin, the earlobes, the shape of the ear, the forehead, the placement of the eyes . . .

■

All of this programming by Jensen and Burger was to be culminated, however, in a most extraordinary discussion class conducted by Burger in a small Texas town very close to the Louisiana border. This material came out on tape in early November 1974, and is contained in the transcripts of a hypnotic session between John Nebel and Candy Jones.*

The hypnotic session began with Candy discussing Arlene. Arlene then emerged and said she was waiting for word from someone that would send her into action. Candy had complained at the very beginning of the session that her stomach hurt. Arlene told Nebel that Candy had been poisoned, and Arlene suggested that the poison was in something Candy had recently eaten. Nebel was unable to elicit further information about this, and the session proceeded to other topics. There was also a regression back to Candy's childhood.

Nebel commented into the microphone that Candy had the most severe pain in her abdomen that he had ever witnessed, and that she was almost crying. She had also complained of leg pains. Nebel worked to take away the pain, and succeeded after three minutes. Suddenly, Arlene's voice came through, and she told Nebel about the severity of the pains Candy had just experienced.

"I can't stand that stuff," Arlene said.

Nebel assumed she was referring to something she had been drinking, perhaps orange juice in Jensen's office, and asked her about it.

"It tasted just like boiled laundry," replied Arlene. "I ate the food in the test kitchen."

Arlene then mumbled something that sounded to Nebel like "ugly."

"Who is ugly?" he asked.

"All of them. They eat this stuff. Maybe that's why they look like they do. They say you are what you eat. Can you come up with something that I could order and that I could eat? Something I can stand. . . . Can you have plain rice? Would that be suspicious? Would it look strange? I could say I have a bad stomach or something." [Candy returned]

■

JOHN: Where are you now? What building are you in?
CANDY: I'm in the test kitchen. In the test lab.
JOHN: What city are you in?
CANDY: There's no city.

*Tape # 18 "A," Sides A and B.

JOHN: What country then?
CANDY: *(laughing)* You mean what state.
JOHN: Yes.
CANDY: Texas.

■

John reinforced the trance and tried to get more from her at this point, but she was unresponsive. He commented into the microphone that he was exhausted and was going to end the session.

When they resumed later on that same day, they discussed a gun that Candy had carried with her during her CIA days. It was, according to her, a .22-caliber pistol, and she also commented during this portion of the session that she was given a .45-caliber pistol but found it too heavy to carry. Nebel tried to get the name of the person who gave her the gun, but she refused to name him. (In subsequent sessions she claimed that Gilbert Jensen had an extensive collection of weapons in his Oakland office and had provided her with both the .22 and the .45. Jensen had also taken her to a firing range near or on Travis Air Force Base in northern California, where she had been taught to fire the pistols.)

The segment about the guns ended, and when Nebel resumed working with Candy later that day, he was confronted with Arlene rather than his wife. Arlene claimed she was trying to help Candy by giving her strength.

Moments later, Candy, who was lying in bed throughout these hypnotic sessions, sat up and began yelling, "Caucasians are not the concubines of the blacks."

Nebel was shaken by this sudden outburst and tried to calm her.

"It is revolting and it is disgusting," Candy screamed.

■

JOHN: Who told you to say that?
CANDY: Gil said to just look around and I'd see it, and I do see
    it. *(Her voice still strident)* Does a lion mate with a tiger?
JOHN: Do you know where you are right now?
CANDY: Yes, I'm in the discussion class. In the building outside
    of ... I don't know where it is ... Texas ... Louisiana, Texas
    ... on the border ...

JOHN: Who is your instructor?

CANDY: Dr. Burger.

JOHN: That's the man you met in Chicago.

CANDY: I met him years ago. *(Suddenly whispering)* I'm not supposed to say that.

JOHN: And he's the one that . . .

CANDY: Ssssssssh.

JOHN: Why should I be quiet?

CANDY: I met him once before, but he pretends he doesn't know me.

JOHN: And he's the one giving you instructions in class?

CANDY: It's just his discussion class.

JOHN: Is it about blacks and whites?

CANDY: Blacks, and whites, and yellows . . . and the whole thing. Integration is one thing, but mixed breeding is another. He is so right.

JOHN: You agree with him?

CANDY: Oh, yes.

JOHN: What else has he said in today's discussion class?

CANDY: He said it is always the minority group that tries to get the majority group to go with them. It'll be the blacks trying to get the whites to go with them, and the yellows trying to get the whites to go with them. It will always be that way. Those people are very strong.

JOHN: Where did you learn that, from Dr. Burger?

CANDY: Uh-huh. And I read it in the literature they give you.

JOHN: What were some of the things they gave you? Do you remember?

CANDY: "World Power" . . . "World Peace" . . . "Peace Is Not a Color," or something like that. *(Becoming animated)* You go to the back of the room there and they have the booklets on that little table. It's all free and you can just take any ones you want.

JOHN: How many people were in the discussion class?

CANDY: Eight or nine of us today.

JOHN: And Dr. Burger is the main speaker?

CANDY: Yeah . . . they expected a whole lot of people, but something happened to the bus.

JOHN: Has Gil Jensen been here?

CANDY: Oh, yes. He introduced him.

JOHN: He introduced you to Burger?

CANDY: No, he introduced Burger to the class. He was the moderator of the class and introduced Burger.

■

There is a break in the hypnotic session at this point. When it resumes, it appears to be Candy speaking, but her voice has taken on Arlene's familiar militant, grating tone.

■

CANDY: The black people will take over as much as they can. They will first get their white women and bring in as many offspring as they can. These people . . . are going to be taking the white women and it will be integration. It is wrong.

JOHN: Is that what Dr. Burger said?

CANDY: Oh, yes, and it is wrong. It will happen. Burger told the whole thing and it makes sense.

*(Nebel comments into the microphone that Candy is sitting up in bed, her face twisted into a hateful sneer.)*

JOHN: It makes sense to you?

CANDY: Of course it does.

*(Nebel asks whether she is asleep. He repeats the question three times, and she eventually answers, "Uh-huh." Her voice has softened to the normal tones associated with Candy Jones. Nebel now asks her whether Dr. Burger is still in the room.)*

CANDY: No.

JOHN: *(commenting into the microphone that she is looking around the bedroom)* He left the room?

CANDY: I don't see him.

*(Nebel whispers into the microphone that Candy is still looking around the room and is pointing at their television set. As he comments, Candy interrupts.)*

CANDY: I want to talk to Gil.

JOHN: You want to speak with Gil Jensen?

CANDY: About what?

JOHN: I don't know. You said you wanted to talk to Gil.

CANDY: *(still pointing toward their television set)* He's up there at the blackboard.

*(Nebel agrees that he sees Jensen at the blackboard, and asks whether she wants to say anything else.)*

CANDY: I don't say anything, I just listen. He is telling us all the truth. I know it's true because of all those pictures they show us, and it was disgusting.

JOHN: Who gave you the pictures?

CANDY: They didn't give them to us, they showed them on the screen. They were up there, all those black men with white women. It was revolting, disgusting. Those white women going after the black men. It's going to be a bad scene.

JOHN: It's a bad situation, huh?

CANDY: It sure is. It's all true.

JOHN: Is that what they're teaching in the organization?

CANDY: They show you.

JOHN: Is that what the CIA . . . what Dr. Burger taught you?

CANDY: Marshall said that everybody knows a white who's going with a black. He said it is going to be some big problem. Marshall said that it is going to be tough on the children and that they should be sterilized. I think that's so.

JOHN: And that's what Burger taught you?

CANDY: Uh-huh. *(Becoming vehement)* They should be sterilized. They should not be allowed to bring in children. They should stick to their own kind. Does a tiger mate with a lion?

JOHN: Wasn't that what Dr. Burger said?

CANDY: He sure did.

JOHN: Is Dr. Burger paid by the CIA?

CANDY: He *is* the CIA. He's important out here in discussions, but I don't know how big he is.

■

As mentioned earlier, this CIA programming to hate most people with whom she was likely to come in contact had a profound effect upon Candy's daily life.

But even more upsetting for Nebel was Arlene's shifting attitudes toward *him.* A love-hate relationship developed between them, both emotions causing considerable upset and concern.

# 14

# Viewing Each Other

As Arlene Grant intruded with greater regularity and impact into John Nebel's life, it became obvious to him that she was not to be simply dismissed as a psychological phenomenon. She was very much her own lady, physically and mentally, and made it known that she was not content with her secondary role in Candy's life. Day after day she demonstrated her own unique characteristics—strength, sarcasm, testiness and even violence —the same characteristics Gilbert Jensen found so appealing in terms of the CIA work he planned for Candy.

There are numerous examples taken from the hypnotic-session tapes that point up the differences between the two women. One of them had to do with smoking. As with most of the recorded hypnotic sessions, few tapes are confined to a single issue. And often, a hypnotic subject will be subtly influenced by events around him or her, even though the subject is presumably unaware of peripheral influences while in deep trance. In this session, Candy, under hypnosis, regressed to Jensen's office.*

*Tape #3, Side A.

She commented to Jensen that she smelled smoke, and reminded him that he had told her that neither she nor Arlene should smoke because it wasn't good for them.

"Arlene smokes," Candy said.

"You smoke, too," Nebel, playing Jensen, reminded Candy. (Candy had been a smoker during her days with the CIA, but quit in 1970.)

"Arlene smokes more than I do," Candy commented to Jensen. "If Arlene is around, there are more cigarettes smoked."

Candy is concerned in this session that someone else is in Jensen's office, but Nebel, playing the role of the doctor, assures her that it is only the lingering smell of cigarette smoke left by a neighbor who had been there earlier. Candy was surprised to hear that anyone else had been allowed in the office; she had often questioned Jensen as to whether he had any other patients.

This hypnotic session also contained Candy's comment that she didn't know why she kept coming to his office. "I feel so sleepy after I get the phone call that brings Arlene here," she told him. "How do you transmit those sounds on the phone? I've never heard sounds like that before." She is referring to the mechanical sounds that Jensen had used in his office and, according to other recorded material, played for Candy on the phone as a code which would spur her into some form of action.

Arlene's overall attitude toward Candy was one of scorn. She constantly commented on Candy's weaknesses, often referring to her as dumb, slow and stupid. Nebel and Arlene often found themselves in long discussions in which Candy was the center of attention. Arlene enjoyed calling Candy "goody two-shoes" and snickered at those aspects of Candy's character that made her soft and pliable.

In an undated tape,* Arlene, using her most contemptuous voice, called Candy "the mother of her country," referring to Candy's track record as a volunteer for the military in World War II. Arlene added during this session that Candy had made a mess of her business because of this willingness to donate her time and energies. There is some truth to this; Candy's involvement with the CIA began to take so much of her time that she

*Tape #77, Side A.

was unable to devote the necessary energy to her businesses in New York.

Arlene also accused Candy of being a poor judge of character, and pointed to some of her relationships as examples. Arlene had never been fond of Mel Heimer, and maintained that Mel fostered the relationship with Candy in order to borrow money to pay his gambling debts.

Arlene's reaction to Harry Conover was one of disgust, and it is difficult to fault Arlene for having that reaction to Candy's deceased husband.

Candy, on the other hand, is more defensive and positive in her feelings toward Arlene. She often talks of how grateful she is to Arlene for having bailed her out of a number of messes in her life. It should be remembered, however, that Candy's childhood dependency on her little imaginary friend who could run faster, swim better, and perform other physical feats with greater skill and stamina was seized upon by Jensen to create in Candy an adult dependence upon Arlene.

On an undated tape, Candy and Arlene discussed the differences between them.*

"I'm Candy Jones," Arlene told Nebel during that session, her tone mocking. "I have a lot of scores to settle up, and if Candy can't settle her scores for herself, I'll settle them for her. I've made a list."

"Who is on the list?" Nebel asked.

"Wouldn't you like to know?" Arlene replied. "It goes from the garbage man right on up to the top."

"Does Candy want you to do this for her?" Nebel asked.

"Who cares? Candy is too dumb to know. Candy has been screwed so many times, and I'm going to help her unscrew her life because she is just too goddamn dumb."

Arlene went on to say that Candy is scared of everything and sits back like a nice girl. "I'm sick of watching it," Arlene said. "I'll do something about it when the times comes. I'll be like a rapier."

Nebel, as he began to do in the later stages of his relationship with Arlene, talked tough with her. In this session he told her that he would get rid of her.

*Tape #7 "A," Side B.

"The only person who can get rid of me is Gil Jensen, and you can't reach him," Arlene said. "I listen to Jensen."

"Would you listen to me?" Nebel asked.

Arlene laughed. "You're a pussycat. You wouldn't get rid of me, because your curiosity is whetted."

Further along in this same session Candy emerged and agreed that Arlene was much stronger than she. She told Nebel, who was playing her alter ego, that Gilbert Jensen had brought Arlene out and liked her very much. "Jensen said that Arlene was a sublime woman," Candy said. "He liked Arlene better than me. It was easy for him to bring Arlene out because she was eager to speak with him."

Nebel questioned her as to how Jensen brought Arlene out in his office.

"I was very tired from the trips and I took naps. Just before I went to sleep he would say something that sounded like tit-tat-toe, tit-tat-toe, tit-tat-toe. He kept repeating it over and over."

Nebel asked what the code meant, and Candy said she didn't remember, except that it made her sleepy. Nebel later ascertained that it was this same code that was used by Jensen on the telephone.

A little later Candy said that Arlene was more Jensen's type. She called Jensen a creep, but added that Arlene saved her life many times by running fast for her. She also claimed that Arlene was capable of withstanding much more pain than she was, an advantage, she claimed, when intercepted in Taiwan and tortured with electrodes.

Another difference between Candy and Arlene is in their drinking habits. The tapes indicate that Arlene consumes more than Candy, and prefers vodka martinis. Candy was never fond of vodka martinis, according to Arlene, but has developed a taste for them through exposure to the drink while under Arlene's control. There have been episodes in the recent past in which Candy, contrary to her normal behavior, has had too much to drink while dining out with Nebel. I can testify that Candy Jones is a moderate drinker in her everyday life, and that for her to have two drinks at dinner is unusual. I have also, however, seen Candy go into the trance state in restaurants and become Arlene. When this happens, she has an increased appetite for alcoholic beverages, particularly vodka martinis.

Another interesting difference between the two personalities lies in their use of obscenities. Candy does not use four-letter words; Arlene, on the other hand, enjoys obscenities, and when you hear Arlene's voice during a trance state, you can be sure that what she has to say will contain a number of spicy phrases.

Candy once referred, while under hypnosis, to having been told by Gil Jensen that she needed Arlene to perform difficult physical tasks.* She claimed during this session that she had taken physical-coordination tests in California, and hadn't scored very high, but that when Arlene took the tests her score was considerably higher. Candy was dejected during this session because although she said she used to be very good at physical activities, including horseback riding and swimming, it had been Arlene who had done those things for her, even as a child.

Whether this is true or not could conceivably have something to do with Jensen's programming of Candy. In convincing Candy that she needed Arlene today, it would have been useful to persuade her that her youthful sports activities had been performed by Arlene. It should be pointed out, too, that Candy's mother seldom praised Candy's childhood activities, which contributed little to her adult sense of self-worth.

"Arlene is good at protecting me," Candy told Nebel during a recorded session that took place on July 2, 1973.** "Arlene is very good at some things, but I don't need her now," she said. Candy also claimed in that session that Arlene was jealous of her, which Arlene herself confessed during a number of recorded hypnotic sessions.

On the whole, Candy's life has been one long process of convincing her that she is not worthy. Her mother instilled this feeling in her from early childhood, and, unfortunately, she spent the 1960s and early 1970s under the control of a man who, it seems, for his and his agency's own purposes, found it useful to perpetuate that negative sense of self-worth. It is especially sad in view of the fact that Candy Jones is actually an extremely talented and capable woman. She is the author of 11 hardcover books and is considered by her editors to be a proficient and talented writer. It was distressing to hear a portion of a recorded hypnotic session in which Candy talked about Arlene taking over

*Tape #40, Side A.
**Tape #58, Side A.

in every difficult situation she faced in her life.* She told Nebel during this session, her tone melancholy, "I can watch the work that Arlene does. I can see the work she does coming out of my typewriter every day." Obviously she'd reached a point of even believing that her books had been written by Arlene.

There are many wrenching sessions in which Nebel attempts to break down these beliefs and convince his wife that she is a worthwhile person in her own right. This is more easily said than done, for he is dealing with a woman who has been purposely fragmented, and who has been programmed to believe that she is a nonentity, and that Arlene is to be the dominant force in her life. Jensen, according to material contained in the tapes, wanted to build Arlene to the point where she eventually took over. If he had been able to accomplish this, Candy Jones would, in effect, have ceased to exist; in her place would have been Arlene Grant, wearing her black wig, her dark makeup, and ready to perform on cue for Jensen and the CIA for the rest of her life.

Had Candy Jones not married Long John Nebel, there is every likelihood that Arlene would have succeeded in becoming the dominant personality. Candy had little quarrel with Arlene early in the game, and easily accepted her presence. It was only through Nebel's repeated attempts to convince her that there was no Arlene, or that if there had been such a person, she would no longer play a role in her life, that Candy's attitude toward her second personality changed from sympathy to anger.

There is an interesting tape recorded on July 9, 1973, in which Candy expresses concern that Arlene will be injured unless she runs away.** This session was fascinating for a number of reasons, one of which was an experiment that John Nebel attempted in dealing with Arlene.

At the start of the session Candy complained of a severe headache. She mumbled, "Go away, go away."

"Are you talking to Arlene?" Nebel asked.

Candy said she was.

Nebel then asked her if she wanted him to tell Arlene to go away and to stop bothering her. At first Candy did not want this, but eventually agreed that if John could reach Arlene and con-

*Tape #66, Side B.
**Tape #74, Side A.

vince her to go away, her headache might disappear.

Nebel called for Arlene. "Arlene, can you hear me?" He repeated the question. Finally, Candy's face became distorted, her lips drawn into a thin line, and when she spoke, it was in Arlene's voice.

"Yes. I hear you," Arlene said, and began to laugh.

■

JOHN: Is the laughter necessary, Arlene? Don't you want to talk to me?
ARLENE: No.
JOHN: We talked yesterday morning, didn't we? . . . Why don't you want to talk to me, Arlene? . . . Are you afraid of me?
ARLENE: Not of you.
JOHN: Who are you afraid of?

■

Candy began whimpering, displacing Arlene for the moment. Nebel, unaware that Arlene was no longer there, asked Arlene why she was giving Candy a headache. Candy answered, and said her headache was almost gone.

"Are you leaving, Arlene?" Nebel asked, still not realizing she'd already departed.

"Don't let her come near me," Candy pleaded. He realized he was talking to Candy, and decided to attempt to reach both personalities simultaneously.

"Arlene, don't do this to me," Candy begged.

"Candy, tell Arlene to talk to me," Nebel said. "Arlene is intelligent and I would like to talk to her more."

"She won't talk to you," Candy said.

"We talked before," said Nebel.

Candy suddenly sat up in bed and warned, "Go away fast, Arlene. Run! Run! They'll catch you." Her voice was filled with urgency. "Oh, hurry, Arlene."

"Is she going?" Nebel asked. "Is she going away?"

"She's hiding," Candy said, sounding satisfied.

"Who do you think will catch her?" Nebel asked.

"I will," Candy said.

"What would you do if you caught her?" Nebel asked.

"Lock her up."

"Where?"

"It would be a secret."

This segment of the session ended when Candy told Nebel, her alter ego, that Arlene couldn't talk at the moment because she was frightened. Candy added that Arlene bragged about being strong but was really very afraid.

The only genuinely harsh words Candy has had for Arlene, aside from those that came after John Nebel began working with her, were the result of her physical discomfort, which she blamed on her other self. She blamed her frequent stomachaches on Arlene's trying to come out, and she often pleaded with Arlene to stop bothering her.

There is a certain irony in the situation in which John Nebel found himself following his marriage to Candy Jones. Nebel is by nature a man who seeks control of the lives of those with whom he comes in contact. Candy is, on the other hand, someone who seems quite receptive to being controlled. This is conceptually the best marital pairing. When one party in a relationship needs to control, and the other is willing to *be* controlled, there is the potential for forward movement and achievement as a couple.

But while John Nebel married a woman who, through her basic personality, was susceptible to being controlled, she presented him, in Arlene, with quite a different story. Arlene was the controlling side of Candy's personality, which she lacked in her everyday life. Perhaps this is the reason why a strong second personality ever develops at all. Each of us has a need to be able to override our basic personality when a situation demands it. In Candy's case, Arlene provided certain physical and emotional strengths which, Arlene claims, helped carry Candy over the rough spots. What it meant for Nebel, however, was that he was faced with another controller, and a particularly formidable one at that.

The day-to-day relationship between John and Arlene progressed from fascination to antagonism. As Arlene developed into a more determined personality, during both induced and spontaneous trance states, her thoughts and needs were laid on the table for Nebel, and he often had trouble dealing with them. There are a number of recorded examples in which Nebel, frustrated and upset, threatened to do away with Arlene in physical, often sadistic terms.

Nebel's threats to Arlene became frequent, and I have transcripts of seven hypnotic sessions in which the threats were detailed and lengthy. Since they are all basically the same, however, one will serve to illustrate what actually occurred during these difficult days and nights in Nebel's apartment.*

In this session Arlene spent a great deal of time criticizing Candy for the way she had conducted her life. She accused Candy of wanting to get rid of her, but said that whenever Candy tried to do this, she, Arlene, was capable of scaring her away.

"I find it amusing," Arlene told Nebel, referring to the times she had purposely frightened Candy.

"Why do you find it amusing?" Nebel asked.

"I don't know."

"Maybe Candy will scare you?" Nebel suggested.

"She couldn't scare me because she wouldn't know how," Arlene said smugly.

Nebel went on to suggest, in a fit of pique, that Candy was the one capable of articulating, and that Arlene was not.

■

ARLENE: You'd have trouble articulating too, if you weren't a whole person.

JOHN: Is Candy a whole person?

ARLENE: When I let her be. I can control Candy as long as I want to.

JOHN: *(in a threatening voice)* Suppose you were burned to death?

ARLENE: I wouldn't like that.

JOHN: I don't care what *you* like.

ARLENE: Candy wouldn't like that.

JOHN: Maybe Candy will request it sometime.

ARLENE: She wouldn't want to burn. What happens to me will happen to Candy.

JOHN: *(angry, frustrated)* Your knowledge in this area, Arlene, is extremely limited. I can exorcise you. One way I can do it is with flame.

ARLENE: *(laughing scornfully)* I wouldn't advise you to try it.

JOHN: You're treading on dangerous ground, Arlene.

ARLENE: *(becoming louder, continues to laugh at Nebel's threat)* I've felt flames before.

*Tape #4, Side A.

JOHN: Would you like to feel flames again?
ARLENE: Do you really want to burn me?

■

Nebel answered by repeating over and over his desire to rid Candy of Arlene's unhealthy presence. Arlene reluctantly agreed that Candy didn't need her, but admitted that she needed Candy in order to live. Nebel appeared to be winning this dialogue until Arlene summoned up strength and took the offensive. She told Nebel that he would never burn her because, she said, with the rising inflection of someone who has suddenly discovered a truth, "You find me too fascinating to get rid of me." She giggled, and began playing the coquette.

Nebel changed tactics and told Arlene that she was nothing more than a reflection in a mirror. This sudden shift in emphasis upset Arlene, and she told him that she didn't want to hear that kind of talk. Once Nebel had her back on the defensive, he returned to his threat to burn her, describing how he would first put her in a box.

Arlene became hysterical and pleaded with him not to carry out his threat. Nebel became concerned for Candy and terminated the session.

The hours John and Arlene spent together were not always so filled with anger, threats and fear, however. Arlene indicated, at times, a romantic and even sexual interest in John Nebel.

In a hypnotic session that took place on September 5, 1974, in the bedroom of Candy and John's apartment, Arlene emerged as soon as the session began. As in a previous session, Arlene delighted in the fact that Nebel was not sure to whom he was speaking. He asked whether she was Arlene, and she laughed and told him she thought it was very funny that he couldn't tell the difference between them.

"This is a funny situation," she said. "Arlene just keeps coming in and out."

"Is Arlene out now?" Nebel asked, still not sure.

"I don't know whether Arlene is out, but if I did know I wouldn't tell you," she replied. "I don't want to confuse myself."

"You had better tell me who you are," Nebel threatened.

"I am Arlene, but don't you think I sound like Candy?" Arlene asked, giggling. "I can sound like namby-pamby Candy."

"Why are you so angry, Arlene?"

"I'm not mad, but I don't have a chance to live like Candy does."

"Do you think Candy is lucky to have married John and to have him in her life?" Nebel asked.

"*I* want to be with John," Arlene replied, her voice teasing. "I'd like to know what it would be like to be with John."

Nebel asked her why she wanted to be with him and inquired whether she thought he was a nice man.

■

ARLENE: He's fascinating, but he doesn't like me.

JOHN: All right, Arlene, do you want to go to sleep now?

ARLENE: I'd like to go to sleep with John sometimes.

   (*Nebel ignores the comment and again suggests she go to sleep.*)

ARLENE: When I wake up, who will I be?

JOHN: (*disgusted*) Goodnight, Arlene.

ARLENE: (*in a sexy voice*) Goodnight, John.

JOHN: Should I say goodnight, Arlene, or goodnight, Candy?

ARLENE: Say "Goodnight, Arlene." Do you want to kiss me goodnight?

JOHN: I wouldn't do that because my wife is Candy.

ARLENE: I'm your wife.

JOHN: Well, are you Arlene or Candy?

ARLENE: Does it matter?

JOHN: It does to me.

ARLENE: We're all alone.

JOHN: I happen to be very honest and sincere with Candy. That
   doesn't put you down or anything, Arlene.

ARLENE: But I'm Candy.

JOHN: No, you're not.

ARLENE: How do you know?

JOHN: I know.

ARLENE: You wouldn't know unless you kissed me.

JOHN: Goodnight.

ARLENE: Goodnight. You're pretty smart, aren't you? Someday
   I'll trick you and I'll make you think I'm Candy.

■

Arlene dozed off at this point. Ten minutes later she began talking in her sleep, and Nebel turned on the tape recorder.

"Are you sleeping, Arlene?" he asked.

"I'm just dreaming," she answered. "Dreaming and plotting. I just wanted to make sure you were here."

"Where's Candy?" Nebel asked.

"I don't know."

"Have you taken over Candy again?"

"I'm just taking over until Candy gets strong again. She has a bad stomachache. Don't you ever wear clothes to bed?"

Nebel laughed at her reference to his usual sleeping attire, a pair of bikini shorts. Arlene rolled over in bed and began running her hands over his chest.

"Why are you doing that?" Nebel asked.

"Just to make sure it's you," she said, affecting a kittenish voice. She added that she intended to go to work with him today.

"Do you intend to make a disturbance?" Nebel asked.

"No."

During another recorded hypnotic session, Arlene again asked Nebel to kiss her goodnight. This time he gave her a light kiss on the cheek.

"I bet you don't kiss Candy that way," Arlene said sarcastically.

"That's none of your business, Arlene."

"Are you going to kiss me goodnight again?"

Nebel kissed her lightly, this time on the lips.

"That's much better," Arlene said. "I could get you to like me a little bit if you weren't such a creep. You are a creep at times."

And on still another tape in which Arlene displayed affection to Nebel,* she emerged at the 20-minute mark and said, "I need you." She stretched, yawned and said, "It is good to be out."

"What do you need me for, Arlene?"

"It's good to be out."

"You're already out of Candy, Arlene. What do you need me for?"

"I need you to help me," Arlene told him.

"To help you do what?"

*Tape #34, Side A.

"To help me come out."

"You're already out. What do you need me for?"

"To help me stay around. Stay around with me," Arlene said.

"Are you saying I should drop Candy?"

"Why not?"

"She's no good?" Nebel asked.

"She's been dropped before."

"By whom?"

Arlene laughed at the question. "Her queer husband dropped her," she snickered, referring to Harry Conover.

"Who else?"

"Her writer friend." Arlene laughed again. "It was so funny. I used to sit and watch them and laugh and laugh." (She is referring to Mel Heimer.)

"Who else dropped her?" Nebel asked Arlene.

"She didn't have the nerve to try and find a man again."

"Why did she marry me?" Nebel asked.

"She thought she could make it work."

Nebel asked, "Do you think Candy took advantage of me?"

"She's not smart enough," Arlene said sneeringly.

"Are you saying that you're smart enough to take advantage of me?" Nebel asked.

"I would keep you with me."

"Was it good that Candy married me?"

"Marrying you was a good thing for Candy and it made her happy," Arlene said. "But I'm going to make her sadder than she has ever been in her life."

There was little more of substance during this segment, and Nebel ended it by having Arlene put her hand on the paneling in their bedroom.


Arlene often exhibited jealousy of Candy's new radio career, as well as of her new husband. There are frequent references to Arlene wanting to go to the studio with Nebel and to do the show with him.

One session found Arlene complaining belligerently of not having a life of her own.* Nebel told her to calm down and to

*Tape #42, Side A.

stop playing games with him. He told her that if she didn't behave herself, he would break her arm. Arlene countered by accusing him of being afraid of her, and suggested that he let her do the show that night instead of Candy.

"You're not competent, Arlene."

"Try me."

Arlene then suggested that Nebel try to get to know her better. "You might find you like me better than Candy."

"I happen to be very much in love with Candy," Nebel replied.

"But why don't you try? . . . You might like me better. . . . Some people like vanilla ice cream, but then they try chocolate and they find they like that even better."

"I happen to have one woman, Candy, and I love her very much."

"But we're the same."

"No, you're not. You're just using the same body, that's all."

"You know," Arlene said, "no one would ever believe you if you told them about this."

Nebel declined to argue the point and brought Candy out of the trance.

Whenever Arlene appeared to be making a play for John, she would begin by trying to confuse him as to her identity. She would also often begin those hypnotic sessions by complaining that she had no life of her own. Her message seemed to be that Nebel provided for her the potential for being able to take over Candy's body and role in life, as had been hoped for by Gilbert Jensen.

In one session Arlene told Nebel that she had some rights, too. "I just want to get a breath of living," she said, and reminded him that he had just told her that he loved her.*

"No, I said I love Candy, not you," Nebel said.

"No, John, you told me you loved *me.*"

Nebel pointed out to her that he was married to Candy.

Arlene smiled and said whimsically, "But here you have two for one." She evidently pondered the morality of this unusual triangle for a moment, and then began to imitate Candy. She stopped, however, when Nebel challenged her to continue the

*Tape #86 "A", Side B.

imitation. Arlene often displayed an obstinate streak during hypnotic sessions.

Quite frankly, John Nebel found much of the interplay between him and Arlene Grant to be fascinating. He had no way of knowing, of course, that Arlene's hateful side would eventually result in a physical attack upon him.

On Christmas Day, 1974, Arlene complained bitterly about not having a Christmas of her own. She further stated that she wanted to spend Christmas with John, and did not want Candy to have that pleasure.

In July 1973 Nebel asked Candy, while she was in the hypnotic trance state, whether she thought Arlene would ever try to harm him. The inference in his question was not that Arlene might harm him physically, but that she might do something to hurt his career, or his standing with his friends.

Candy answered by saying, "Arlene won't hurt you if I'm here." Her answer, in retrospect, had a ring of warning to it, but one cannot fault Nebel for not recognizing it at the time.

In August 1973, during a hypnotic session in which Nebel and Arlene had a long talk about her relationship with Candy, and about the fact that she was seldom allowed to come out and enjoy life, she warned him that he had better keep himself ready at all times in case she came out unexpectedly.

"Don't make any moves you can't control, Arlene," Nebel told her.

"I don't intend to," Arlene said menacingly. "But I might make some moves when no one is awake."

# 15

## The Attack

"It was about seven o'clock at night and Candy was sitting up, her back against a pillow and a foam-rubber wedge," John Nebel recalls of an evening in September 1973, two months after Arlene had made her identity known to him.

Nebel continues: "Candy seemed calm and relaxed. She was reading the *New York Post* and I was browsing through a book written by an author I was to have on the show that night. All the lights were on in the bedroom. Candy was wearing a very pretty blue negligee, and appeared to me to be very contented. All of a sudden, her features changed. So did her voice.

"Now bear in mind, I had not hypnotized her. This was a spontaneous change on her part. I looked at her and asked, 'Who are you?' She just sat there staring at me, her eyes wide open and looking as though they were going to fall out of her head. I waved my hand back and forth in front of her face, but there was no response. She didn't even blink, because she couldn't see my hand while she was in the trance state. I moved closer and again asked what her name was."

"I'm Arlene," she answered Nebel.

"What are you doing here?"

"I don't have to talk to you because *I don't like you,*" Arlene said to Nebel, her eyes still wide and focused on an unseen distant object.

Nebel decided to turn on the tape equipment and record whatever might occur during this spontaneous regression. But as he fumbled for the switch and untangled the microphone cord, she let out a sigh and sat back against the pillow, her face again that of a serene Candy Jones. Nebel told her that Arlene had just appeared, but as usual when in the conscious state, Candy didn't believe it.

"Are you all right?" John asked her.

Candy laughed. "Of course I'm all right, John. Why shouldn't I be?"

Nebel turned on his side and closed his eyes. Last night's show had been a difficult one, and various appointments around the city had kept him from sleeping that day. He hoped to get some rest before they left for the studio that evening.

As he tried to relax, he felt Candy shift positions on the bed behind him. He raised his head and turned to see what she was doing. But before he could turn all the way around, she was on top of him, the distorted, twisted face of Arlene looking down into his, her hands at his throat.

Nebel twisted and brought the edges of his hands down on her wrists. "Drop your hands!" he yelled. He hit her again, harder this time, and she loosened her hold on his neck. Nebel pushed her off and scrambled to his feet at the side of the bed.

"I don't think I'd ever been as frightened in my life," Nebel recalls. "It wasn't just the physical attack on me, because living in a large city like New York, you almost expect to be attacked on the street, particularly during the nighttime hours I keep. But this was my wife! And she had turned into a monster, a woman with strength I didn't know she had, and whose face had taken on a mean, vicious expression like something you'd see in a horror movie. I stood at the side of the bed and shook, and looked at her, my eyes as wide open as hers had been. She was on her knees, and she looked confused, about to cry. I instinctively reached out and touched her face."

After he and Candy had calmed down, Nebel questioned her about the attack. Candy denied having done it, and denied even

being aware that there had been such an attack. Nebel found this
difficult to believe, which only added to his confusion. Was it
possible, he wondered, for a person to attack another person
and have absolutely no recollection of it, even minutes following
the act? Nebel was distrustful of those tales about drunks who
wake up in the morning and cannot remember their actions of
the night before; he tended to believe that such selective loss of
memory was a device to avoid responsibility. Could it be that
this other woman with whom he was living, Arlene Grant, a
figment of his wife's childhood imagination, dredged up from
her past by a California doctor, could have attacked him as she
did without the *real person* having any knowledge?

It was all too bizarre for Nebel to deal with, and he dropped
the subject, although he made a mental note to bring it up the
next time he talked with Arlene. A second mental note he made
was that when such a discussion did occur, the tape recorder
would be rolling.

The opportunity to have such a discussion with Arlene arose
during the next hour when Candy slipped into another spontaneous trance.*

A number of things occurred during the first 15 minutes of
this recorded session, including Candy's regression to childhood. But about halfway through the half-hour tape she became
the adult Candy Jones again and brought up the question of
whether she had attempted to strangle him in bed an hour
earlier. She was upset at this point, and pleaded with John to
believe that she would never try to hurt him. He pointed out that
it was not she who had attacked him, but Arlene. Candy became
upset and denied that there was such a person as Arlene. In fact
Candy spent four minutes trying to get John to believe that she
would not have attacked him. At one point, John became angry
with her for refusing to accept the facts, and harsh words ensued.

This is one example of many in which John Nebel's frustration
reached large proportions. Candy invariably refuses to acknowledge the fact that her personality has changed at any time,
particularly when that personality change is labeled Arlene. She
will listen to a tape and react with horror to what she hears

*Tape #6, Side A.

coming from her own mouth, but philosophically she cannot accept that there is this second person living within her.

Many psychiatrists and psychologists would agree with her, for there is considerable skepticism in the psychiatric fraternity about the existence of a true split, or multiple, personality. Few deny that within each of us there is the capacity for personality change, depending upon the situation with which we are faced. Most of us have at least two sides to our nature, perhaps a flamboyant personality when that is pleasing to us, and a more conservative one when placed in a more conservative milieu. It is when these personalities are extended to a point where one personality is able to function independently from the other that such cases as the one reported in the best-selling book, *Sybil,* occur.

In the August 1975 issue of *Psychology Today,* Dr. Emanuel Berman, a clinical psychologist, reported on a case that had first been presented by him and Frederick Coplon at a meeting of the American Psychiatric Association. It concerned a black woman, whose name was changed in the article to Veronica, who had a second personality within her, given the name Nelly. Berman says: "Two women showed up alternately in the same body, usually after sleep, and were very different on personality tests. Veronica is afraid that Nelly is getting out of control. Small wonder; Veronica acted like a little girl, emotional, animated, often tearful. Nelly was aloof, arrogant, sexually provocative. With therapy and time, the two merged into a whole woman."

Dr. Berman goes on to say at the end of the article: "With such a theory of personality, full-scale multiple personalities such as Eve [*The Three Faces of Eve*], Sybil and Veronica would be seen not as curious freaks, but as extreme examples of a normal human phenomenon. What is extreme and probably pathological about the true split personality is not the differentiation itself, but its rigidity; the obliviousness by each side to the other; and the impenetrable wall between contradictory aspects of one's self.

"Being capable of varied and sometimes contradictory roles and feelings is an asset; their rigid separation is a burden. Recognizing the potency of existing splits may be a crucial step toward ultimate integration."

Dr. Herbert Spiegel, too, is skeptical of the existence of a true

multiple personality. He appeared on the "Long John Nebel–
Candy Jones Show" on WMCA on January 4, 1975, and discussed the subject with Nebel, Candy and me.

I asked Dr. Spiegel whether, since hypnosis can be used to
*treat* a multiple personality, it could be used to *create* one.

"Oh, sure. It works both ways. . . ."

"You could deliberately create a second personality?"

"Yes . . . it's done. . . . I once had occasion to do that with a
woman who was a Grade Five [highest on the Hypnotic Induction Profile developed by Dr. Spiegel]. . . . We had to deal with
certain different points of view she had about herself. . . . Although she didn't spontaneously have multiple personalities,
which is a debatable thing anyway, and we can go into it later
if you wish in order to make the point clearly and to make it
quickly, we assigned a certain point of view towards her family,
towards her mother, towards sex and towards her husband, to
different names. . . . We had four different people to which we
assigned these roles. . . . We had group-therapy sessions with the
four of them. . . . If someone had observed us through a one-way
mirror and looked at me talking to this one woman who'd been
divided into four, I think I would have been put away. . . .

"For example, the girl who was sort of mischievous and sexy
and seductive was named Sonya . . . the patient gave her that
name. . . . Then there was another name, Phyllis, who was the
proper housewife. Every time Phyllis tried to talk, Sonya would
butt in. It got so that they started arguing with each other, and
I had to stop it. I said, 'Now Sonya, that's enough. I want you
to get out of here and wait outside until I tell you to come in.'
I got up and opened the door and told her, 'Get out and stay
out!' . . .

"When I came back to the patient, she said, 'Oh, God, am I
glad we got rid of her.' "

Dr. Spiegel went on to explain the psychological theories
behind such a treatment strategy, and pointed out that once
Sonya was gone, Phyllis was able to analyze what Sonya's presence had meant in her life.

I asked the obvious question of Dr. Spiegel: "Were you able
to get rid of the other personalities once they had served their
purposes?"

"Oh, yes," Dr. Spiegel replied. "The patient and I openly

acknowledged that it was only a technique, and she was fused into one whole person again.''

Dr. Spiegel then brought up the question of multiple personalities in general. He said, "I knew Sybil very well. She was one of our research subjects, and was kind enough to come to our classes at Columbia several years in a row while still in treatment with Dr. Wilbur [Dr. Cornelia B. Wilbur, Sybil's psychoanalyst]. Dr. Wilbur and I often discussed Sybil's case, and when Dr. Wilbur was away I would take over because there were times that Sybil was in such a fragile state that Wilbur didn't feel comfortable leaving her alone.''

After a discussion of Sybil and of Dr. Spiegel's role in her case, he went on to say, "In my view, multiple personalities are more a fiction that is made into a pseudoreality by the way we deal with the patient. When you consider that the highly hypnotizable person, which Sybil was, is suggestible . . . and if we keep reinforcing a point of view, or an aspect of ourself, and we start calling it a name and we say this is another person, such is the compliance of the highly hypnotizable person that he or she will say, 'Okay, if you want to call it another person, it's okay with me.' So we can now carry that fiction on and we call it a multiple personality. Think about any person . . . think about yourself . . . you think of yourself in different roles. . . . Highly hypnotizable persons are very imaginative, very affable, very easygoing and very willing to go along with suggestions. . . . You come along with the idea that you'd like to call them a name, and then they test you out by calling a point of view a name. . . . The doctor approves, which pleases the patient. . . . 'Hum,' says the patient, 'I'm getting Green Stamps from the doctor.' . . . Indirectly, the doctor is training the patient to call a personality change by another person's name.''

Dr. Spiegel said that he was not against the concept of multiple personality, but feels we're kidding ourselves if we take it too literally. "Sybil did not have, in my view, sixteen or seventeen different personalities. What she had were sixteen or seventeen different points of view, and they were named,'' Spiegel concluded.

Dr. Gilbert Jensen seems to have done exactly what Spiegel refers to in his evaluation of the multiple-personality concept. Jensen wanted a different point of view from Candy, one that would be more closely aligned with his and The Company's goals. The fact that Candy brought to Jensen a ready-made "second personality" named Arlene, who had functioned for Candy from that second, stronger viewpoint in childhood, made Jensen's job all the easier.

To return to the hypnotic session following Arlene's attack— after Candy and John's argument the discussion went on to other areas until the 25-minute mark when, with her usual suddenness, Arlene took over from Candy.

■

JOHN: Are you Arlene?

ARLENE: *(playfully)* I could be.

JOHN: Where is Candy?

ARLENE: She hasn't gone far.

JOHN: *(speaking to Arlene as though she were a third person)* Do you know that Arlene put her hands around John's neck? Do you know that, Arlene? Were you there?

ARLENE: *(smugly)* I was watching.

JOHN: What did she do?

ARLENE: Felt for the jugular.

JOHN: Do you think she wanted to kill John?

ARLENE: No. She just wanted to . . .

JOHN: To frighten him?

ARLENE: Of course.

JOHN: Why would she want to frighten John?

ARLENE: To show him her power and strength.

JOHN: *(still speaking to Arlene as a third person)* Is there something wrong with her that she would want to do that with John?

ARLENE: She's jealous.

JOHN: She's jealous of Candy? *(Arlene shakes her head)* Then who is she jealous of?

ARLENE: She wouldn't hurt anyone, including herself, or Candy.

■

Arlene told Nebel to stop talking this way because it "makes it all sound so strange." Nebel asked her whether she liked Gilbert Jensen, and she said she did.

■

JOHN: Why do you like Jensen, Arlene?
ARLENE: Because he likes me. But he doesn't like Candy.
JOHN: Did Candy try to strangle John, Arlene?
ARLENE: She didn't.
JOHN: She didn't?
ARLENE: She didn't do it.
JOHN: If she didn't do it, then did you do it, Arlene?
ARLENE: I showed her where.
JOHN: You did it?
ARLENE: Yes.
JOHN: Did you want her to kill John?
ARLENE: She's weak.
JOHN: Did you want Candy to put her hands on John's jugular
     vein?
ARLENE: I just wanted to show her what to do.
JOHN: Why?
ARLENE: They weren't *her* hands.
JOHN: Whose hands were they?
ARLENE: Mine.

■

Arlene repeated that she felt Candy was weak, and agreed that
she didn't like Nebel or anyone else getting too close to her,
meaning herself. Nebel asked her whether she'd kept Candy
from talking earlier in the session. Arlene's response to this was
to laugh heartily and to agree that she had, indeed, kept Candy's
voice inside. She told Nebel that she had done it before and
would do it again. Nebel went back to the question of the hands
around his neck.

■

JOHN: Why did you put your hands around John's neck?
ARLENE: They were *her* hands. I controlled her hands. Candy
     couldn't even squeeze a fly, and Candy loves everything that
     is alive, including animals. (*Arlene sounds very disgusted about
     Candy's weakness for animals.*)
JOHN: Do you want to do John harm, Arlene?
ARLENE: Not unless he tries to do me harm. I was just looking

for the pressure points on his neck, that's all. I wanted John to know how strong I am.

JOHN: What are you going to do now?

ARLENE: *(sounding considerably weaker)* I'm losing strength.

■

As Arlene weakened, Nebel kept up the questioning about why she had put her hands on his neck. She pleaded with him to stop talking, saying she didn't feel well and that she was having trouble breathing. Nebel, concerned for Candy's health, quickly brought her out of the trance.

There were other hypnotic sessions in which the same subject came up, but they resulted in Arlene basically repeating what she had said in the above session. In both the conscious and hypnotic states, Candy continued to deny that such an attack took place.

There was a long period of time during which this subject did not come up again, but in August of 1974 there was an exchange between Arlene and John Nebel that was indicative of the entire relationship between them.* It found Arlene discussing, with envy, Candy's freedom to move about. She had asked Nebel who he thought she looked like.

"You look like a vicious Candy," he replied.

"What do you mean by vicious?" Arlene asked.

"Candy is a beautiful woman, and you hate Candy's guts, don't you, Arlene?"

"I envy Candy," Arlene said.

"You envy Candy because she found someone to love and to marry."

"I envy her because she can move around and has a life of her own," Arlene said. "Why can't I have a life of my own?"

Arlene was still seeking that independent life as recently as the summer of 1975.

*Tape #42, Side A.

# PART II

# 16

# The Missions

Although the programming of Candy Jones was a continuing process, there was a point at which Jensen presumably felt she was ready to begin performing services for him and for the CIA. He sent her out on assignments, and she undertook them with the exuberance of a third-string ballplayer entering the game for the first time.

Originally, her assignments were confined to simple messenger duties. These were conducted in conjunction with her normal business travels, and included the delivering of sealed envelopes to unnamed persons in Philadelphia, Washington, Boston and New York. Through descriptions that had been given to her, she delivered the envelopes in restaurants, hotel lobbies and in offices. Usually she was alerted that there was a message for her to carry by a telephone call from Jensen. He seldom spoke, and what she routinely heard was a series of electronic sounds that triggered a reaction within her. She knew, subconsciously, from the sounds, that she was to make a return call to Jensen through a New York telephone exchange. Candy's call was automatically fed through a tie line to Oakland, and

Jensen verbally gave her her instructions during the second call.

In New York, the envelope to be delivered was received by mail, either at her office at 52 Vanderbilt Avenue, or at the Grand Central post office box, the smaller envelope enclosed within a larger one.

Jensen was a methodically careful man. Every scrap of paper received by Candy, with the exception of those to be delivered, was to be saved by her and given to him in Oakland. He conducted thorough searches of her handbag on each visit to his office, and maintained a list of all written materials sent to her.

He was especially careful about Arlene Grant. In the early stages of her work for Jensen, it was Candy who took the trips and made the deliveries. But as her scope widened and included travel abroad, Arlene began to assume more of the responsibility. Candy, as mentioned earlier, carried two passports, one for herself and one for Arlene. Arlene's passport was most often held by Jensen in Oakland and given to her just prior to the taking of a trip.*

It's difficult to ascertain precisely when Candy's foreign travels for the CIA began. She believes that she took her first trip abroad for The Company in 1965, although she isn't certain of that date. Since she'd been trained to keep nothing in writing, it is understandable that her memory of a date ten years ago without written aids would be vague. But, as with other aspects of her amnesia about her work with Jensen and the CIA, it was Jensen's skilled use of hypnosis and drugs that is responsible for her gross and global loss of memory. Amnesia is one of the most potent manifestations of deep hypnosis and is, in fact, a test used by hypnotists to determine the depth of trance in a good subject.

Dr. Lewis R. Wolberg states in his book, *Hypnosis: Is It for You?:* "In deep hypnosis, induced amnesia may produce a forgetting of entire segments of experience. . . ."

Drs. Leslie M. LeCron and Jean Bordeaux, authors of *Hypnotism Today,* state: "It [amnesia] will almost always be evidenced after deep hypnosis if forgetfulness is suggested, while on the other hand there will be no amnesia if suggestion to remember

*Candy inadvertently held onto a passport photo taken of Arlene Grant (Candy wearing a black wig, dark makeup, etc.) in San Francisco, as well as the envelope in which the photos were delivered. A reproduction of them appears in the photos and documents section.

on awakening is given. Thus, the operator may cause or inhibit amnesia at his discretion."

After months of combing the transcripts of the recorded hypnotic sessions, I have determined that Candy's first foreign travel for The Company occurred in the fall of 1966, and consisted of at least two and perhaps three trips to Taiwan. It's possible that there were other trips out of the country prior to this time, but the material gained through John Nebel's hypnosis of Candy doesn't indicate it.

Before tracing Candy and Arlene's foreign travels, however, there is an incident that took place during Candy's initial message-carrying chores within the United States that warrants telling.

During a hypnotic session with John in which Candy had been regressed to Jensen's office,* Nebel, playing Jensen, brought up her lack of friends and asked questions about her New York social life.

"Do you go to cocktail parties?" Nebel asked, as Jensen.

"I go to screenings, that's all," Candy replied.

"Have you been following my suggestion not to mix with people?"

"Yes," she answered, her voice sleepy. "But I went to that cocktail party, just like you told me to do."

"Which party was that?" Nebel asked.

"The party at '21.' Bill Buckley's."

"Why did you go to that one? Who told you to go?"

"You did," she replied, annoyed that he'd forgotten. "I had the picture taken."

Nebel paused to collect his thoughts. "What happened to the picture?"

Candy was even more annoyed at his question about the picture. "I brought it to you. You've got it!"

"Why did I want the picture?" asked Nebel, still in the role of Gilbert Jensen.

"I don't know. I don't know anything."

Nebel was at a loss for a moment. Finally he asked, "Did Bill Buckley treat you nicely?"

"Yes," Candy answered with a pleased chuckle. "Very nicely.

*Tape #36, Side A.

He's a very nice. . . . That man came in and insulted him just like you said he would. It was . . . wow, I couldn't believe it."

"What happened?"

"That man . . ."

"Tell me about it again. Let's see if you remember. The man insulted him?"

"He came right over . . . he's standing to the right of me in the picture . . . he called Buckley names . . . he told him what a fink he was, but he used bad words. . . ."

Nebel asked, "Who did that?"

Candy didn't respond.

"Who do you think that man was?" Nebel asked.

Candy made a series of sucking sounds before answering, "I don't know. *You* know who he is. I don't know him. I never saw him before. It's right there in the picture, out on your desk."

"What did the man do then?"

"He left."

No further information on this scene was gathered during subsequent hypnotic sessions, most likely because what Candy reported to Jensen during that regression was the extent of her knowledge.


The 1966 trip, or trips, to Taiwan, turned out to be terrifying for Candy, although it was Arlene who functioned on them as the Company representative, and it was Arlene who bore the brunt of the resulting physical and mental anguish. Candy's travels to Taiwan were preceded by a series of visits to Jensen's office in the spring of that year, one of which was for the purpose of delivering an envelope for Jensen to an unidentified man in San Francisco. During a taped regression, Nebel slipped into the role of Gilbert Jensen and attempted to gain more information about the envelope.* He was unsuccessful. Candy complained to him (Nebel playing Jensen) that the assignment was keeping her away from New York for too long a time and that she could make more than the $500 fee by attending to her own business.

The session concluded with Arlene making an appearance and accusing Jensen of deliberately ruining Candy's life. This is

---

*Tape #20, Side A.

one of the few times Arlene rose to Candy's defense. She told Jensen that he was trying to get rid of Candy so that she, Arlene, would be the only living person. Nebel picked up the cue and said that *they* didn't need Candy.

"Her children need her," said Arlene. "She's never hurt me, but I've hurt her plenty. Leave her alone!"

Candy returned to Oakland in the fall of the year. There appear to have been two visits, one in September and one in October, and it was during the latter month that she made her first visit to Taiwan.

In reality, *Candy* never took the trip. She'd entered Gilbert Jensen's Oakland office, but the woman who emerged from it and who was driven to the airport by the doctor walked with greater confidence, spoke in a lower-pitched voice and wore a black wig, dark makeup and carried with her the passport that matched her appearance. It was Arlene Grant.

Candy had been given a "vitamin" injection in the office to "give her strength for the long flight," as Jensen often said. Arlene emerged following the shot, as he must have planned. The black wig had been carried to Oakland by Candy in her large tote bag, along with the makeup. Once Arlene announced to Jensen she was ready to go, he handed her the passport and also the envelope that she was to deliver to the Taiwan contact who, Jensen assured her, would be at the airport with his car and would watch over her in Taiwan.

"What's his name?" Arlene asked Jensen.

"You don't have to know his name. He'll know yours."

It took repeated efforts by John Nebel to learn the name of the Taiwan contact, and even when he did, there was uncertainty. The names Nebel managed to extract while dealing with Candy and Arlene in the hypnotic mode were a compilation of the names Chin, Yang and Chen. He was identified as a prominent Chinese businessman and a former president of the Taipei Chamber of Commerce.

Chin Chen, as we shall call him, met Arlene Grant at the airport as promised. She offered to hand him the envelope on the spot, but he insisted that she accompany him to his home. She was wary of this but went with him, keeping in mind Jensen's instructions to cooperate fully with Chen.

Arlene's fears proved groundless, at least during that first mission to Taiwan. Chen, whom Arlene has described while under hypnosis as being heavy, well dressed in a conservative business suit and "oh, so polite," drove them approximately 20 miles outside of Taipei. His home, large and institutional, was situated on what Arlene recalls was a surprisingly large plot of country land. A long, symmetrical row of slender trees lined the narrow road leading to the driveway. A lush, freshly cut green lawn sloped away from the house and down to wooded areas that surrounded the house on three sides. In the distance could be seen other houses, separated from Chen's property by the woods and by other open spaces beyond the trees.

Chen parked in front and escorted Arlene into the house. As they passed through a large entrance foyer, Arlene noticed two young Chinese women dressed in white laboratory frocks.

"Who are they?" she asked Chen.

"Household help," he replied, and invited her to join him for tea and a snack. Arlene accepted the invitation and sat with Chen on an enclosed porch at the rear of the house.

Arlene stayed at Chen's house on Taiwan for three days, and was the guest of honor at a small but elaborate dinner party on the final night. Her stay proved extremely pleasant. The weather was superb, and Chen personally took her on sightseeing trips into the lush and exotic countryside, during which time Arlene took numerous photographs. She slept late in the mornings, feasted on bountiful and well-prepared food and was the center of attention during every waking moment. In fact, she was never without someone at her side, in the house and out, day and night.

Arlene departed from Taiwan contented and relaxed. Gilbert Jensen met her at San Francisco International Airport and drove her directly to his Oakland office where he fed her intravenous drugs and restored her to Candy Jones. The black wig, dark makeup and the clothing worn on the return flight were placed in a closet in his office.

"Give me the passport," he said.

She handed him Arlene Grant's passport.

"The rolls of film, too."

Candy handed him the rolls of exposed film from her purse.

When Jensen was satisfied that he'd received everything pertaining to the trip, including the used airline ticket in Arlene's name, he drove Candy to a hotel in San Francisco. She rested until that night when she caught her return flight to New York. She'd been gone almost a week, and the fact that she hadn't specified to anyone in New York where she was going and how long she'd be gone had caused concern with the girls in her office, and with Mel Heimer. Heimer called her office many times during her absence and was met with confused, honest answers: "We don't know when Miss Jones will be back."

Jensen contacted her again shortly after her return to New York, and she was pleased to hear from him. She did not, of course, recall any of the specifics of the trip; Jensen had seen to that during his drug-induced debriefing of her in Oakland. What sense she did retain of the trip was pleasant. Of course by this time there is every possibility that Candy Jones was actually incapable of resisting a command from Jensen. Or, should Candy balk, Jensen had only to pull Arlene from within her and issue his orders to her instead. Either way Jensen was in control, which was, after all, the apparent purpose of the exercise from the start.

Candy's second trip to Taiwan began as the first one had, with a visit to Jensen's office, during which she received an intravenous feeding of his alleged vitamins. Again, it was Arlene Grant who emerged from the office on Cyprus Street and was driven to San Francisco International Airport.

Mr. Chen, the well-dressed Taiwan businessman, was again at the airport to greet Arlene. They drove to his country home, and Arlene became his houseguest for a second time. This time, however, Chen, the host, became Chen, the torturer.

What occurred at his home during this second visit, and during a possible third visit, is not precisely clear from the hypnotic-session tapes.* What is certain is that Arlene was detained by Chen for at least two days, possibly three, during which time he and his associates attempted to extract information from her by various methods of physical torture. What it was that they felt

*There are indications on the hypnotic tapes that Candy and/or Arlene made a third trip to Taiwan, and that torture was again used in an attempt to gain information from her. It is not clear, however, which form of torture was used during which visit, and the possibility does exist that the torturing of Arlene and Candy took place during the first two visits to Chen's home.

Arlene knew, or possessed, is unknown. But it was apparently valuable enough for them to use torture in an attempt to get it. She'd handed over the envelope to Chen as instructed, and every hypnotic tape dealing with this experience contains repeated denials of having any of the information asked for by Arlene's torturers.

Specific information about Chen's torture of Arlene was discovered by John Nebel in hypnotic sessions conducted with Candy in November and December 1974.* There had been painful sessions prior to that in which vague reference to torture had been made by Candy. I found it of interest that although Arlene had undergone the actual torture, Candy was also capable, under hypnosis, of reliving the experience. Now, for the first time, Nebel was to discover the details.

One of the sessions began with Candy referring to a girl who was about to push a button. Nebel asked who the girl was, but Arlene answered and said she didn't know her name. Candy returned and sounded frightened, apprehensive.

"That girl," Candy repeated. "She works here. Are you going to do it again to me?"

Nebel assumed, as did this writer, that she was talking to Gilbert Jensen during the regression. He played Jensen's role for over four minutes until he realized that she was speaking with someone in Chen's house in Taiwan.

"She's going to do it again. You tell her to do it all the time."

"What is she doing?" Nebel asked.

"Shocking. . . ."

"*I* tell her to shock you?"

"Yes."

"You're not getting any shocks."

"Yes, I am. You do it to my shoulder all the time and you know it."

"Whose office are you in now?" asked Nebel, now aware that he might have been mistaken in assuming she'd been talking to Jensen.

"I'm in no office."

"Where are you then? You're not out in the street."

"In the house."

*Tape #2, Side A, and Tape #18 "B," Sides A and B.

"Whose house?"

"I don't know." She moaned. "Please don't do it again. It's so sore."

"No one is shocking you. You're sound asleep."

She took a deep breath.

"What town are you in?" Nebel asked.

"It's outside."

"And somebody is *shocking* you?"

"You've got that thing strapped to me."

Nebel asked her to describe "that thing." She told him that it was a small box on the table from which wires led to her wrist and to her shoulder. Nebel offered to remove the wires from her, and placed his hand on her left wrist. She informed him that the wire was attached to the opposite wrist. He eventually followed her instructions and removed all the imaginary wires from her body, as well as the tape that had held them to her skin. The removal of the tape was felt by her, and she reacted when the adhesive was stripped away.

"That hurt awful," Candy said, rubbing the spots where the wires had been.

"I don't know who told anybody to do that to you."

"*You* did," she responded, annoyed. "*You* told her. And I don't know anything. Nobody here believes me."

Nebel asked the date, but Candy repeated that she didn't know anything. He reinforced the trance and suggested to her that when she awakened she would feel relaxed and rested. He asked her whether she believed that.

"I'm afraid to say yes and I'm afraid to say no. Whatever I say is wrong anyway . . . that's the story of my life."

"I don't know the story of your life."

"Well, you've asked me enough. You should know. . . . Why don't you just kill me?"

"Kill you? Why? You've done nothing wrong."

"I know that, but why do you keep me here like this? . . . I don't know any Dr. Jensen." Nebel had said nothing to prompt this comment from her, and she obviously was responding to what had been said to her in Taiwan.

Candy began to groan. "Oh, why can't I just fly out of here. I want to go back to New York."

"Why did you come here?" Nebel asked.

"I don't know anymore. I really don't know."

"You must have had a reason."

"Just to give the paper, the envelope, that's all."

"Who was the letter for?"

"The name's on the envelope. I can't pronounce it. They have it. . . . If I ever get out of this I'll . . . oh, I don't know what I'll do."

Further details of the torture by electrodes were uncovered in subsequent hypnotic sessions, although these sessions differed in that they found Candy recalling a regression that had previously taken place. This particular regression had been experienced silently—a dream form—and Nebel, after suggesting to her while in that trance state that she would recall the events, interviewed her about them.

■

CANDY: They put a solution first on the skin. . . .

JOHN: A saline solution?

CANDY: I don't know . . . a solution . . . they put it on with gauze on a long stick . . . like a Q-Tip . . . they stuck a wire on the wet area. . . .

*(She pointed to various parts of her body, including her breasts. Nebel asked whether they'd ever attached the wires there, and she replied that they had threatened to place the electrodes on her breasts if she didn't cooperate.)*

CANDY: They put the wire on your finger and . . .

JOHN: Wait a minute. Let's take it step by step. Do they wrap the wire around your finger?

CANDY: They just touch it to the area where the solution is.

JOHN: Is the current on?

CANDY: Of course.

JOHN: And the wire is attached to a box?

CANDY: Yes, like a manicure set, or an electric hair roller. A little box with a few dials on it. And there are two little wires and they touch them . . .

JOHN: They don't touch the two wires to you, do they?

CANDY: Oh, yes, they do. They touch both wires.

JOHN: Did it spark?

CANDY: I didn't look. But I heard it. It hisses.

JOHN: And it hurts.

CANDY: Momentarily. It's a shock. It makes a blister.

JOHN: Then they stop it?

CANDY: Yeah.

JOHN: What did you do with the blisters?

CANDY: I opened them myself . . . with a sterilized needle.

JOHN: How many blisters were there?

CANDY: Let me see. There was one here and . . .

JOHN: *(observing her)* Wait a minute. That's the right hand, fourth finger.

CANDY: Yeah. That was a big one.

*(She also pointed to the little finger of her right hand, and indicated that the blister had run all the way down the little finger to the palm, and that her right thumb had also been badly blistered from the electrodes.)*

CANDY: They like to get to your joints, or to your fingernail because that's more painful.

■

At that point there was a discussion between John and Candy about the fingers on her right hand, and about the fact that there were physical signs on them of actual blisters. This phenomenon, usually termed "memory tissue" in the field of parapsychology, was discussed during the preparation of this book, and is one of its more bizarre and debatable aspects. Research over the years has shown that a good hypnotic subject is sometimes capable of exhibiting so-called memory tissue when regressed to a point in time when a physically traumatic experience took place. An example might be a child burning his or her hand at the age of five. When the child has reached adulthood, all traces of the burn have disappeared. But it is possible, say some researchers, to raise the same blister on the same hand during hypnotic regression many years later.

Dr. Robert London, when asked on the Nebel show whether he could accept the theory of memory tissue, replied, "I'm in conflict. From a scientific point of view, I would have great difficulty believing that I could see blisters [in a hypnotic subject], or to believe that blisters could occur . . . the blisters are there for a reason when you are truly burned. Yet, there is another part of me which says . . . which would lead me to give potential credibility to the theory of memory tissue. There is a memory bank in cells."

Nebel brought up the fact that a good hypnotic subject will drop a cold object if told by the hypnotist that it is, in fact, red-hot, because he has accepted that suggestion while in the trance state. Dr. London agreed with this and then went on to elaborate on his statement that cells have a memory. Citing the field of immunization, he commented that researchers are pointing in the direction of recognizing that body cells do have a memory system of sorts, and that immunity might be linked, in some way, to this system.

The question of whether the body is capable of reproducing physiological symptoms through hypnotic regression will be debated for many years to come. Research is always open to question, and the myriad variables inherent in hypnotic research further complicate the problem.

I recently interviewed a New York neurologist, Dr. Kenneth Jordan, who is assistant chief of neurology at the Staten Island public health hospital. We discussed the theory of engrams, theoretical memory structures created at the time a new piece of information is learned. I asked Dr. Jordan his feelings about the possibility of memory tissue manifesting itself as reported by Candy.

"First of all," Jordan said, "a more apt term would be memory tracings. And a reasonable inference would be that because of the tremendous affective input surrounding the real physical input, these engrams, these components of memory tracing have not developed the same inhibitory components that less traumatic experiences have developed. They thus continuously remain more accessible to conscious recall. It may take only a small clue, an experience that is faintly similar to the previous experience to eliminate the remaining tenuous inhibitory pathways and to allow the memory not only to come forward, but to rush forward with a vengeance.

"We also know that the temporal lobe of the brain is intimately connected with the autonomic nervous system. This is part of the nervous system which controls blood pressure, intestinal emotion, muscle tone, etc. It is conceivable, but by no means proved, that at least anatomically and psysiologically, the same area of the brain that is involved in the vengeful recall of the initial traumatic experience can, without too much difficulty, be simultaneously involved with the autonomic, involuntary physical phenomenon going on within the same person."

I have personally been present in the Nebel apartment when memory tissue seemed to display itself in Candy. On this day, the memory tissue involved concerned the area in the crook of her arm in which Gilbert Jensen had injected the IV. After Nebel brought Candy out of the trance state, we closely examined her arm. There appeared to be distension of the vein, as well as a mark that could have been made by a needle. Whether I saw these things because I wanted to see them is a question I cannot answer. I accepted what I believed I saw and report it here.

Candy claimed under hypnosis that the torture had occurred in what she termed "the sick bay" at Chen's country home on Taiwan. The sick bay was located in the basement, according to Candy.

"His house is on an estate. Very beautiful. I don't know the name of the town."

■

JOHN: How did you get there?
CANDY: In a car.
JOHN: Were you forced?
CANDY: No, I went willingly.
JOHN: For what purpose?
CANDY: I went there to give something.
JOHN: To somebody who was expecting it.
CANDY: Yes.
JOHN: Then why were you tortured?
CANDY: Because I didn't have what they wanted. I didn't give them what they wanted.
JOHN: What did you give them, an envelope?
CANDY: Yes.
JOHN: Sealed?
CANDY: Yes.
JOHN: You had no knowledge what was in it?
CANDY: No.

■

After establishing that Candy, in reality Arlene, had handed the envelope to a man and woman at the country home, presumably Chen and an unnamed female associate, Nebel asked what they'd said to her.

"They said this wasn't it. They wanted to know where the rest of it was."

"What did they hope to accomplish with the electric shocks?" asked Nebel.

"They said that I knew more," Candy replied.

"In your head?"

"Yes."

According to Candy, the torture stopped only after Chen spoke with someone on the phone. Following the conversation, they released her from the chair in which she was strapped and became very friendly and apologetic. They told her that the electrodes were not to torture her but to help jog her memory in a scientific way. They insisted that she stay for lunch, which she did, and they drove her to the airport that night.

"I wore gloves on the flight to California because my hand looked so terrible," Candy says. "And there was a smell from my fingers, like sulfuric acid."

Gilbert Jensen met her plane and took her to his office, where he gave her an injection.

"It was all a mistake," Jensen told her, "a typographical error." Candy assumed he meant that a word in the message was wrong and had led the Chinese man and woman to assume that she knew more than she was acknowledging. These conscious thoughts have come to Candy only in the very recent past. When she left Jensen's office that day and returned to New York, she literally had no memory of what had happened on Taiwan.

Candy had lunch with her friend and editor, Joe Vergara, a day or two after returning, and wore gloves throughout the meal. When Vergara asked why she wore the gloves, she lied by telling him she'd burned her hands while making fudge for her children.

Mel Heimer, although not specifically aware of her adventures on Taiwan, sensed a growing fear in Candy following her return to New York. He urged her to call a friend of his in California, film publicist Joel Preston, now an executive with the New York public-relations firm of Rogers and Cowen. Preston at that time was studio publicity manager for Columbia Pictures in Hollywood, and was Heimer's close friend.

"Why should I call Preston?" Candy asked Heimer.

"In case you ever have any trouble while you're traveling."

"I don't have trouble," Candy insisted.

"I know, but I'd feel better if you had Preston's number." He handed it to Candy and she put it in her purse.

I talked with Joel Preston in the summer of 1975, and asked whether he recalled Heimer mentioning that he'd given Preston's number to Candy.

"Yes, I do," he replied. "Mel called me and said that I might be hearing from Candy Jones some time." Preston asked Heimer why he might receive such a call, but Heimer evaded the question.

I asked Preston whether he ever came to know Candy Jones.

"Yes, through Mel."

"Did you find anything unusual about her behavior?" I asked.

"Well, I suppose so. I always had the feeling that something very strange was going on. There was a tension with her that led me to believe this."

Preston also recalls having numerous telephone conversations with Candy following Mel's death. At that time Preston was in the process of putting together a package to produce a film of Heimer's last book, *Dark Wood*. Candy was acting as the New York liaison between Preston and Heimer's agent, who was proving balky in the negotiations.

"Every time I spoke with her I heard strange noises on her end of the phone," Preston says. "I suggested to her that her line might be tapped, and offered to approach a good friend of mine who was, at that time, head of the FBI's operations in Los Angeles. She was surprisingly upset at the suggestion and made me promise I wouldn't."

"Anything else?" I asked.

"No. Just that I always had the feeling that she was involved with something that she wouldn't talk about."

And *couldn't* talk about. Gilbert Jensen had seen to that.

# 17

---

# The Return to Taiwan

Under normal circumstances, returning to Taiwan after her experiences there would be a remarkable and inexplicable decision for Candy Jones to make. The fact that she did return illustrates the extent to which Gilbert Jensen had succeeded in placing her, through Arlene, under his control. He told her to go back and she went, without question, without debate. And although one of two subsequent trips to Taiwan again resulted in her being tortured, she returned even once more, making her final trip to the Chinese island sometime in 1968.

This final Taiwan trip brought her into contact with others besides Mr. Chen. She was to first deliver an envelope to a young, unnamed Chinese girl in a Taipei art gallery. The girl was there as promised, and after accepting the envelope she stepped back and spat in Arlene's face. By the time Arlene recovered, the girl had fled the gallery. Candy's recollection of this incident came during a recent hypnotic session with John Nebel. She has no explanation for the girl's behavior, and although it is an insignificant event in the overall picture of her final trip, it is indicative of the problems Nebel has faced in each hypnotic session as he attempted to pull from his wife a tidy presentation of a given event.

Arelene was again met by Mr. Chen upon arrival. He had with him another man whom he introduced as a business associate. The three of them drove to Chen's country home, apparently without protest from Arlene. She had received an intravenous injection from Jensen prior to leaving San Francisco and he had evidently been successful in reinforcing her amnesia concerning previous unpleasantness at Chen's house. If Arlene did exhibit memory of that previous event during the final Taiwan trip, there is no evidence of it on the tapes.

Perhaps no other aspect of *The Control of Candy Jones* has been as difficult to chronicle as Candy's reporting while under hypnosis of her torture on Taiwan. The hypnotic sessions in which she so keenly relived and felt the pain inflicted upon her on Taiwan were especially arduous and moving. She invariably became hysterical during these sessions, and whatever frustration John Nebel and I might have experienced because of our inability to pin down specific times and places was appropriately overshadowed by her agony. After much deliberation I've determined that the most effective way to present this material is to allow the transcripts to speak for themselves. Any uncertainty that might arise from their content should take secondary position to the apparent truth that torture was, indeed, inflicted upon Candy Jones, and was inflicted upon her on more than one occasion.

It has been known for many years by researchers in the field of hypnosis that terror, especially when created by physical torture, is brutally effective in enhancing the power and control of the hypnotic trance. The subject's suggestibility increases, and he becomes more compliant in order to bring an end to suffering.

Dr. Herbert Spiegel has commented to me that in his opinion, based upon observations of Candy, she had been terrorized in some form. He also said, "I have no doubt that she's been brainwashed."

There is one theory that I would like to introduce, however, before proceeding with the tape transcripts covering Candy's subsequent trips to Taiwan. The possibility has occurred to me that Mr. Chen and the others involved in torturing Candy Jones might well have been employees of our own Central Intelligence

Agency. I do not have any tangible evidence that this was the case, but the thesis nags at me as I deal with the material. After all, the value of Candy's and Arlene's messenger services to America and to the CIA must be questioned. To have put her through such nightmarish ordeals for the sole purpose of having an envelope delivered challenges my imagination or, at best, causes me to view with an incredulous eye those making such decisions.

Therefore I have asked myself if it is possible that the torture of Candy Jones on Taiwan was another aspect of the testing program instituted by Gilbert Jensen. Putting her to the test, as it were, would have given tangible proof to Jensen and to his superiors that the so-called perfect messenger could be created through drugs and hypnosis. Such a test would have been of dubious value had Candy known ahead of time that she was to be tested. But sending her on what appeared on the surface to be legitimate and useful messenger runs and having her intercepted and tortured would, it seems to me, have constituted a test that would satisfy the most demanding of scientists. If she broke under the mental and physical pressure, Jensen and his colleagues would know that the experiment had failed. But a favorable report from Chen would be a reason for rejoicing in Oakland, and in Langley, Virginia, the home of the CIA and its Science and Technology Directorate.

There is little question that the government was interested in testing Jensen's success in establishing control over Candy Jones. According to the tapes, Jensen personally escorted her to headquarters in Langley and demonstrated to his colleagues, in a brutal and degrading manner, the effectiveness of his project. That demonstration at Langley is covered in detail in Chapter 18 of this book, but if such an incident did occur, it would give credence to the idea that Chen, acting as an agent of Jensen, might have been testing Candy. There were other tests as well, and those are detailed along with the Langley experience.

Another aspect of the Taiwan adventures that causes me to question Chen's actions is the use of electrodes. Electrodes have long been the standard device used to test pain tolerance in hypnotic subjects. As reported by Dr. G. H. Estabrooks in his book, *Hypnotism,* a device known as a variac is plugged into a light socket (or any source of electrical current), its leads placed on the subject's hands. A saline solution is used to establish the best possible contact. According to Estabrooks, 15 volts of current would be very painful, 20 unbearable. But a good hypnotic subject in deep trance could withstand 60 or even 120 volts without flinching.

Jensen could have administered such tests himself, but their value would have been considerably diminished. He would have been testing his own work, a dubious procedure. Too, by having others test the effectiveness of his work, he brought about a greater measure of personal glory for himself. Gilbert Jensen's ego, which according to Candy and Arlene was sizable, may have driven him to operate beyond the limits of CIA blessing. At any rate, there is the possibility that it was the CIA itself torturing its own operative, Candy Jones.

That it took place on Taiwan comes as no surprise. Taiwan has been and continues to be a hotbed of CIA activity. It has been reported by various former CIA agents, now authors, that Taiwan has more foreign intelligence operatives than any other nation in the world. It would also follow that, being California-based, Jensen's contacts would be in the Far East.

Candy discussed Arlene's greater tolerance for pain during an undated hypnotic session with John Nebel, and eventually began to relive her experiences with torture on Taiwan.* Candy claimed that it was Arlene who felt the pain of the electrodes on her fingers, not her, and told Nebel that it was Arlene's hand that carried the blisters. "She [Arlene] had such blisters she couldn't even put her fingers together," Candy said while in a trance.

■

JOHN: Did they threaten you with anything else? Or her [Arlene]?
CANDY: They put her hand in the thing.
JOHN: In what?
CANDY: In with the scorpions. She didn't know whether it would be the scorpions or the coral snake.
JOHN: You mean into a box?
CANDY: Uh-huh. The scorpion was in there.
JOHN: What did they do after the scorpion bit her?

*Tape #7 "A," Side B.

CANDY: Gave her all sorts of antibiotics and . . . they all got very excited because they didn't know it was alive.

JOHN: Did the antibiotics work?

CANDY: Sure, but you could see where she was bit. On her thumb and her index finger. It clung to her and they thought it was dead. They were trying to scare me.

JOHN: Scare *her,* you mean.

CANDY: The two of us. They didn't know me. They just knew her.

JOHN: What name did she use?

CANDY: Arlene Grant.

*(Candy had been sitting during this session in a bedroom chair, her hands hanging at her sides. She suddenly pulled them up and held them in her lap.)*

CANDY: I don't like to let my hands hang down like that.

JOHN: Well, don't.

CANDY: I'm always afraid they'll be bitten.

JOHN: Don't worry, I'll protect you.

CANDY: Why?

JOHN: Because I think you're a lovely lady.

CANDY: That isn't true. You just want to win some medals or something.

*(John realized at this point that she'd been talking to Gilbert Jensen. He slipped into Jensen's role and began chanting the code, "tit-tat-toe, tit-tat-toe, tit-tat-toe.")*

CANDY: That's not the way it's done and you know it. *(She says the code herself, rapidly changing inflection and pace with each repeating of the phrase.)* It's a rhythm.

JOHN: When you hear that, do you do something?

CANDY: Uh-huh. Call you, Gil.

■

Nebel brought her out of the trance and she slept. When she awoke an hour later, he played the previous portion of tape for her. Candy screamed in terror. Nebel switched on another recorder.

■

JOHN: Tell me, do you feel uncomfortable now?

CANDY: I don't like to think about it, because it really happened . . . and it wasn't dead, it was alive. It was worse than a snake because I could have picked a snake up.

*(Nebel asked her why she was searching under the bed and chairs in their bedroom.)*

CANDY: Because it was creepy. . . . Look! You can see the scar on my finger.

JOHN: That's memory tissue. You weren't just bit, Candy.

■

She became frantic as her search of the floor intensified. She was actually looking for real scorpions, and evidently believed the scene had just taken place. Nebel tried to convince her that nothing had happened, but his words were useless.

■

JOHN: There is nothing here to be frightened of.

CANDY: *(pointing to her finger)* Look! That's not memory tissue. That's a real scar!

*(Candy does have a small scar at the point where her right thumb intersects with the fleshy web between the thumb and index finger. Whether it was caused by a scorpion bite is open to conjecture.)*

CANDY: *(very upset)* That's where it hung on to me. Right here! They said it wasn't alive, but it was. *(She's almost crying.)*

JOHN: Candy, please. There is nothing under the bed and nothing under your pillow. Come on now, where are you?

CANDY: I know where I am. I'm in bed with you.

JOHN: All right. I know that it was shocking to hear, but . . .

CANDY: I'd forgotten all about that.

JOHN: I know.

■

Nebel managed to change the subject and again asked about the code used by Jensen on the telephone. Candy had little more to offer except that the word "tat" was always emphasized when she heard it over the phone. As Nebel pressed his questioning, she appeared to slip into another spontaneous hypnotic trance.

"I don't know anything," she began to chant.

"Do you know Gil Jensen?" Nebel asked.

"I've heard the name. I don't know anything."

"What about Arlene Grant?"

"I don't know anybody by that name."

The session ended.

But later the same day, Candy again went into a spontaneous trance and rapidly moved her feet on the bed.

■

JOHN: Is something wrong?
CANDY: I have to hurry.
JOHN: Where are you going?
CANDY: To catch a plane.
JOHN: To where?
CANDY: New York.
JOHN: Where are you now?
CANDY: San Francisco.
JOHN: Where have you been?
CANDY: *(quietly)* I've been away.
JOHN: What do you have to get back to New York for?
CANDY: I have to be back by Monday.
JOHN: For your business?
CANDY: Uh-huh. *(She begins to squirm and whimper.)*
JOHN: Are you uncomfortable? What's wrong?
CANDY: My thumbs.
JOHN: Your thumbs? What's wrong with your thumbs?
CANDY: I'm hiding 'em.
JOHN: Why?
CANDY: They got crushed.
JOHN: Oh. On the journey?
CANDY: Yes.
JOHN: How did it happen?
CANDY: *(muttering)* I don't remember.
JOHN: Was this on Taiwan?
CANDY: I don't know where it was.
JOHN: Don't you even have an idea what country it was?
CANDY: Yeah. I had to take a booster shot.
JOHN: How did that effect your thumbs?
CANDY: They got smashed, but I'm hiding 'em.
JOHN: Yes, but how did it happen?
CANDY: Because they look funny.
JOHN: Yes, but why?
CANDY: They cut the nails so short.
JOHN: Who?
CANDY: I don't know what her name is. She's an assistant.
JOHN: Who is she an assistant to?

CANDY: To the doctor.

JOHN: Which doctor?

CANDY: In the house.

JOHN: In the big house?

CANDY: Uh-huh.

JOHN: That's on Taiwan, isn't it?

CANDY: Uh-huh.

JOHN: Well, why did they cut your nails?

CANDY: They just cut my thumbnails. They were going to keep cutting them down unless I told them . . .

JOHN: Told them what you knew?

CANDY: *(panicked)* I don't know anything. I gave them the letter. . . . They cut it right down into . . . it's all raw. . . .

JOHN: Do you know what the date is today?

CANDY: It's January . . . twenty-fourth, I think . . . 1968.

JOHN: Do you feel uncomfortable now, or are you all right?

CANDY: My thumbs hurt me. Both thumbs. I have to cover them up.

JOHN: All right. Are you going to get on the plane now?

CANDY: It hurts so much to hold my bag.

JOHN: I'm sorry.

CANDY: How could your thumbs hurt so?

JOHN: Because they cut the nails short. Did you tell Gil [Jensen] about it?

CANDY: I couldn't because I didn't have time. I just made the connection.

JOHN: Are you going to call him when you get to New York?

CANDY: *(like a little girl)* No. He wouldn't care. He'd just tell me that these were the chances I had to take.

JOHN: How much is The Company paying you for this trip?

CANDY: *(animated)* It's got to be five thousand. I owe it to the hospital.

JOHN: What hospital?

CANDY: Gracie Square.

JOHN: For your son?

CANDY: Yeah. Cary.

JOHN: Do you get the money and give it to the hospital?

CANDY: No. They said they'd arrange for it to be paid to the hospital directly. . . . The bill is forty-seven hundred, and that's not even all.

■

Nebel then turned his attention to the code sounds that were used over the telephone to spur Candy to action, and tried to learn more about them, but the attempt was not fruitful. The remainder of the session was devoted to a personal discussion of Candy's children.

In another undated hypnotic session between John and Candy, Candy sat on their bed, her hands tightly pressed against her ears. Nebel told her to lower her hands.*

"Please don't put anything in my ears again," she pleaded, her voice ringing with fear.

Nebel questioned her about her ears.

*"You* put straws in my ears," she replied, pleading with him not to do it again.

"What town are you in?" asked Nebel.

"I don't know. I don't know."

Nebel questioned her further about the straws in her ears, but she would only repeat what she had already said. He asked her her age and she replied, "Forty, or forty-one." She then told him that she was in Taiwan, but did not know the name of the town which, she claimed, was on the outskirts of Taipei.

As she became more hysterical, Nebel attempted to bring her out of the trance. He thought he'd succeeded, and told her that he had just brought her back from an unpleasant scene in Taiwan. That comment sent her back into a hysterical state, and she pleaded with him to believe her when she told him that she'd delivered everything and had nothing more to give. Nebel again ended the session.

The final reference to being tortured on Taiwan occurred at the end of one hypnotic session and carried forward into another.** Rather than inject John Nebel's comments, I've elected to simply allow Candy's words to describe the scene.

I was in this place that wasn't too far from the second airport. It was on Taiwan, but to the south. I can't think of the name of the airport, but it's where you go out of Taiwan, not come into it. It was a house about a ten- or fifteen-minute drive from that airport.

*Tape #11, Side B.
**Tape #87 "B," Sides A and B.

I was coming back [to the United States] and you don't always leave from the same airport. The weather was bad and the flight was not going to be taking off. A man told me to come back to the house with him and wait for the flight. I can't think of his name. He was American, and he was going to be on my same flight. . . . I met him at the airport. He came over to me. He told me that I looked very familiar and asked whether he had seen me there before.

I was Arlene Grant when he came up to me. The flight was going to be delayed two hours, and he told me the house he was going to was actually part of an American installation, like an officer's club or something like that. I stupidly said, "Okay, okay."

So we went outside and he got us a rickety-tin old cab. We chatted in the cab and he told me he was in Taiwan surveying American business interests there, and had done a report on American holdings. He was wearing civilian clothes, and was very pleasant.

The house was very nice and looked like a club. Lots of entertainment went on in houses on Taiwan that were turned into nightclubs. I don't like the look of those big Chinese houses, but some people do. It was a tacky place. We walked in and the same goddamn Oriental music was playing. There were little tables in the lobby; it was like an inn. There were a few people around. He asked me what I wanted to drink, and they served anything you wanted. They even had American drinks. We were sitting talking and he asked me whether I would like to see the rest of the place. I agreed. He told me there was a beautiful view that he enjoyed every time he stopped there. There was a very large and beautiful staircase leading upstairs.

We went into one large room that could have been a dining room or a conference room. He asked me whether I knew a certain man, who had his offices in that house. I don't know what his name was. He told me this man was an old friend of his and suggested we step in and say hello.

I followed him into a room. The man behind the desk was middle-aged—forty-eight or forty-nine. He introduced me to the man. The man looked Chinese to me. He was sitting and reading a magazine.

The man with me told his friend that he had adopted me

like an orphan and taken me out of the storm. The man behind the desk spoke English quite well. He invited me to sit down, and told me he had heard about me. I had been introduced as Arlene Grant. He asked me where I had been, and obviously I couldn't tell him the truth. He offered me tea, but I declined. He insisted, however, that I have a drink. I pointed out that I had one downstairs at the table. He suggested I have a fresh one and asked me what it was I was drinking. I told him vodka on the rocks. He served a fresh drink. He talked a great deal about San Francisco and how wonderful it was that the American woman was free to travel and do things.

I don't know what was in that drink but I suddenly became very dizzy. He asked me what was wrong, and I told him that I was dizzy and hot. He asked me if I wanted to relax, but I told him I had to leave because I had to catch a plane. I thought I was going to get sick, and told him that. He called in a woman who took me to the ladies' room. It looked more like an infirmary to me than a ladies' room. There were two beds in the room. There was a bathroom, but the beds were in a little room separated from the toilet by a curtain.

I was drenched with sweat, and very weak. The woman, who was Chinese and spoke very little English, told me that she would take care of my clothes. The sweat was pouring from me, and I could feel my heart beating a mile a minute. I was wearing a suit, and she asked me to give her my jacket. Even the shoulders of my jacket were wringing wet with sweat. I took off my skirt, jacket and blouse and handed them to the woman. She said she would bring me a gown, and suggested I lie down on the bed. I did and waited for her, but she didn't come back. She had also taken my shoes. My foot began to ache in the spot where I had broken it a few years before. I was wearing an Ace bandage on it as I often did when I traveled.

A man came into the room. He introduced himself as a doctor. Right behind him was the man who had given me the drink in his office. The doctor told me I looked terrible. I must have because my hair was soaking wet. I said I thought something had been put into my drink, and the man became very offended. The man introduced to me as a doctor took my pulse. He seemed very professional, and he looked into my eyes. He told the other man that I was going to go to sleep and that I needed rest. The doctor had a much heavier Chinese accent than the other man.

I asked them what had happened to me. The doctor said he didn't know but asked if I had ever had malaria. I agreed that I had, but said that this was not malaria and I knew that it wasn't. He assured me that I would shake and get chills, just like malaria. I asked them for my pocketbook, and told them that I had to get the plane back to the United States. They brought my pocketbook to me, and when I looked into it I knew someone had gone through it. I began to become very frightened.

The doctor asked if I felt sick to my stomach. I said that I did, and he began to pull the covers off me to examine my stomach. I told him not to. My sheets and pillowcase were soaking wet, and the doctor suggested I get into the other bed so that they could change this one. I refused to move. A woman entered the room and grabbed my arms and literally dragged me out of one bed and into the other. I was embarrassed at only having my bra and pants under the gown. Someone asked me what was wrong with my foot, and I told them that I had tripped.

The man who had given me the drink asked me who I had seen while I was in Taiwan. I could barely answer because I was so sleepy. Suddenly, the doctor gave me a shot in my arm. He tried to roll me over on the bed, and although I tried to fight him, I was too weak to resist. He told the woman to pull me over, which she did. I suddenly was afraid that I was going to be murdered right there. They had me on my stomach and examined my buttocks, and the doctor commented that I hadn't received any injections there.

My voice was growing very weak. The man told the doctor to let me sleep it off, and said he didn't think I knew anything. He then asked me where the papers were. I told him that I didn't have any papers. He asked me who I had given the papers to. I didn't answer, and the men left the room. The woman asked me if I wanted to sit up, but I was so weak I couldn't manage it, and my muscles felt like jelly. The woman tried to pull me up by my arms, and although I wanted to hit the woman, I couldn't muster the strength.

The woman pinched me, and asked me where the papers were. She kept pinching me all over my body. She eventually began pinching my breasts, and I fell back on the bed from the pain. She kept pulling me up, and every time she did, she continued to pinch me viciously. I felt myself passing out, and I believe I did actually black out. The woman left the room and I tried to get up, but I simply fell on the floor. I tried to reach up to pull the sheet down over me but I couldn't raise my arm. The last thing I remember was trying to crawl underneath the bed.

I must have been out for a long time, and when I woke up I was again in the bed. The doctor came in and gave me a shot in my other arm. I had stopped perspiring, and I fell into a deep, deep sleep, waking up the next day. My clothes were in the room and had all been cleaned. I never saw that woman again. A younger girl came into the room, asked me how I felt and gave me some orange juice. I was afraid to drink anything, but asked the girl for some water. When she brought the water, I made her drink some first before I would take it. She also brought me coffee, which I had her taste first. The girl told me that I had better hurry if I was going to make my flight home. She could barely speak English. The girl said I'd had a bad dream and had been very sick. I pulled up the sleeve on my gown and looked at my arms. There was an injection mark on each one.

The girl left the room, and when I tried to get up, I had to grab a chair to support myself on my wobbly legs. I used the chair like a crutch to move across the room. I locked the door, got dressed, rinsed out my mouth in the bathroom, washed my face and looked into the mirror. I don't think I'd ever seen myself look quite so terrible. I realized that I was not wearing the black wig any longer, and discovered it lying on the other bed.

After I was cleaned up and dressed, I unlocked the door and went to the staircase. I looked down and saw there were people having drinks at the small tables. They didn't pay any attention to me as I started to come down, but then I tripped and tumbled down the entire staircase. People ran over and picked me up and put me in a chair. I told them I was all right and had just had a fainting spell.

Someone drove me to the airport and I flew home. I immediately went to see Gilbert Jensen and told him about the incident. He seemed very concerned and wanted to see my arms. My breasts were all black and blue from being pinched, but I refused to show them to him.

Jensen sent Candy on other missions, as reported by her during hypnotic sessions. None involved torture, as far as the tapes indicate, although physical abuse did result on at least one occasion. As always, Candy's instructions were to carry and to deliver an envelope, which she did without hesitation or reservation, at least until toward the end of her relationship with Jensen and with the CIA. If Gilbert Jensen ever had any fears that his "perfect messenger" was not a total success, they were without grounds. There is nothing in any of the research to hint that Candy, or Arlene, betrayed his trust—until her marriage to Long John Nebel and his use of hypnotism to counteract Jensen's control.

But Jensen could never be sure. And there was his ego to be dealt with. He took Candy to Langley, Virginia, as mentioned earlier, to satisfy both weaknesses and became, quite deliberately, another of her torturers.

# 18

# The Subject on Display

Once Gilbert Jensen had established a level of control over Candy Jones with which he felt comfortable, he proceeded to expose her to various aspects of training and testing within the Central Intelligence Agency's official structure.

She was taken on two occasions to a leading San Francisco public-health institute where she was tested for acuity of senses. Jensen was present during the testing; Marshall Burger was, too, on at least one occasion. Similar testing took place, as previously reported, at Burger's California institute.

She was also trained at "the Farm," described by Victor Marchetti as the CIA's West Point, located 15 minutes outside Williamsburg, Virginia, on the road to Richmond. To the outside world, the Farm is known as but another military installation— Camp Peary. But its primary function is to train CIA operatives in the tools and techniques of their business.

Candy, and Arlene, were at Camp Peary in November 1971, according to an undated taped hypnotic session.* At the start of

*Tape #8 "A," Side A.

the session Nebel asked her where she was, and she responded by muttering, ". . . next door."

■

JOHN: What about next door?
CANDY: They're all mock-up rooms.
JOHN: What are they used for?
CANDY: To teach you how to destroy.
JOHN: What do you use to destroy?
CANDY: You put a thing like a brick on your shoe . . . you kick . . . you kick forwards first, then backwards . . . kick through [the wall].

■

Nebel then asked if anyone was with her, and she replied, "My teacher."

After a lull, Candy said, "The whole place is a mess 'cause they teach you how to smash 'em up."

"Who teaches you?" Nebel asked.

"Guerrillas."

"How are they dressed?"

"In fatigues."

Nebel learned through questioning that Candy was staying overnight in Washington, D.C., approximately an hour's drive from the Farm, and had come to the training facility as Arlene Grant. She complained to him that she'd hurt her side by kicking improperly, and had had great difficulty in smashing dresser drawers against the floor.

"This is terrible the way they destroy all this good furniture," Candy said while in the trance. "It's all smashed up."

"Do they call you Arlene here?" Nebel asked.

"They call me Arlene, yes," Candy replied. "See my wig?"

"Yes," Nebel said. "Do they treat you nicely here?"

"Yes."

"Is Gil Jensen here with you?"

"No. . . . I'm maybe going to go in a helicopter."

"Where? Back to Washington?"

"Uh-huh. I'll land at the air force base."

Nebel asked how she was feeling.

"I have pain," Candy answered.

"Did you tell them that?"

"No, because I don't think I'm going to pass this test anyway."

"What does that mean?" Nebel asked.

"I guess it means they won't give me any assignments like this. It's just as well. I don't like this anyway."

She then told Nebel, who was playing her alter ego, that she had learned to break through a partitioned wall, and to take apart chairs and sofas. Nebel asked how she was taught to take apart a sofa.

■

CANDY: You do that with your razors.

JOHN: Suppose you don't have your razors with you?

CANDY: You take a sharp piece of the lamp.

JOHN: And cut up the upholstery?

CANDY: Uh-huh.

JOHN: Why would you want to do that?

CANDY: To find it.

JOHN: To find what?

CANDY: *(annoyed)* To find whatever you're looking for. They hide things there.

■

She elaborated by saying that the razor was used to cut an X in the upholstery, thus creating flaps that could be pieced back together.

Nebel asked what she was doing at the moment.

"Sitting on the floor in the corner." She sounded disgusted.

Nebel told her he would take away the pain in her side, and handed her an imaginary pill. She placed it in her mouth, and as she sucked he told her to count from one to ten. She counted with him, and as she reached seven, her voice became that of Arlene.

"Are you a doctor?" Arlene asked. "Are you going to tell anyone?"

"Absolutely not."

"The medicine was good," Arlene said in her low voice. She tilted her head in response to sounds she evidently heard coming from the next room. "Some student is really going at it," she muttered, chuckling at the thought.

"Do you like this work, Arlene?" Nebel asked.

Her voice was flat, unemotional. "I don't like this stuff. I don't want to get involved in this. I'm not equipped for this."

"Candy's not equipped for it either."

"No. She has a terrible side. She shouldn't continue."

"That's right."

"I've never seen you before," Arlene said. "Why don't I see your face?"

"I don't know."

"I don't either."

"Can you see my body, Arlene?"

"Are you behind the chair?"

"Yes."

"Are you afraid of me?"

"Why should I be afraid of you?"

"I don't know. Are you Chinese?"

"Yes."

"Then why don't you stand up?"

"Why? Would that make it better for you?"

"What are you hiding for?" Arlene asked. She was on the offensive and enjoying it, a situation Arlene always seemed to savor.

"You were in trouble and I was trying to help you," said Nebel.

"Are you American-born?"

"Yes. Does it make a difference?"

"Somewhat."

"I just thought you might be peeved because I called you Arlene instead of Miss Grant."

"Why should you call me anything else? It says it right here." She pointed to where a name tag would be pinned. "It says it right here. Arlene G."

"Yes, that's right." Nebel was going along with anything she said, his only alternative if he wished to discover what was occurring during the regression.

Arlene told Nebel that she didn't like working in the smoke room. He questioned her about it and discovered that there was a room in which agents learned to set fires.

"I'm afraid of fire," she said.

"Did you actually see the fire or just the smoke?"

"The fire. You have to set it. That stuff goes up fast."

"Why do you think they teach you that?" asked Nebel.

"It's a guerrilla tactic. You know, I don't know why I'm in-volved in this nonsense. I don't even know why I'm here."

"Because you're involved. Right?"

"Well, I know what I'm going to be involved in, and it won't be this."

"You can't be selective all the time," Nebel said.

"Well, I intend to be."

"I think you're assuming too much, Arlene. You're employed by them."

"I am not employed," she said emphatically. "I am an inde-pendent contractor. I am not on full-time. I am per-assignment. These others are full-time but not me."

Nebel asked her for the time.

"Four, isn't it?" she said. She then asked him about the medi-cine he'd given Candy for her pain. "I hope you know what you gave her," Arlene warned.

"Don't worry, I did."

"What was it?"

"A Demerol combination."

"Why'd you call it a Number Ten?" (Nebel had told Candy earlier that the pill was called a Number Ten, to explain his having had her count down.)

Nebel began a long and involved explanation. Arlene cut him off with, "You and Burger."

"What's wrong with Burger?" Nebel asked.

"Everything is count, count, count."

"Did you see Burger here today?"

"No, but I heard he was here."

"You don't like him much, do you?" Nebel asked.

"He's okay. What time is it?"

"About four-ten."

"I have to be out of here at four-fifteen," Arlene said.

The session was over.


Nebel subsequently learned in other sessions with Candy that the section of the Farm used to teach operatives to destroy furniture as a search technique was known as the 3-D facility. It stood for Detect, Destroy, Demolish. There were numerous rooms available for the training sessions, although according to Candy the facility was still in the final stages of construction.

She and the other students had worn army fatigues and she mentioned that a number of Chinese Nationalists were among the trainees. The razor referred to in the previous session was worn on a ring, much the same as those worn by newspaper deliverymen for cutting the cords that bind the bundles. Arlene had to wear adhesive tape on her finger beneath the ring because the one issued to her was too large.

It was at the Farm that Candy/Arlene was introduced to such devices as a lipstick containing a poisonous substance. A female agent could end her life if captured by simply biting into the stick. She was also taught that an effective way to kill another person was to insert a hatpin into the lipstick and then jab the pin into the intended victim.

She was taught how to use acid as a defensive and offensive weapon, and how code numbers could be painted on her nails and covered with nail polish. She fired handguns, climbed ropes and engaged in a variety of physical exercises. She disliked every aspect of the training but went along with it because she was told to by Gilbert Jensen.

There are references to still other training received by Candy over the course of her involvement with the CIA and Gilbert Jensen. She trained at the now infamous Florida center from which the invasion of Cuba (the Bay of Pigs) was choreographed. That same Florida training facility was also used to prepare for the surprise parachute drop into the North Vietnamese prison camp of Son Toy in November 1970. The mission was a failure, for there were no American prisoners in the camp at the time of the raid.

Candy claims to have almost played a role in that mission. It was arranged for her to lead a USO troupe to Vietnam just prior to the attack. While in South Vietnam she was to feign illness and leave the troupe, and was to be transported by military helicopter to the North Vietnamese border where she would deliver a message to an unidentified man. The USO tour was canceled at the last minute, and it is Candy's assumption that a leak, originating at the highest level of the USO, not only caused the tour to be canceled but was responsible for the North Vietnamese evacuation of American prisoners from Son Toy only days before the attack on the prison camp.

 

The training of Candy Jones did not seem as important to the CIA as the testing of her did to Jensen and his medical colleagues. There are a number of significant tapes dealing with these testing episodes, one set of which was recorded in my presence.

I was at the Nebel apartment on a Sunday afternoon when John induced a deep hypnotic trance in his wife and began to question her about trips she'd allegedly made to various CIA installations. When the session began, Candy was in the conscious state, and, with gentle probing by her husband, tried to recall certain details of one of her visits. She talked of having been taken to what appeared to her to be a research facility which, she claimed, was very near to a marine camp. My assumption is that she was at the Farm—Camp Peary.

"The rooms were white," she told us, "like little examining rooms. But there was also an auditorium. It was round, and people could sit up high and watch what was going on in the middle."

Nebel asked her whether it was like a surgical auditorium in which medical students observe operations.

"Yes," Candy replied. "That's exactly what it was."

Candy also mentioned an unusual set of sliding doors, and in response to Nebel's questions she described them as being very thick and made of metal. It was at this point that Nebel induced the trance and suggested that she was actually standing before those metal doors in Virginia.

"What do you see when the doors open?" he asked.

"A hall. A corridor and a desk. There's a soldier sitting at the desk. He has a book in front of him, and a clipboard."

"Is it a long walk from where you are at the doors to the desk?"

"About ten feet."

Nebel told her to walk down the hall and approach the soldier at the desk. I watched as Candy, deep in a trance and leaning against the back of the couch in their living room, mentally followed her husband's instructions.

"What are the walls like?" he asked her.

"Gray."

"Are you at the desk?"

"Yes."

"What is the soldier saying?"

"Grant. He said my name. He asked for my ID and I gave it to him."

"What else?" Nebel asked.

"He gave me the holder to put the ID card in. I pin it to my clothes."

"What's the soldier doing now?"

"Calling . . . on the phone."

"Who's he calling?"

"Jensen."

"Gil Jensen?"

"Yes. He's coming down the hall. See?"

"Yes, I see. Is he coming to greet you?" Nebel asked.

"Yes."

"What's he saying?"

"He asked me if I had a good trip."

"How is Jensen dressed?"

"He has on a white coat."

"A uniform?"

"No, civilian clothes, and his white coat."

Candy continued to provide John, and me, with a description of events as they took place. Jensen introduced Candy to another doctor. She described him as being shorter than Jensen, and older. He had mousy-gray hair and wore steel-rimmed eyeglasses. Nebel attempted to get the other doctor's name but to no avail.

After the other doctor left them, Jensen led Candy to what she described as a cafeteria where they sat at a table and had coffee. Jensen told her she was looking pale and asked whether she'd recently had a vitamin shot. Candy told him that her internist in New York, Dr. Childs, had given her a shot a few days before. Jensen suggested that she might need a booster shot.

They left the cafeteria and went to one of the small white examining rooms. There was a cot, a small chest of drawers and a mirror. Jensen told her it might be a good idea if she stayed overnight in the room and returned to Washington the following day.

"Had you planned to stay overnight?" Nebel asked.

"Yes . . . I had a bag . . . just a shoulder bag. . . . Oh, no, I was definitely planning to go back to Washington that night."

"Did you fly here from Washington?"

"No, they drove me."

"Who's *they?*"

"A driver."

"Was it an official car?"

"No, just a car."

"What time is it?" asked Nebel.

"Eleven-thirty."

"At night."

Laughing. "No, in the daytime."

According to Candy, and under questioning by Nebel, Jensen prepared to give her a booster shot. She sat on the edge of the cot and watched as he took out a needle and readied the IV apparatus.

"Why don't you lie down?" Jensen suggested, as reported by Candy.

"Do I have to take my shoes off?" Candy asked.

Nebel wasn't certain for a moment whether she was asking him or Gilbert Jensen. He decided her question was part of the regression and assumed the role of Jensen. "Yes, I think you'd be more comfortable," Nebel said.

"The floors are so cold," Candy told him, thinking she was speaking to Jensen.

"Are they?"

"Yes. Concrete is always so cold."

This role-playing between John and Candy carried right through the process of inserting the IV in her arm and waiting for the contents of the bottle to empty. Nebel attempted to have her read the label on the bottle, and after repeated tries she said, "CIBA. I think it says New Jersey." CIBA is a leading pharmaceutical company, and one of its chief products is reserpine, a component of the Indian snake-root plant, *Rauwolfia serpentina.* It is used in various combinations to treat high blood pressure, and does so by depleting the body's store of an important nerve-transmitting chemical. As noted earlier, the Soviet Union has been extremely interested in reserpine for some years and has actively been experimenting with it as a mind-controlling substance.

Interestingly enough, Arlene emerged following the intravenous feeding and took over from Candy. Although it had been Arlene from the beginning (it was her name tag and ID), Candy's voice had been describing the events. Now, with the needle taken from her arm, Arlene was fully in control.

(The change in Candy's personality when Arlene emerges never fails to cause me to feel uneasy and unsettled. There is an implied viciousness in Arlene that comes through each time, a tacit threat of danger, of action, of a person who might act irrationally because there is so little to lose. Arlene upsets me, and I have never enjoyed being in her presence during the research portions of this book. I can imagine the effect it has had on John Nebel, who locks horns with Arlene on an almost daily basis.)

I entered into the regression at Nebel's invitation. He introduced me to Arlene as a medical associate, a Dr. Murphy. I questioned Arlene about her recent activities for The Company and she became antagonistic. While it was a fascinating experience for me, and served to heighten my understanding of the entire hypnotic process and of the dual personality with which I was dealing as the writer of this book, not much new information of substance resulted from the scene.

The session that Sunday in Nebel's apartment lasted for over an hour. Nebel eventually counted Arlene out of the trance and restored Candy to the room. She began to weep.

"Why are you crying?" Nebel asked, placing his arm around her.

"I'm so sad," she said.

"Why are you sad?"

"I don't know."


As destructive as Arlene might have been to Candy over the years, she also served a positive function. When things got rough for Candy as a child, and later with Harry Conover and Gilbert Jensen, Arlene stepped forward and did battle with these controlling forces. And if ever Candy needed Arlene, it was when she was placed before 24 doctors at CIA headquarters in Virginia and subjected to tests to prove that Jensen had truly created a puppet.

The event to which I'm referring may have taken place during that same trip to Virginia. It is possible that after receiving Jensen's booster shot she was taken to the amphitheater where the doctors had gathered to witness Jensen's CIA-sponsored work. If so, her sadness at the end of the previous session is particularly understandable.

In July 1974 John Nebel put Candy into a hypnotic trance and waited for her to spontaneously regress. She did, and asked him whether he had found her. He didn't know to what she was referring, but agreed that he had, indeed, found her.

"I'm very weak," she said, and her voice reflected it. "They kept me over the weekend."

"Who kept you?" Nebel asked.

"They wouldn't feed me. No water. I got sick."

Nebel did not know what event in Candy's life was being relived, and asked questions that he hoped would illuminate the situation. She ignored his questions and continued what was basically a monologue.

". . . Where's Captain Birch? . . . My stomach hurts so . . . they pushed me down." She struggled on the bed against unseen persons.

"Who pushed you down?" asked Nebel.

"The nurses." Candy was becoming more upset, and thrashed about the bed.

"Where are you now?" asked Nebel.

"Virginia."

"At the big place?" Nebel asked, meaning CIA headquarters. Candy had referred to the Langley facility as "the big place" on a few occasions in the past.

"Uh-huh," Candy replied. She sounded weary, almost drugged.

"Why did the nurses push you down?"

"I don't know. I don't think they even knew who I was."

"Was Gil Jensen there?"

"Uh-huh."

"Dr. Jensen?"

"Yes."

"I see. Who put you in the bed?"

"Gil."

"Why did he do that?"

There was no response. Nebel probed and she told him she had been present at a meeting at which Jensen displayed her to his colleagues. There were eight subjects on the program, and Jensen scheduled Candy first. "Being first is worse than being number eight," she moaned.

Further questioning by Nebel brought the following comment from Candy: "Gil said that there were those people in the room who could stand up and make all sorts of accusations, but that if they were loyal Americans, their comments would be very valuable and would contribute to the case histories."

Nebel asked Candy if she had spoken to the group, and she said she had.

"What did you say?" he asked her.

"I told them they were all phonies, hoodwinkers."

"You told them that?"

"Uh-huh. And I told them not to be taken in by all of this."

"What did they do when you told them this?"

"They applauded all of a sudden. It was funny."

"Did Jensen take a bow?"

"No."

"Was he pleased with what you'd said?"

"No. He asked me what I was trying to pull. I asked him who all the people were and what *he* was trying to pull. He had people all over the place."

"How many people were there?"

"About twenty-four."

Nebel asked the purpose of her being there. "Was he trying to prove what a success he was?"

"Yeah, I think he was."

"Trying to prove it?"

"I think he was successful."

"What name did he use for you when he introduced you?" Nebel asked.

Candy fumbled for a name as she tried to recall the incident. Finally she said, "Something like Laura Quidnick. Something like that. Laura something. . . ."

"Did you have on a wig?"

"Uh-huh."

"Which one?"

"The black one."

Nebel questioned her in an attempt to learn whether Jensen had done anything prior to introducing her to the group that might have acted to induce a hypnotic trance in her. He asked whether Jensen had used his hands, or held a watch on a chain or lighted a candle.

"A candle," Candy said. "He held it down . . . low . . . very low." Her voice began to display anxiety.

"Did he light the candle?"

"Yes." She was at the verge of tears as she recalled this moment from her past.

"He lighted it in front of the people?"

"Yes . . . I don't know . . . I don't know anything."

"What did Jensen say to you when the candle was lit?"

"He asked me questions . . . I don't know. I don't . . ."

Nebel reinforced the trance at this point. As he did, Candy began to moan.

". . . he tried to put the candle . . . he tried to . . ." She began to cry as she muttered these statements about Jensen and the candle. ". . . he tried to put the candle . . ."

"Where did he try to put it?" Nebel asked.

"Oh, no . . . I almost killed him. . . ."

Nebel pressed her as to where Jensen had attempted to put the candle, but she fought against answering him, repeating, "Oh, no, I don't know anything. . . ." Her movements on the bed became violent as she twisted to escape Nebel's words.

At this point in the session, and in a subsequent session in which this same scene was related, Nebel switched to the role of Gilbert Jensen in an attempt to break through Candy's reluctance to discuss it.

"I don't know anything," Candy said again.

"Oh, yes, you do," Nebel responded. "You can tell me everything, and you know it. Where did I try to put the candle?"

"I don't know anything." She said it over and over.

"Yes, you do. This is Gil Jensen."

"I don't like you."

"Come on now, tell me where I tried to put the candle."

"You hurt my arm. It hurt. I couldn't help it." She was almost hysterical.

"Come on, tell me."

"You tried to stick it into me." It was a child's exclamation, filled with hatred and sorrow.

"Where did I try to stick it?" Nebel asked as Gilbert Jensen. He kept at her, narrowing down areas of the body: "Below the knees? . . . Above the waist? . . . *Where?*"

Candy continued to plead with him to believe her when she'd said that she didn't know anything. "You *told* me I wouldn't remember," she screamed.

"All right," Nebel said. "Then tell me *why* I did it."

"To show them that you could do anything with me."

"Did I hurt you?"

"No. You said it wouldn't hurt, and it didn't."

"Then tell me, where did I try to stick the candle?"

Candy continued to resist. She told him she hated him and wished him dead.

"Where?"

"You know, you know," she screamed. "You gave me the shot and I couldn't move my arm because you had it taped down."

"Where did I put it?"

"I don't know anything."

"This is Gil. Tell me!"

"I . . ."

"I'm going to count from five down to one. When I reach one, you'll have complete memory. Five . . . four . . . your memory is coming back . . ."

"No! Stop it!"

". . . three . . . clear memory . . . two . . ."

"I hate you!"

". . . one . . ."

"Take your hands off me!" She was screaming at Jensen; Nebel was at least two feet from her on the bed and was not touching her.

"You have your memory."

"You pushed it . . . into me." Her voice sagged, and she sighed.

"Between your legs?"

"Yes." She cried uncontrollably and Nebel ended the session.


Arlene discussed the candle incident in a session with Nebel recorded on July 6, 1974.* She said that some of the doctors at

*Tape #59, Side B.

the seminar had tried to break through Jensen's control of Candy but had failed, much to Jensen's satisfaction.

"Candy is perfect," Arlene told Nebel. "Jensen proved in Virginia how impossible it was to break his control."

# 19

---

# Attempting To Quit

When Arlene made her statement that Jensen's control over Candy was total and irreversible, there was every reason to accept it as an unfortunate fact. Candy seemed without the inner resources to balk, despite the fact that she desperately wanted to disengage herself from Jensen and The Company. The trips, the tests, the demonstrations to colleagues, the physical and mental abuse had taken their predictable toll. But she was unable to divorce herself from Jensen's domination.

There were tangential factors that entered into Candy's inability to break away. One was money; Jensen's payments had kept her afloat. She never saw any of the money directly, but benefited from it nonetheless. Her sons' private schooling was paid, in part, by direct payments from The Company to their schools. Large hospital bills were paid in full in the same manner.

The role that money played in Candy's involvement with The Company came up on a number of tapes.

During one recorded hypnotic session, Nebel, playing the Jensen role during the regression, asked Candy whether she'd ever discussed her CIA work with anyone else. She assured him that she had not.*

"What about Mel?" Nebel asked, meaning Mel Heimer.

"I told Mel that if I ever needed help he should come fast," Candy replied.

"That wasn't very smart," Nebel told her.

"I think it was. I have no one to help me and I'm scared."

"Are you sorry you got involved?"

"Yes," Candy replied. "I wish I'd never started, and it's all your fault."

"My fault? How is it my fault? You wanted to work for us."

"Yes, that's true, but it's your fault that I got in so far. I thought I was going to make a lot of money, but it never works out that way."

Nebel chided her for her lack of patriotism. "I thought you were doing it for your country."

"I am," Candy said, her voice a plea for him to understand. "I love my country and that's why I started in the first place. But . . . why am I explaining anything to you? It's none of your business. Who are you to ask me about it? Could you do what I'm doing? Go ahead. You go and do the things I've been doing. You couldn't do it."

On another occasion Candy muttered to Nebel, again playing Gilbert Jensen, "There must be a better way to make money than to work for you. If I could sell my business and get some collateral . . ."**

She told Nebel during another regression that she was working on a new book and hoped it would be successful enough to allow her to stop working for The Company.*** This particular regression took her back to October 14, 1971, and into the apartment she shared with her mother at 1199 Park Avenue. She told Nebel, who was playing her alter ego at the time, "My mother and I are going away for Christmas."

"Will you be seeing Gil [Jensen]?" asked Nebel.

"Not if I can help it," was Candy's response.

It's obvious from the tapes that Jensen not only was unhappy with Candy's threats to cease working for him and for The

*Tape #36, Side A.
**Tape #84 "A," Side B.
***Tape #80 "A," Side B.

Company, but found his fears of such a move intensifying as her threats became more frequent and forceful.

But there was more for Jensen to fear than the simple likelihood that Candy might one day expose his and The Company's macabre experimental project. Over the course of her involvement, she had naturally been privy to other information that could prove damaging to Jensen and, perhaps, to others with whom he was associated. Jensen had worked hard to prevent such information from filtering into Candy's sphere of knowledge, but even the most careful of men, which Gilbert Jensen was, cannot guarantee that someone in Candy's position would not, over such a prolonged period of time, sense a mood, observe a face or hear a whispered telephone conversation. An even more frightening possibility was that the careful man himself might one day slip, particularly should the longevity of the association breed a relaxation of the rigidity of the roles. And that is exactly what happened between Gilbert Jensen and Candy Jones.

There is evidence from the tapes that Jensen displayed an active sexual interest in Candy, which was not returned by her. The recorded hypnotic sessions are sprinkled with brief scenes in which Candy fights off his advances while in the hypnotic mode. Most people are aware of the stale debate over whether a hypnotist can force a subject to act against his or her ingrained moral code. The answer is yes *and* no. To use an example on the level of the high-school locker room, let us say that a young man wishes to use hypnosis in order to convince his girl friend to strip away her clothing in his presence. No matter how deep in a trance she might be, a direct order to remove her clothing would invariably prove ineffective. The young man's only hope of success would lie in creating the hallucination that the room had become insufferably hot. Or, the young man might try suggesting that he is the girl's trusted family doctor. If he succeeded in either of these strategies, the young lady might disrobe, convinced that her actions were appropriate and well within her moral code.

Jensen's approach with Candy was direct, and he leaned heavily on the fact that he was, indeed, a medical doctor. Many tapes find him attempting to remove her clothing while she was in a hypnotic trance and was on his small examining table. But

Candy was forever aware that although he was *Dr.* Jensen, his function was to prepare her for intelligence work and not to perform physical examinations. She constantly rebuffed him, which angered him. Often he attempted to approach her through Arlene who, by her own admissions, liked him better than did Candy. But even Arlene was not interested in any sexual relationship with Jensen, and her rejection of him was harsher and more to the point, very much in line with Arlene's basic personality.

Whether or not Jensen's sexual overtures were successful is less important than that he made them at all, for to have done so signals the sort of human frailty that has doomed more than one covert agent. Jensen was an aloof and meticulously careful man, but there were times when those attributes were nudged aside by a more relaxed and personal quality.

Like a number of incidents in Candy's secret past, the plan to have her commit suicide was told to Nebel over a long period of time as the hypnotic sessions progressed in the bedroom of their apartment. At first Nebel did not connect Jensen with Candy's early comments about ending her life. He assumed, with sound psychological justification, that her state of mind was such that suicide would be a possibility. She was under great pressure; Arlene was interfering in their marriage with increasing and annoying regularity. The day-to-day tension was also taking its toll on Nebel, and Candy often burst into uncontrollable tears when the realization of what Jensen's work was doing to the marriage hit home.

In an undated hypnotic session, Candy regressed to childhood and began to cry.* Nebel realized she'd gone back to her earlier years and called her Doll.

"Why are you so sad?" he asked.

"I want to die," she replied, sobbing softly. "I want to die and go with you." It was apparent that she was speaking to her grandmother, Ma-Má, and was referring to Ma-Má's impending death.

"But why do you want to die?" asked Nebel.

*Tape #87 "A," Side A.

"It's too hard to live," Doll answered. "I can never do anything right."

After a few moments of tender dialogue, Candy, as Doll, said, "I want to jump off the cloud. I don't want to be alone on the cloud anymore."

Nebel tried to calm her, but she became even more upset and continued to threaten to jump from the cloud. He had her place her hand on the wood paneling in the bedroom and she seemed to come out of her hypnotic trance.

"You told me you were going to jump off a cloud," Nebel told her, assuming now that he was speaking to her in the conscious state.

"I should be dead," Candy replied.

"Why do you keep saying that, Candy? Did someone tell you you should be dead?" Nebel was referring to Candy's mother because there had been references on past tapes to episodes in which the mother, in a depressed or angry mood, had told her small daughter that she would be better off dead.

"*They* said it. There's no point in continuing."

"Who said it?"

"The one I was speaking with at the time."

"Where were you? What office were you in?" Nebel assumed that the conversation to which Candy was referring had taken place in the Oakland office of Gilbert Jensen.

"I was on the telephone," Candy muttered.

"Who was the person you were speaking to?"

"I was talking to a man in California."

"Oh. Was he . . . ?"

"He's a doctor."

"What's his name?"

"Oh, I don't know."

"You know his name. Let me hear it."

"He was right." She sounded very sad at admitting it.

"Come on now, what was his name?"

"I don't know anything." It was the singsong automatic response Nebel had heard hundreds of times on the tapes.

"Was it Gil Jensen?" Nebel asked.

"I don't know anything."

"Don't tell me you don't know anything," Nebel snapped. He'd found in the past that getting tough occasionally prodded Candy to drop her denials and open up. Now she began to sniffle and to move about on their bed. "Stop it!" Nebel said in a firm voice. "You know everything." He placed his hand on her arm.

"Don't do that to me!" It was Arlene's voice, and she yanked her arm from his grasp.

"Nobody's doing anything to you," said Nebel, not aware that Arlene had taken over.

"You be careful," Arlene warned in her ominous voice. "You just be careful of what you do to me."

"Don't tell me to be careful," Nebel said. "No one's doing a damn thing to you, and you know it." He now recognized that he was now dealing with Arlene. "Cut it out, Arlene. No more nonsense. Did you hear me? If you want to talk like a lady, fine, but . . ."

"How would you know a lady?" Arlene asked.

Nebel was angry, but checked his temper. "Did Jensen tell you you'd be better off dead, Arlene? Did he tell Candy that?"

"She told him," Arlene replied.

"And what did Jensen say?"

"He agreed."

"Was she sitting in her office talking on the phone to him?"

"Yes."

Nebel asked, "What else did he say to her?"

"He told her not to talk about it to anybody else."

"To talk about what? The fact that she felt bad?"

"He told her she didn't need to go to any other doctor. He told her there was nothing wrong with her."

Nebel attempted to get Arlene to agree with him when he called Jensen an incompetent jerk. She refused to play along, saying instead, "There was nothing wrong with her mentally or physically. She didn't need any other doctor." Arlene turned away from Nebel on the bed and pressed her fist against her mouth.

"Why do you have your hand in your mouth, Arlene?"

"So I don't call out for help." Her voice cracked.

"What kind of help do you need?" Nebel asked. "We'll get it for you right away."

She began to cry, and Nebel put his arms around her. It was Candy again, his wife, and she cried herself into a natural sleep.

Nebel learned more about Candy's conversations with Jensen

about suicide on another undated tape. He played the role of Jensen and asked Candy whether she agreed with him that she felt stronger whenever Arlene came out.

"Yes, I am stronger," Candy responded.

"Do you still think about killing yourself?" asked Nebel, as Gilbert Jensen.

"I didn't think about it," Candy said, believing she was back in Jensen's office. *"You* thought about it. You're always asking me questions about it. You're very strange."

"Why do you say that?" Nebel asked. "I never tell you to commit suicide."

"No, but you talk about suicide all the time. You're always asking me how I would do it and . . ."

"All right, tell me how you would do it," Nebel challenged.

"Oh, not again."

"Come on, tell me."

"I don't remember."

"Do you ever get so depressed that you think about suicide?"

"No, no, no. Only when I think of you."


In still another undated hypnotic session, Candy told Nebel that he shouldn't listen to "that woman who tries to come out of me and tells you silly things."*

"You're strong, Candy Jones," Nebel told her. "You don't have to let that woman come out."

"She's trying to push her way out now," Candy said, her voice reflecting some pain. She was doubled up and holding her stomach.

"No, she's not," Nebel said. "You're stronger than she is."

"I know. I am. But I can't keep fighting like this anymore. I'm tired of fighting. I can't fight anymore. He's going to make me give up."

"Who's going to make you give up?" Nebel asked.

"Dr. Jensen."

"What's Dr. Jensen going to do to you?"

"He's not going to do it to me. He's going to make me do it to my own self. Give up."

"Give up what, Candy?"

*Tape #16, Side A.

"I don't know. Whatever he says."

"Did he tell you you should give up?"

"No. He says that he'd help me work it out if I ever had to do it."

"What do you mean by give up, Candy? End your life?"

"He didn't say that, but that's what he meant."

"What do you think of Dr. Jensen now?" Nebel asked.

"I think he did me bad. I used to think he did good for me." She paused, then said, "He wanted me to go down there and jump off the rock."

"Jensen said that to you?"

"He told me it would be very nice because I like it down there." [She was referring to the Bahamas.]

"What else did he say?" Nebel asked Candy.

"He said, 'You might as well go, why wait?' "

"That was his suggestion to you?"

"No. He said that if I was unhappy I might as well go and do it."

Nebel worked to convince her that Jensen no longer had any control over her, but his efforts were not effective, at least during that particular session. Candy said that she had to talk to Jensen so that he could "reverse things." She then said, "I tried to call him in California the other day." It was another upsetting reference to having been in contact with Jensen after her marriage to John Nebel.


In yet another hypnotic session, also undated, Nebel was to learn more about Jensen's suicide plans for Candy. In this instance he was filled in by Arlene.*

The session opened with Arlene preparing to leave on a mission, as instructed by Jensen. She was in Miami during the regression, and she told Nebel that *Candy* had traveled to Miami, but once there, Arlene had been instructed to take over, which she had.

■

JOHN: Do you like Candy?

ARLENE: *(insolently)* With almonds.

*Tape #36, Side B.

JOHN: Are you brave, Arlene?

ARLENE: Not brave, just stupid, and strong, and fast.

JOHN: Isn't Candy strong?

ARLENE: She's strong but not as fast as me.

JOHN: Did Jensen ever suggest to you that you commit suicide?

ARLENE: He can't get rid of me that fast. I won't let her, *or* him.

JOHN: Well, if Candy dies, you're dead.

ARLENE: Candy doesn't know that.

JOHN: Do you think Candy would ever kill herself?

ARLENE: It's not called killing. It's stopping what is.

JOHN: What does that mean?

ARLENE: *(condescendingly)* It means stopping the progression of a positive action.

JOHN: That doesn't make any sense.

ARLENE: *(annoyed)* It's the stopping of movement.

JOHN: You mean death?

ARLENE: Yes, of course.

JOHN: Would you like to be dead, Arlene?

ARLENE: I am.

JOHN: If you're dead, how can you talk?

ARLENE: Why don't you die and find out?

■

Nebel and Arlene continued to talk about Candy and her state of mind at the moment. Arlene told him that Candy was in very deep trouble with Jensen, and that Jensen was looking for Candy.

"What will Jensen do if he finds Candy?" John asked. "Make her commit suicide?"

"No," Arlene replied. "But Candy might kill herself. She might."

In another undated hypnotic session, Nebel had an opportunity to ask Candy if she thought Jensen would ever harm her.* Candy had regressed, and John was playing the role of her alter ego.

■

*Tape #40, Side A.

JOHN: Do you ever think that your life is in danger?

CANDY: My life is in danger twenty-four hours a day. And I am exhausted. I just want to lie down and rest.

JOHN: Why do you do this if it puts you in danger and exhausts you? Because Jensen tells you to do it? He's not your friend. He's done you a lot of harm.

CANDY: He won't kill me.

JOHN: Why not?

CANDY: He's not going to do anything unless he can make it look accidental.

JOHN: Are you saying that he would kill you if he *could* make it look like an accident?

CANDY: No. He wouldn't do it yet because it could be traced to him. . . .

■

Nebel was unable to gain any further information during this session, but was successful at a later date in learning more about his wife's supposed "last assignment."

As session after session unfolded, more details of Jensen's plan to have Candy commit suicide surfaced. It was to occur in December of 1972. Jensen had booked a first-class seat for her on Pan Am to Nassau, the Bahamas. She would check into the Paradise Beach Hotel, where she'd been a frequent visitor over the years, as Candy Jones.

But Arlene Grant would meet her there. That was part of Jensen's plan. He told Candy that she would receive a call during her second day on the island. She asked him who would be calling her, but he refused to tell her. I assume it was to be Jensen himself who would call, and his call would cause Arlene to take over from Candy and guide her to a steep bluff overlooking the sea. Arlene would make the high dive, just as she had done when they were children. And it would be over for Candy Jones.

"Did you know that Arlene planned to kill you in the Bahamas?" Nebel asked Candy during a hypnotic session in July 1973.*

*Tape #58, Side A.

"Yes."

"What had you done to make her that angry with you?"

"It's all too complicated," Candy replied. "I was told to meet her there."

"Where?"

"The Bahamas. The Paradise Beach Hotel."

"When did this happen?" Nebel asked.

"Last November. That's when I was told."

Nebel asked Arlene about the incident during a regression that took place in their apartment on an unspecified date.*

"Candy is just a dragnet around your neck," Arlene told Nebel. "But she needed you. She had all the time in the world to go to Paradise Island in December and take the high dive, but she married you."

"If Candy killed herself, Arlene, you would be dead, too."

"Oh, no," replied Arlene. "I'd be the one who'd survive." Jensen had persuaded Arlene of that.

"What about Candy's marriage to John, Arlene? Have you been deliberately trying to ruin the marriage?"

Arlene laughed her bitter, harsh laugh. "What do you mean tried? I *did* ruin it."

Candy's marriage to John Nebel on December 31, 1972, precluded her taking the trip to the Bahamas. But although it was a heartening incident in that it perhaps indicated that with sufficient motivation, Candy was able to counter certain of Jensen's instructions, it did not signal the end of all control Gilbert Jensen had established over her. His presence pulled at her throughout the early years of the marriage and, on many occasions, threatened to smash it to pieces, as certainly as she herself would have been smashed had she leaped from the bluff in Nassau.

*Tape #68, Side B.

# 20

---

# The Present

Could there ever be a neat and definitive ending to the adventure lived by Candy Jones and John Nebel since their marriage on December 31, 1972? Not without taking vast literary license, · which would be inappropriate. And to expect such an ending would be to ignore the fetchingly complex aspects of their individual personalities, and to deny a basic truth—that we are the sum of what we were.

There is thus no ending to be written to this story. But there is resolution, and rather than dealing with a final chapter in the life of Candy Jones, it more accurately involves that *other lady*— Ms. Arlene Grant.

*"There is no Arlene!"* Candy proclaims with regularity and conviction these days, and John Nebel hails her proclamations. But they both know that there will always be an Arlene Grant in their lives. What is different about her now is that she has become a spinster aunt who occasionally visits on the holidays.

Until very recently, Arlene was intruding into the lives of John and Candy with such ferocity and tenacity that it appeared, for too long a time, that she would succeed in destroying her creator, Candy Jones, and in fulfilling the hopes of her mentor, Gilbert Jensen. Had she done this, she would have undoubtedly destroyed John Nebel as well, for his life depends on Candy's well-being. Ironically, Arlene's destructiveness fostered a closeness between John and Candy that most couples might never experience.

The diminution of Arlene has been a slow and gradual process, hindered by the lingering control exercised by Jensen, and perhaps by the Central Intelligence Agency itself.

There was a period of time when Candy's every movement in Manhattan was observed by a man in a tan trenchcoat. He first appeared on the scene when Candy was living with her mother at 1199 Park Avenue. Usually he sat in a plain, light-blue sedan across from the apartment building, chain-smoking and watching. Candy describes him as being left-handed, of medium height, fair complexion and with dark eyes. He came on the scene sometime early in 1972, shortly after she told Jensen she was through for good, and popped up on an irregular basis through the middle of 1973.

"I told Dr. Jensen about him," Candy told John during a hypnotic session.

"What did Jensen say?" Nebel asked her.

"He said that I shouldn't try to find out who the man was. He said to stay away from him."

Candy did approach the man once. She was walking her German shepherd, Lady, one evening and crossed the street to where the man was standing. He didn't move, and Lady growled and strained at her leash. The man turned and walked up the street without saying anything.

"Why didn't you report him to the police?" Nebel asked during the same hypnotic session.

"I did."

"Didn't they do anything?"

"I didn't want them to. I didn't file an official complaint."

"Why not?"

"Gil [Jensen] told me not to."


There were many incidents to follow in which Candy had to make sudden phone calls. When Nebel would ask whom she had to call, she invariably replied, "I don't know." When asked by Nebel what number it was she wished to call, she would only mutter, "The Murray Hill number."

"I could never figure out what prompted her to make the calls," says Nebel. "Something triggered her. I knew that. Every time it happened, it was Arlene who insisted she had to go to the phone. Candy would become Arlene in a matter of seconds, and my greatest fear was that Jensen and The Company were in some way contacting her, either through a meeting on the street or on a bus. I could never be sure. All I was certain of was that it was happening too often to be comfortable, and it was driving a stake into our relationship."

There is some evidence from the tapes that Nebel's fears about Jensen or the CIA making contact with Candy might have had validity.

During a hypnotic regression that occurred one evening, Candy relived what she had done that very afternoon.* She believed she was talking to her alter ego, and was concerned that her husband, John Nebel, would find out where she'd been. Nebel, as the alter ego, assured her that John would never find out. Relieved, Candy began to tell of her actions after she'd left the apartment, ostensibly to buy a pair of boots.

"... I called him but he wasn't there," she told Nebel during the regression.

"Who did you call?" he asked.

"Colonel Paxton.** He's back. He retired but he's back."

"Why were you calling him?" Nebel asked.

"To ask him . . . to straighten things out. . . . I have to know about those phone calls."

"What phone calls? Your business is closed."

"I still get them. They're crazy calls. I don't want to get them anymore. Paxton can fix that."

Further probing by Nebel as her alter ego resulted in Candy telling him about a New York office from which Paxton operated. It was, according to Candy, a CIA front. Nebel failed to obtain a location during this session, but on a subsequent hypnotic tape Candy told him that the office was located at 90 Park Avenue, a large Manhattan office building.*** This taped ses-

*Tape #72, Sides A and B.
**A fictitious name.
***Tape #89 "A," Side A.

sion also found Candy reliving her actions of another recent afternoon. Again she had attempted to contact someone from The Company in the hope that she could resolve the problems of her present life. And she was aware that John might not be happy with what she was doing.

She told her alter ego, "My husband was sleeping when I left the apartment. He doesn't know what I did."

"Don't you think your husband would be mad, and hurt, if he knew?" Nebel asked.

"I don't think so," Candy replied. "I'm only doing it to protect us. He'd understand that."

On July 3, 1973, more than six months after they'd been married, the following message was left on the telephone-answering machine in their apartment:* "Japan Airlines calling on the 0-3 July at four-ten P.M. . . . Please have Miss Grant call 759–9100. . . . She is holding now reservation on Japan Airlines Flight 5, for the sixth of July, Kennedy–Tokyo, with an open on to Taipei. This is per Cynthia that we are calling. Thank you."

A check through Japan Airlines confirmed that the phone number 759–9100 is the reservations number for that airline. But because the trip was never taken, and the tickets were never picked up, there is no record in the airline's computer of who made the reservation for Miss Grant.

The term "per Cynthia" in the recorded message is interesting. The message did not say that Miss Grant should respond to a reservations clerk named Cynthia. In fact, there is no reservations clerk named Cynthia in Japan Airlines' New York offices. The message said, "This is per Cynthia that we are calling."

Friends in the reservations offices of other airlines have told me that Cynthia sounds like a code name for an organization. The airlines book space and bill through a great many codes for large organizations, and I cannot help but speculate that were I with the CIA and looking for such a code, Cynthia would be my hands-down choice for a word to indicate CIA.

The possibility that Jensen or the CIA had been in touch with Candy after her marriage to John Nebel is compelling. But more than a possibility is the reality that the years of hypnotic and drug-induced patterning of Candy had left their dark and heavy

*Tape #37, Side A.

244 THE CONTROL OF CANDY JONES

mark. I have personally been with Candy and John when she has slipped into a spontaneous trance while in a public place, the trance induced by a flickering candle, or by repetitive Oriental music.

Early one evening in the summer of 1975, we dined together at our favorite Chinese restaurant. We'd worked that afternoon on aspects of the book, and the mood at the table was carefree and relaxed. As the meal progressed, however, I began to sense a rising tension within Candy. Nebel, of course, who has been so much closer to the situation, sensed it even quicker than I did.

"Excuse me," Candy said, rising and walking from the table. We watched as she silently passed one of the hosts at the restaurant and a very close and dear friend of Candy and John, and ascended the graceful staircase to the second floor where the rest rooms are located.

Nebel and I began talking about things unrelated to Candy and to the book, but after 15 minutes I asked whether he considered her absence to be unusually long.

"Of course it is," he answered rather angrily. "But what do I do, make a scene? Do I ask one of the women here to go upstairs and check on her?"

We sat silently and waited for Candy to return. When she did, she was a totally different person. She was Arlene. She glared at me as she took her seat and sat stoically, her face solemn and rigid, eyes fixed across the vast dining room, each breath slow and deliberate. Nebel knew immediately what had happened, because it had happened so many times in the past. He quickly paid the bill and hustled us to the nearest cab.

We drove home to the apartment, the three of us—John, Arlene and me. Once inside she immediately went to bed.

What had happened in the ladies' room that evening had happened in other rest rooms around the city, and in the tiny bathroom in their apartment. *The mirror.* Candy can feel Arlene struggling to come out, and when she goes to a mirror and peers into it, she sees not herself but that dark, foreboding person with whom she shares a common body, Arlene Grant.

A flickering candle can often cause a spontaneous trance as well. Another restaurant that has been a favorite of John and Candy is a West Side steak house. It is an intimate dining spot, with soft, flickering candles on each table. John and Candy stopped going there because of the frequency with which the candles induced a trance in Candy and caused her, or Arlene, to act unconventionally. On one occasion the flickering candles caused Candy to regress while in the trance state. It was an extraordinary experience in that the regression took her back to San Francisco and into the Mark Hopkins Hotel, where she had had dinner one evening with Gilbert Jensen many years ago. Nebel describes what happened:

> I knew from past experiences in this restaurant that the candles were a problem, so I took a menu and attempted to cover the one at our table from her view. But I noticed that she had fixed her eyes on candles on adjoining tables, and I began to become concerned. . . .
>
> We ordered steak and salad for dinner, and we sat without speaking for about fifteen minutes. Just as the food was about to be served, Candy announced that she was going to the ladies' room. She stood and proceeded across the room, wobbly, as though she might fall, and actually did brush against the backs of other people who were seated at tables between us and the ladies' room. . . .
>
> When she came back to the table and took her seat, I knew immediately that I was no longer having dinner with my wife, Candy. It was Arlene. I tried to ignore the situation and began eating my steak, which had been served and which I had to send back to keep warm while she was gone. She took a few bites of her steak, looked at me and said, "Let's go home. I'll meet you outside." . . .
>
> I was angry at having the dinner spoiled by Arlene, but was more concerned with avoiding a scene in the restaurant. Candy and I were both known by many people, both customers and help, and I didn't wish to have Arlene create a hassle that would be embarrassing for both of us. I called the waiter and asked for a check. He walked away from the table, and as he did, Arlene looked at me and said, "Give me the gun." . . .
>
> I didn't know what the hell she was talking about, but had learned that it was better to play along with Arlene than to question her and cause her to become angry. I reached inside my jacket and drew out what I represented to her to

be a gun. In fact, it was simply my empty hand curled around an imaginary object the size of a gun. Arlene immediately unzipped the top of her large handbag and held it open. I assumed she wanted me to place the gun in the bag, which I pretended to do. . . .

She quickly stood up and said in that deep, loud voice, "I'll get a cab and meet you outside." The waiter came over with our check. Arlene ignored him and walked very deliberately to the front door. He asked me if anything was wrong. I assured him it wasn't, fumbled for enough money to cover the check and handed it to him, telling him to keep whatever the change was. I stood up as Candy reached a single step that is located just before you reach the front door. She stumbled over it but regained her balance and went through the doors. I quickly followed, aware that a number of other patrons were watching our action. . . .

We got into a cab and I asked her about the gun. She refused to answer me, and we rode silently across Manhattan. Once upstairs in our apartment, I questioned her again, but she slammed the bathroom door in my face and stayed in the bathroom for twenty minutes. I got ready for bed and was sitting on the edge of it when she came into the bedroom. She was a completely different person now . . . she was my Candy Jones. I asked her about what had happened only minutes before, but she had no recollection of it. She remembered going to the restaurant, and was aware that she was in our apartment at that moment. What had occurred in between was a complete blank to her.

Nebel was to discover the genesis of the scene during a hypnotic regression weeks later. According to Candy while in the trance state in their bedroom, she'd begun to feel weak while at the table and suffered abdominal pains. She went to the ladies' room and stood peering into the mirror for a few moments. When she rejoined Nebel at the table, *he* was no longer John Nebel. He was Gilbert Jensen, and she, Arlene, was with him at the Mark Hopkins Hotel in San Francisco.

During that dinner in California, Jensen had been carrying a gun. He was concerned at going through the metal detector that had been installed by the hotel to thwart the theft of silverware from the restaurant. Arlene suggested he put the gun in her shoulder bag. She would carry it by its long handle, low enough to pass beneath the metal detector. And that is evidently what they did that day in San Francisco. In the New York restaurant, Candy's regression had taken her back to that same scene in the Mark Hopkins.

Such spontaneous regressions were to be repeated over and over in the months to come. They occurred on buses, in cabs, in restaurants and, virtually nightly, in the apartment. Arlene seemed uncontrollable, an unassailable and invisible force that had moved in with John and Candy and was capable of taking over all aspects of their life.

Candy withered under the strain. She denounced Arlene, damned the day she first saw her in the mirrored panels of her grandmother's dressing table, threatened her, pleaded with her to go away and to leave them alone. But her protests were empty, for the truth was that inside, intellectually and emotionally, Candy Jones refused to acknowledge that Arlene Grant even existed.

"No, no, that did not happen," Candy would say after Nebel had played a tape for her in which Arlene had emerged during a hypnotic session. "No, I did not say that."

Nebel bent to the strain, too. He was never sure when Arlene would make an appearance, and this constant apprehension ate away at his confidence. He was concerned about the effect the situation was having on the legion of people with whom he was associated, either through his professional career or through long years of friendship. He asked himself every night as he prepared to go to the studio with Candy to do the show, "Will Arlene come out tonight?"

Strangely, and fortunately, Arlene never did interfere with the conduct of the six-hour-a-night talk show. She showed up at the radio station on many occasions prior to air time, flinging nasty comments at Nebel and threatening to cause a blowup. But once the red light came on, Candy seemed to be in command. Or, if Arlene did sit in the interviewer's chair occupied by Candy Jones, she said little. The show, and Candy, prospered, and she has grown into a solid and stimulating radio pro, giving WMCA the only husband-and-wife team on late-night radio.

At home, things did not go so smoothly. Despite his success with Candy as a hypnotist, Nebel was aware that help was needed from the medical fraternity. On occasion, he consulted with those doctors he was close to, and in whom he placed the greatest confidence. Chief among these was Herbert Spiegel. But Candy balked at seeing Spiegel. He was a doctor, and she'd been programmed to avoid all doctors except Gilbert Jensen. Nebel pleaded with her, but to no avail.

There were mornings when Nebel walked into their bathroom and was confronted with desperate messages written in lipstick on the mirror—*Arlene, leave me alone,* or, *Please, help me!* One morning Nebel discovered a towel draped over the mirror. Candy had done it during the night to shield herself from Arlene's mirror image.

A dozen long-stemmed red roses had been sent to Candy by one of her sons for Mother's Day. She placed them in a vase on top of their color television set and went with John to WMCA.

Nebel went to bed immediately upon their return. When he awoke, Candy was sleeping beside him. He got up and fumbled for a cigarette. It was then that he spotted the roses and what had been done to them. The flowers had been carefully cut away from the stems and were strewn on the floor. A pair of scissors was on the television set next to the vase.

Arlene admitted having done it that morning while John slept. She laughed. Destroying the flowers had amused her.

The preparation of this book did not help matters. Nebel eventually ceased hypnotizing Candy, but by the time he did, Candy, through Arlene, had plunged into the book project with verve and determination. I began receiving eight- and ten-page letters each day from her, written immediately upon returning to their apartment from the radio station. Despite her exhaustion, she seemed driven to put down for me every scrap of information she could plumb from the recesses of her mind, and I began to wonder how these details could have been recalled in the conscious state.

But then I received the following letter, written in the broad red strokes of a felt-tipped pen in the apartment Candy maintains for her own work next to their regular apartment.

Don:

To recall trips, Arlene and *those days,* places and experiences for you on paper, I first have to use the mirror—look into it and ultimately, in a form, Jensen's "cute" gimmick —there *she* is: Arlene.

The trouble, however, is that by the time I'm to go back to our living apartment and to bed—which may be noon or later, I'm so exhausted I can't bring *myself* back.

Today must be the last time I use the mirror in here for fear of the above happening again.

Hard for anyone 'cept John to understand and I know it has destroyed much of his regard of me.

I love him very much, and know I'm troubling him—not on purpose, but it's not good.

It's possible that many of the detailed pages I've written you are useless, but I must stop *Arlene* in the mornings, or at any time.

You realize that the more tired I am, the easier it is for that other personality to *push* out. But, as I said, I can't control it after awhile and it wrecks John, and no doubt is physically damaging me.

So—no more morning typings about the past to you or for anything related to Arlene.

I am eager for the book's success—for so many reasons and for everyone's sake—and #1 project now is to re-do, reorganize our living quarters. Neat non-sequitur, huh?

Best regards,<br>C.J.

P.S. There's something vaguely in my head *about a tie* I often wore with suits. I'll try to recall for you.

I sensed a determination in that letter that had been lacking in Candy in the past, a resolve to meet Arlene head on and to take steps to deal with her. I was to learn that this decision by

Candy was not totally self-motivated, for at the time she wrote me the letter she had agreed to begin seeing Herbert Spiegel as a patient. Her willingness to do this was heartening to Nebel. He'd labored hard to break Jensen's hold on her concerning other doctors, and when she announced her intentions to pursue professional help, Nebel was overjoyed.

Candy also began seeing Dr. Frederick Dick, the Manhattan internist who, as a student of Spiegel, uses hypnosis in a variety of ways in treating those of his patients whose capacity for hypnosis is established, and whose problems indicate potential benefits from hypnotic suggestion. Dick was reluctant to deal with Candy on a psychological level. He'd become John Nebel's physician, and Candy initially began seeing him as an internist. But both she and John developed great respect for Dick, as they had long had for Spiegel, and it was respect and faith, which was reciprocated by the doctors, that appeared to be the operative ingredients in dealing with Candy's problems.

Her entire life had been lived with, and under, people who'd destroyed all faith in herself. Her mother, a troubled woman, dashed Candy's spirit at every turn. Harry Conover was a user, and Candy's marriage to him only served to further maim her spirit and self-respect. And Gilbert Jensen deliberately capitalized upon what had gone before, fragmenting Candy into bits and pieces for his own ends.

Small wonder that Arlene came onto the scene in Candy's life. Arlene proved to be a savior of sorts, a device through which Candy was able to cope with the destructive forces around her. Perhaps, without Arlene, there would be no Candy Jones today. Without Arlene, the destruction might have proved to be final and total.

But now that she was surrounded by people in whom she had faith—her husband, Spiegel, Dick—she saw an opportunity to effectively deal with Arlene. In effect, Candy had decided to announce to Arlene that her services were no longer needed.

Candy was run through a battery of tests, including a brain scan, TAT and Rorschach test, to determine whether there was any psychophysical basis for her problems. There was not, according to the test results, which put aside Candy's growing, although unstated, fears that perhaps she was insane. Jensen had cautioned her during numerous brainwashing sessions that if she ever told anyone of their relationship, she would certainly be considered insane. She deeply doubted her sanity as the months progressed, and the positive results of the tests worked wonders in helping her regain some semblance of self-confidence.

Drs. Spiegel and Dick knew they were not dealing with a mentally ill person in Candy Jones. Spiegel's background and eminence in the field of psychiatry and hypnosis, coupled with a most disarming and gentle straight-forwardness, filled Candy with faith and hope, and because her reactions to the men around her were so positive, she was receptive to the strategies they suggested.

Basically, Candy was taught while under hypnosis that since she had created Arlene in the first instance, it would follow that she was capable of controlling her. This is an approach used by Spiegel in a number of treatment situations, particularly those dealing with seizures. A patient suffering from certain types of involuntary seizures can be taught to deliberately bring about a seizure while in a hypnotic trance. Once the patient realizes that he or she is capable of causing a seizure, it follows that he or she is capable of stopping them. This is an oversimplified explanation of this approach, and its success demands the skill and training of a professional to make it work. But the philosophy upon which it is based is sound, and in embracing it for herself, Candy has discovered that she is not subject to Arlene's domination. She, Candy Jones, will call the shots and fight the battles.

In conjunction with this strategy given Candy for dealing with Arlene, all those associated with her have worked to instill a strong sense of self-worth and self-confidence. Confident of her own abilities, Arlene's value to Candy diminishes.

The story of Candy Jones as I have come to know and live it has pointed out to me a selfishness that is ingrained in most of us, myself included.

I recall a meeting with Ed Kuhn and Bob Gleason of Playboy Press shortly after we decided to proceed with *The Control of Candy Jones.*

"What concerns me," said Kuhn, "is that by doing the book we'll in some way perpetuate the problems Candy is having. I wouldn't want that."

Gleason and I agreed, of course, that we shared his feelings.

But as the material from Candy began to dry up once she'd decided to no longer allow Arlene to play a dominant role in her life, I found myself frustrated. There were so many unanswered questions that I wished to pursue, and yet I knew, as did John Nebel, that to do so might bring about the very thing feared by Ed Kuhn.

One unanswered question concerned the postscript to the last letter Candy had written to me. She'd mentioned a tie, and I wondered why she'd mentioned it. She answered that question a month later when, in the conscious state, she recalled that Jensen had given her the tie as a weapon. It was made from a form of rubber, and could be used as a garrote. In addition, it had sufficient heft that a numbing blow could be struck with it. It was but one of hundreds of such items developed by the CIA for its agents.

Other questions have not been answered, but perhaps they will be in the future, not by Candy but by those who are investigating the Central Intelligence Agency and its operations. I have managed to contain the natural inclination to pursue aspects of Candy's story in an independent manner. It is tempting to follow up on the CIA's testing program and to delve deeper into that agency's inner workings. But that would involve another book of the sort being researched and written by investigative journalists as this book achieves publication.

There is also so much more to be learned about the assassination of Robert Kennedy and the possibility that hypnosis was used to program Sirhan Sirhan. Again, that would necessitate a book of its own.

For me, this book was to be the story of one woman and her experiences, as reported by her, as a testing subject and messenger for the Central Intelligence Agency. More important, it was to be the accounting of the married lives of two extraordinary people, John Nebel and Candy Jones, as influenced by her prior experiences with the CIA and its questionable research projects.

For Candy, there is the need to put behind her those aspects of her life that have been unpleasant and to move forward as the beautiful, talented and healthy lady that she is.

And for John Nebel, there is the deep desire that the adventure be over. There was a time when Nebel seriously considered going to California and putting a gun to Jensen's head. Things had reached that proportion in his relationship with Candy.

But now Nebel is content in seeing that the story is told, and that he and his wife can happily progress through the years ahead.

"I hope it's over," were Nebel's last words to me as I finished this final chapter and delivered it to Playboy Press. "I'm confident that it is. But there are times when I wake up and expect to hear a knock at the door. And should I open the door, I expect to see a uniformed policeman standing there and offering his condolences to me for my wife's death. I am still convinced that Jensen and the CIA are attempting to make contact with her. I only hope that I am wrong."

1975  October

After reading this book
I marvel at the author's patience
for the factual reporting of the
vast details involved, his sensitivity and resistance to dwell on
much of the sensationalism contained, and the Herculean task it required to telling my story. Only a
master craftsman, Don Bain, could
do it.  For all of this I am grateful

Had it not been for John
Nebel, I wouldn't have been alive;

Jensen nearly won out. I
almost lost my marriage-which is my
everything.  I won't have to take
<u>that</u>  swim now. *Candy Jones*

# The Hypnotic Induction Profile

The Hypnotic Induction Profile (HIP) developed by Dr. Herbert Spiegel uses the actual induction of a trance to measure the subject's general capacity to enter into the trance state. It is based upon the eye-roll levitation method of trance induction in which the subject, seated comfortably in a chair and facing the hypnotist (operator), is told to do certain things and to comment on his own reactions to them. The subject's comments, coupled with what the trained operator observes, are recorded on a standardized sheet, and the resulting record is the subject's HIP score. The scoring scale runs from zero through five, but since there are few zeroes or fives, the operative scale is from one to four. The higher the score, the greater capacity the subject has indicated for entering hypnotic trance.

There have been other tests developed to test trance capacity, but the HIP provides the first disciplined clinical approach to testing, enabling operators to exchange information based upon a standard understood by all, and applicable to most cases.

On the surface, determining a patient's HIP score would appear to have little value beyond enabling the operator to know how readily the subject might enter the hypnotic mode. But there is, in actuality, much more to be gained by the physician through the use of the HIP. Dr. Spiegel, through years of testing and correlation of his research, has developed a link between trance capacity and personality, or character type. It is a complex and provoking hypothesis, and its impact upon psychiatry is beginning to be felt.

Candy Jones has gone through the entire HIP testing procedure four times. The first time occurred during a break in the seminar at Columbia conducted by Dr. Spiegel. Dr. Robert T. London and Dr. Barbara DeBetz, both of whom presented portions of the program, performed HIP tests on those attending the seminar as a matter of courtesy and to demonstrate for the students the proper way the test should be given. Candy's first test was done by Dr. DeBetz, a psychiatrist in private practice and on the faculty of the New York University Medical Center. She sat facing Candy in a far corner of the stage, on her lap a clipboard holding the single sheet used by the hypnotist to record scores and reactions during the test.

■

DOCTOR: What is your name?

CANDY: Candy Nebel.

DOCTOR: Have you ever been hypnotized before?

CANDY: I don't know if I have been hypnotized. I don't think so.

DOCTOR: Are you wearing contact lenses?

CANDY: No.

DOCTOR: Sometimes we have problems with contact lenses when the person is asked to look up. All right, are you comfortable?

CANDY: Yes.

DOCTOR: Now look up as far as you can to the top of your head, all the way up. Not your head, just your eyes. Now, leave your eyes up and close your eyelids slowly. . . . Close. . . . Take a deep breath. . . . Leave your eyes closed. . . . *(Candy had opened her eyes at this point)* . . . Let's try again. . . . Look up as far as you can to the top of your head. . . . Leave your eyes up and close your eyelids slowly. . . . Take a deep breath and hold it . . . and exhale . . . and concentrate on floating.

*(Dr. DeBetz wrote down on the score sheet her judgment of Candy's upgaze and eye-roll. There are other subtle considerations such as squinting, but it is the ability to roll the eyes high into the head and to keep them there while slowly closing the eyelids that is important.)*

DOCTOR: . . . imagine that your body is very free and light and relaxed, and you feel as though you are floating. . . . It is a very comfortable and relaxing sensation. . . . While you concentrate on your body's sensation of floating, I'm going to concentrate on your left hand and forearm. . . . In a little while I'm going to stroke your middle finger on your left hand, and there will be a moving sensation spreading from your middle finger to your arm, and your left forearm will float upwards until it is bent at the elbow. . . . You'll find something amusing about this whole experience.

*(At this stage of the test, Dr. DeBetz is watching for Candy's arm to rise. If she immediately accepts the suggestion that her arm will rise, the levitation is recorded in the appropriate space on the score sheet. If she doesn't, Dr. DeBetz will make the suggestion again, using more visual language to enhance the feeling of floating—e.g., helium-filled balloons are said to be tied to the arm, or a magnet is pulling it upward. As it happened, Candy's arm did begin to rise immediately following the initial suggestion, and is noted on the score sheet as a four. It should also be pointed out that DeBetz planted a post-hypnotic suggestion when she said that Candy would find the experience amusing. Dr. DeBetz checks Candy's face for a sign of a smile to indicate her acceptance of that suggestion. Questioning following the trance will also help establish whether Candy was amused.)*

DOCTOR: Now that your arm is in this position, you are going into a state of complete relaxation. . . . Every time you do this exercise it will be easier and easier for you to go into this state of relaxation. In fact, your arm will remain in this position even after I give you the signal to open your eyes. If I try to put it down, it will go back into this position and stay there until I touch your left elbow. After I touch your left elbow, you will have your normal controlling sensation in your left forearm and hand. . . . Now, every time you do this exercise and you want to bring yourself out of this pleasant state of relaxation, at the count of three you take a deep breath and roll your eyes up into your head and open your eyelids slowly. . . . Ready? . . . Three . . . take a deep breath. . . . Two . . . roll your eyes and open your eyelids. . . . One!

*(Dr. DeBetz then asked Candy a series of questions.)*

DOCTOR: Are you aware of any tingling sensation in your left hand and forearm?

CANDY: Yes.

DOCTOR: Do you feel that your left hand is as much a part of your body as your right hand?

CANDY: No.

*(Dr. DeBetz then took Candy's wrist between her thumb and first finger and gently attempted to help Candy's left arm rise. It did begin to rise.)*

CANDY: It just wants to fly up.

DOCTOR: Are you surprised about that?

CANDY: *(laughing)* Yes.

DOCTOR: Now for comparison, put your right arm up. *(Candy follows the instruction)* Now put it down. Do you feel any difference in the control you have over your right hand as compared to your left?

CANDY: Yes.

DOCTOR: You feel you have more control in your right arm than in your left?

CANDY: I was aware of bringing my right arm up, but my left just came up without that much awareness, without *making* it come up.

DOCTOR: Okay. What about now? Do you have the same control in both arms?

CANDY: *(pointing to her right arm)* This arm is heavier.

DOCTOR: What about control? Do you feel you have full control now in your left arm?

CANDY: Yes. I suppose so. It's not floating up. *(Laughs.)*

DOCTOR: All right. Now that the hypnosis is gone from your left hand and arm, do you have any idea what made it go away?

CANDY: No.

DOCTOR: Did I tell you how it would go away?

CANDY: No.

DOCTOR: Did I touch your elbow?

CANDY: Yes.

DOCTOR: Did you experience any floating sensation?

CANDY: Yes.

DOCTOR: In your arm and your body?
CANDY: Yes, in my whole body.
DOCTOR: Did you feel relaxed throughout the whole experience?
CANDY: Lovely.

■

Dr. DeBetz had Candy repeat her upgaze and eye-roll because it had registered lower than might be expected when compared to Candy's performance on the rest of the test. She scored higher the second time, although the original upgaze and eye-roll score remained on the sheet.

"You are pretty high on the scale of hypnotizability," Dr. DeBetz told Candy.

Candy's second HIP test came during the early morning hours of February 6, 1975, and was performed by Dr. London at the WMCA studios. Dr. London was the guest on the show that night, and he took Candy into an empty room during a long commercial break. Dr. London found her to test even higher than had Dr. DeBetz.

Dr. Spiegel's Hypnotic Induction Profile of Candy is reproduced in the photos and documents section. A full explanation of its workings and meanings would be impractical here. The importance of it is that Candy rates extremely high on the scale of hypnotic trance capacity, and only those subjects who do score this high are capable of the experiences reported by her.

Candy has also been tested by Dr. Frederick Dick, the Manhattan internist who studied therapeutic hypnosis with Dr. Spiegel and has become Candy's and John's family doctor. In addition to being their internist, he has worked with Candy during long hypnotic sessions to implant a strategy for dealing with Arlene. This strategy is discussed in Chapter 20.

# Report to the President by the Commission on CIA Activities Within the United States

## *Domestic Activities of the Directorate of Science and Technology*

In the past two decades, the CIA has placed increasing emphasis upon gathering foreign intelligence through technical and scientific means.

In 1963, Director John McCone sought to coordinate the scientific development of intelligence devices and systems by creating the Science and Technology Directorate within the CIA. Most of the scientific and technological endeavors had been previously undertaken by the Plans (now Operations) Directorate.

The Science and Technology Directorate is presently responsible for all of the research and development engaged in by the CIA in all fields of science and technology. Projects range from complex satellite systems to the development of miniature cameras and concealed listening devices.

The Directorate also is engaged in developing countermeasures to neutralize new scientific and technological devices developed by foreign intelligence services.

Private industry provides much of the research and development of new intelligence gathering devices on a contractual basis.

In addition to engaging in research and development, some branches of the Science and Technology Directorate provide operational support in the field for use of intelligence gathering devices developed by the Directorate.

Other branches of the Directorate themselves engage in the task of foreign intelligence-gathering abroad, utilizing technical intelligence gathering devices not developed for use by operations agents.

The Commission investigated a number of projects of the Science and Technology Directorate which have affected persons living within the United States.

Most such activities were lawful and proper, although there have been scattered improprieties described below.

## A.   The Testing of Scientific and Technological Developments Within the United States

While the research and development of new CIA scientific and technical devices is naturally undertaken within the United States the evidence before this Commission shows that with a few exceptions, the actual devices and systems developed have not been used operationally within this country.[1]

However, the Agency has tested some of its new scientific and technological developments in the United States. One such program included the testing of certain behavior-influencing drugs. Several others involved the testing of equipment for monitoring conversations. In all of the programs described, some tests were directed against unsuspecting subjects, most of whom were U.S. citizens.

## 1.   The Testing of Behavior-Influencing Drugs on Unsuspecting Subjects Within the United States

In the late 1940's, the CIA began to study the properties of certain behavior-influencing drugs (such as LSD) and how

[1] A few audio-surveillance devices developed by the Science and Technology Directorate have been used by the Office of Security in the course of investigations of persons within the United States. In addition, several devices developed by the Agency have been used by other federal agencies in operations conducted within the United States.

such drugs might be put to intelligence use. This interest was prompted by reports that the Soviet Union was experimenting with such drugs and by speculation that the confessions introduced during trials in the Soviet Union and other Soviet Bloc countries during the late 1940's might have been elicited by the use of drugs or hypnosis. Great concern over Soviet and North Korean techniques in "brainwashing" continued to be manifested into the early 1950's.

The drug program was part of a much larger CIA program to study possible means for controlling human behavior. Other studies explored the effects of radiation, electric-shock, psychology, psychiatry, sociology and harassment substances.

The primary purpose of the drug program was to counter the use of behavior-influencing drugs clandestinely administered by an enemy, although several operational uses outside the United States were also considered.

Unfortunately, only limited records of the testing conducted in these drug programs are now available. All the records concerning the program were ordered destroyed in 1973, including a total of 152 separate files.

In addition, all persons directly involved in the early phases of the program were either out of the country and not available for interview, or were deceased. Nevertheless, the Commission learned some of the details surrounding several tests of LSD conducted on unsuspecting subjects between 1953 and 1963.

The possibility, and the importance, of testing potential behavior-influencing drugs (including LSD) on human subjects was first suggested in 1953. It was also suggested at that time that Agency trainees might be utilized as test subjects. Any such testing was to be carefully supervised and conducted only in the presence of a qualified physician.

Following laboratory testing of LSD and other potential behavior-influencing substances, a few tests were run on voluntary participants. Commencing in 1955, under an informal arrangement with the Federal Bureau of Drug Abuse Control, tests were begun on unsuspecting subjects in normal social situations. Testing was originally conducted on the West Coast. In 1961, a similar testing program was initiated on the East Coast.

In 1963, the Agency's Inspector General learned of this program and questioned the propriety of testing on unsuspecting subjects. The Inspector General reported that in a number of instances, test subjects became ill for hours or days following the application of a drug. There was one reported incident of hospitalization, the details of which could not be learned by the Commission because of the destruction of the records and the unavailability of witnesses.

The Commission did learn, however, that on one occasion during the early phases of this program (in 1953), LSD was administered to an employee of the Department of the Army without his knowledge while he was attending a meeting with CIA personnel working on the drug project.

Prior to receiving the LSD, the subject had participated in discussions where the testing of such substances on unsuspecting subjects was agreed to in principle. However, this individual was not made aware that he had been given LSD until about 20 minutes after it had been administered. He developed serious side effects and was sent to New York with a CIA escort for psychiatric treatment. Several days later, he jumped from a tenth floor window of his room and died as a result.[2]

The General Counsel ruled that the death resulted from "circumstances arising out of an experiment undertaken in the course of his official duties for the United States Government," thus ensuring his survivors of receiving certain death benefits. Reprimands were issued by the Director of Central Intelligence to two CIA employees responsible for the incident.

As a result of the Inspector General's study of this drug program in 1963, the Agency devised new criteria for testing substances on human subjects. All further testing of potentially dangerous substances on unsuspecting subjects was prohibited. Between 1963 and 1967, some testing of drugs continued, but only on voluntary subjects, primarily inmate volunteers at various correctional institutions. In 1967, all projects involving behavior-influencing drugs were terminated.

It is presently the policy at CIA not to test any substance on

[2]There are indications in the few remaining Agency records that this individual may have had a history of emotional instability.

unsuspecting persons. Current practice in all experimentation is to adhere strictly to Department of Health, Education and Welfare guidelines concerning the use of human subjects, and all current CIA contracts carry language to that effect.